Detailed notes on adult books
for use with young people

Doors to more mature reading

Compiled for the
Young Adult Services Division
by
Elinor Walker
Donald W. Allyn
Alice E. Johnson
Helen Lutton

American Library Association
Chicago   1964

Copyright © 1964 by the American Library Association
Manufactured in the United States of America
Library of Congress Catalog Card Number 64-8298

Preface

Doors to More Mature Reading is an outgrowth of the publication, *Book Bait*. *Book Bait*, prepared by a group of young people's librarians, was eagerly greeted by librarians everywhere.[1] Although it is still widely used, it does not meet the need of school and public librarians who work with more mature readers. The demand for a new list above and beyond *Book Bait*—a list that would reach the older teen-ager who was ready for more mature books—resulted in the appointment of the *Book Bait* Sequel Committee.

This committee, originally composed of seven members, worked hard and long, reading, rereading, and screening hundreds of titles to find those adult books that bring challenges to young people, that widen their horizons, and that deepen their appreciation of language, of truth, of beauty, of life itself. Each member of the group was disappointed not to have every one of his favorite titles included, and some would have eliminated a few titles which were included. At least four votes were required for every title listed. Any book to which at least two people definitely objected was rejected. The committee made no attempt to produce a balanced list. The choice of books was based on value, not on date of publication. The librarian should note that the date of first publication for a classic title is given in brackets immediately after the title, to call attention to the fact that these titles are choice items from a different era.

This book has been prepared with loving care for the busy librarian or teacher who may not be—at least in his early years—conversant with all that is fine in adult literature and who is not sure which books are usable with young people. Here the committee takes the librarian on a tour of his own collection to point out books which are well-worth taking down, reading, and suggesting to young people. The titles are suitable for class collateral

---

[1] *Book Bait*, compiled for the Association of Young People's Librarians and edited by Elinor Walker (Chicago: American Library Association, 1957). 88p.

reading as well as for recreational reading. The book is only incidentally for the rare teen-ager to whom the librarian wishes to hand it.

Doors to More Mature Reading includes plays, poetry, science, and history as well as fiction, biography, and travel. These are books which the members of the committee have used successfully with young adults and which represent "touchstone titles" against which to judge similar books. *Doors to More Mature Reading* is a gateway through which the librarian and his patrons can explore many fields of information, adventure, and romance.

The annotations are long and attempt to give the flavor of the stories. Publishers have been generous in giving permission to quote from many of the books. The notes will give the librarian a working acquaintance with the titles until he can gain a first-hand knowledge by reading them. The persons to whom each book will appeal are usually suggested in the second paragraph. The pages or chapters which lend themselves to book talk presentation and similar books to be used as follow-up titles are included in the last paragraph. An asterisk on a follow-up title indicates that an annotation on the title appears on another page, as indicated by the Index.

A few titles are out-of-print in their original editions, but most can still be found on library shelves or are available in paperback editions. When the librarian finds that he cannot obtain additional copies of an out-of-print book, he should write to the publisher stating that he has a demand for the book and would like to have it reprinted. Publishers say that otherwise they have no way of knowing how great the need for a reprint might be. When the pages for book talk suggestions are given for out-of-print recent books, they are those in the original hard-cover edition. The pages given for classics are those in the edition named in the bibliographic information following the title.

Because book prices change frequently, they have been omitted from the bibliographic information. Librarians interested in currently available paperbound editions should check *Paperbound Books in Print,* published monthly by the R. R. Bowker Company.

Acknowledgment is gratefully made to the following persons for help in compiling and completing this list:

Mrs. Audrey Biel, Public Library, Detroit, Michigan; Eugene Hatch, Public Library, Lakewood, Ohio; and Mrs. Mary Spradling, Public Library, Kalamazoo, Michigan—who were members of the original committee but were unable to continue; Jane Manthorne, Public Library, Boston, Massachusetts; Pauline Winnick, Public Library, Boston, Massachusetts; Gloria Anderson, La Follette High School Library, Madison, Wisconsin; Gladys Cavanagh, University of Wisconsin Library School, Madison, Wisconsin; Mrs. Cordelia Smith, Lucas County Library, Maumee, Ohio; Grace Jones, High School Library, Snow Hill, Maryland; Mrs. Sabra Kittner, North Carroll High School Library, Greenmount, Maryland; Caroline Arden, Arlington County Libraries, Arlington, Virginia; Mrs. Florence Sanborn, Public Library, Los Angeles, California; Mrs. Priscilla Bower, Public Library, Denver, Colorado; Robert Dumas, Public Library, Dedham, Massachusetts; Elizabeth Keen, Free Library, Philadelphia, Pennsylvania— all of whom contributed to the annotations.

A special thank you goes to Mrs. Alice Waddy, Carnegie Library, Pittsburgh, for doing all of the typing of manuscript and correspondence.

Donald W. Allyn
New York Public Library

Alice E. Johnson
Evanston Township High School

Helen Lutton
South Hills High School, Pittsburgh

Elinor Walker, Chairman
Carnegie Library, Pittsburgh

Doors to More Mature Reading

ADAMSON, JOY

Born Free: A Lioness of Two Worlds

1960. Pantheon.

The stellar role in this real-life drama is played by a young lioness, Elsa. The setting is the Northern Frontier Province of Kenya where the author's husband is Senior Game Warden. The drama is provided by Elsa's very colorful personality and by her half-wild, half-domesticated existence as the Adamsons' household pet. George had brought her home when she was just a few days old, and soon she was romping and playing as if she had been born to no other life. Like most youngsters, Elsa enjoyed automobile rides, playing games, and being cuddled by loved ones. Her reactions to the world around her were a constant source of study and amusement, and she often displayed remarkably human behavior, such as sleeping on a cot, seeking human consolation when frightened, and refusing to walk when transportation was available. Elsa learned to hunt and retrieve game and even had a native boy, Nuru, to look after her. Concerned about the future of this near-human creature while they were on overseas leave, her "parents" began the heartbreaking task of transforming a tame lion into a wild beast. By teaching Elsa to kill animals and forcing her to stalk from hunger, Joy and George slowly trained the lioness to return to the wilds. Eventually she was accepted by other lions and had the problem of her own cubs to solve.

This rambling, delightfully simple story has no real plot except the unique relationship between man and beast. As a study in animal psychology or an episodic tale of Africa, it appeals to most young adults as soon as they glance at the photographs.

Elsa's encounters with other animals on pages 50–55, for example, could be used as book talks, but a brief introduction coupled with a showing of a few of the excellent photographs should   7 make further description unnecessary. Similar titles include *Circus Doctor* by Henderson, *My Zoo Family* by Martini, *Serengeti Shall Not Die** by Grzimek, *No Room in the Ark* by Moorehead, *Operation Noah* by Lagus, and *The Lion* by Kessel. *Living Free* by Adamson provides a sequel about Elsa's offspring.

ANDERSON, MARIAN

My Lord, What a Morning

1956. Viking.

Marian Anderson was born in Philadelphia of working-class parents. She began singing as a child and came slowly to the understanding that she had an unusual talent. Gradually the encouragement of friends made her realize that a career in the concert world might be possible if she were willing to work hard and face great obstacles. After devoting years to the study of both music and foreign languages, the young Negro contralto made a premature debut in New York, but it was actually in Europe that her voice and art were first recognized and appreciated. After her European success, people at home came to hear her, and since then she has sung in many parts of the United States, Mexico, South America, Europe, and the Orient. This autobiography acknowledges her debt to her teachers, accompanists, and managers and discusses the problems of wardrobe and tour planning. The happiness of her early home life with her devoted mother and sisters, and the joy she has found in her marriage and home in Connecticut, permeate the story.

High on the list of books that will promote racial understanding is this one by and about one of America's greatest singers, to whom Toscanini said, "Yours is a voice such as one hears once in a hundred years." Proud of being a Negro, Miss Anderson is aware of the problems she faces. She is not a militant worker for the rights and recognition of the Negro, but in her quiet way she tries to help her people. Happily, she feels that the picture is changing and concludes optimistically, "The United States could set a shining example and could reap rewards far beyond any expectations. All the changes may not come in my time; they may even be left for another world. But I have seen enough changes to believe that they will occur in this one." Older girls interested in singing or a stage career enjoy this anecdotal autobiography.

An incident that might be used for a book talk is the time Miss Anderson lost her music roll and her letter of credit when she

8

arrived in England to study, pages 118–24. *Angel Mo' and Her Son, Roland Hayes* by Helm, *American Daughter* by Thompson, and *George Washington Carver** by Holt are true life stories of other Negroes. *Subway to the Met* by Crichton tells a similar story of Risë Stevens' rise to fame as a singer.

ANDERSON, WILLIAM R., and BLAIR, CLAY, JR.

Nautilus *90 North*

1959. World.

At 11:15 P.M., Sunday, August 3, 1958, the first under-ice crossing of the North Pole by a nuclear-powered submarine was completed. Commander William R. Anderson, U.S.N., former instructor in submarine tactics, informed the world by sending the message: "*Nautilus* 90 North," thus making a reality of the dreams of men like Lyon, Wilkins, Eisenhower, and Rickover. Initial probings under the ice in 1957 had brought the *Nautilus* within 180 miles of the Pole. Then in June, 1958, the first attempt at a transpolar voyage, "Operation Sunshine," had failed because the ice was too thick and endangered the submarine by forcing it too close to the ocean floor. The ship had turned around and headed for Pearl Harbor. Hurried conferences at the Pentagon and with Admiral Rickover, enthusiastic support by President Eisenhower, and the secret installation of new, revolutionary navigating equipment enabled the *Nautilus* to leave again in July, 1958, for a second and successful try.

The book appeals to boys and some girls who wish to relive a bit of history in our own time, as well as to those interested in contrasting the hardships and disasters encountered here with stories of earlier polar voyages. It is packed with details about the structure and operation of the *Nautilus,* life aboard the submarine, and the problems of secrecy and rumor. Commander Anderson recreates the day-to-day events, hours of suspense, tension, even practical jokes and, finally, recognizes the accomplishment and implications of this voyage.

Material for book talks will be found in Chapter 1, which reveals information about Commander Anderson's professional and personal life as well as his interview with Admiral Rickover, pages 20–29, stressing the importance of reading. Descriptions of the crew and the ship in Chapter 5, plus a few facts about the hazardous trip through the narrow ice straits in Chapter 16, could lead up to the historic event itself as told in Chapters 21 and 22.

Other high spots are the serenade to "heroes" on page 39; repairing the damaged periscope on pages 85–89; the fire on pages 122–29 and 133–35; and the North Pole party on pages 225–26. For the reader who wants "something else like this," try *Operation Deepfreeze* by Dufek, *Challengers of the Deep** by Cross, *Surface at the Pole* by Calvert, *Around the World Submerged* by Beach, and *Seadragon* by Steele. Suggest, also, *Little America* by Byrd, *Come North with Me* by Balchen, and *The Atomic Submarine* by Blair.

ARNOLD, ELLIOTT

Blood Brother

1950. Duell.

"It was late fall, the time that is called Earth is Reddish Brown." Thus begins this story of the tribe of the Chiricahua nation of the Apache Indians and their brave, revered chief, Cochise. In 1856, after the United States had taken over from Mexico the territory which was to become the southwestern states, Cochise decided that his people should adopt the ways of the white man to avoid extermination. He reached an understanding with Major Steen, commander of the U.S. troops, whom he respected and who admired him. When a stagecoach line was established across Apache territory, Cochise promised to protect the stages when they were on land under his jurisdiction. Neighboring tribes were unfriendly, however, and several times Cochise's men rescued the stage when it was attacked by these Indians. Some of the white men honored and trusted Cochise, but others believed that he was treacherous, though clever. This was the situation when a brash, young lieutenant falsely accused Cochise of stealing a part-Indian boy, and by his pigheadedness managed to turn a slight incident into the bloodiest war in the history of the Southwest. Cochise swore vengeance—ten white men for every Indian killed—and the desert ran with blood. During these years a young white man, Tom Jeffords, had been working in and out of this area. Tom ran the post office in Tucson, but was having difficulty getting his riders through the Apache territory. A man of great courage, he went to see Cochise, who was impressed with his integrity and sincerity. A mutual feeling of respect and admiration developed at their first meeting. In the Indian camp Tom met and fell in love with a young Indian girl, Sonseeahray. Soon they were married, and Tom spent as much time as he

10

could with her in Cochise's camp. Although it was necessary for him to leave her from time to time, he remained true to her until her untimely death. Tom's grief was so great that only the blood brotherhood ceremony between him and Cochise gave him comfort. Tom had always hoped to bring about peace between the white man and Cochise and he did achieve it, but on the condition that he become their Indian agent. The bond of faith and trust between Tom and Cochise continued, and before the Indian died, Tom was able to convince him that although conditions for his people were bad, the future would bring improvements.

This is a fine historical novel of the old West which appeals to mature readers. The motion picture and the television series, "Broken Arrow," were based on this book. A good adaptation for younger readers was done by the author; it also is entitled *Broken Arrow*.

In a book talk describe Cochise and his relationship with the white man in 1856 and then tell what happened to change the agreement. Introduce Tom Jeffords and indicate his part in the story, pages 22–35, 40–54, 83–96, 162–77, 182–88. *Laughing Boy* by La Farge, *Ramona* by Jackson, *The Loon Feather** and *The Shining Trail* by Fuller are good follow-ups. *America's Concentration Camps* by Embry gives a picture of the condition of the Indians today. *When the Legends Die* by Borland tells of an Indian boy caught in the conflict between the traditional life of his people and life in the modern white man's world.

BALZAC, HONORÉ DE
Eugénie Grandet [1833]
1962. Heritage.
At the age of twenty-three, it appeared to Eugénie that strict economies of food, heat, and clothing were necessary for what she assumed was a family of moderate means. The demure, naive girl had no real understanding of her father's extensive wealth, some of which he kept in a locked room where he could gloat over it privately. While the townsfolk of Saumur gossiped about the incredibly sly financier and the monetary prize represented by his daughter, Eugénie and her meek mother led almost cloistered lives, interrupted only by occasional visits from prospective suitors and their envious families. Accepting frugality for herself, Eugénie was not willing to impose it upon Charles Grandet, her handsome cousin, who appeared unexpectedly from Paris to visit   11

his provincial relatives and won the affection of the gentle Eugénie. Awed by his poise and beautiful clothes, Eugénie managed to provide a real wax candle for his room and schemed to get extra eggs, sugar, and other luxuries for his menu. When it became known that Charles's father had committed suicide rather than face bankruptcy, the young man grieved. Fearing that Charles might win his daughter's hand and seizing the opportunity to make more money by manipulating his dead brother's losses, old Grandet, in an outwardly generous gesture, financed Charles's passage to the Indies, where he might make a fortune. When Grandet learned that Eugénie had given her cousin a large sum in gold accumulated from gifts received over the years, the old man demonstrated the extent of his monomania by reducing her rations to bread and water—an action which scandalized the community and led to his wife's premature death. In time Eugénie learned to manage the vast financial holdings and upon her father's death assumed control of the estate. Her hope to marry Charles was shattered by his fickleness, and a brief marriage to a long-time suitor left Eugénie widowed at thirty-three. She became a recluse living on rationed food and fuel; only by giving money to charity was she able to undo some of the mischief begun by her father.

A good introduction to the realism and satire typical of Balzac's writing, this melodramatic novel appeals to older girls who want a "story to cry over."

Open a book talk by describing the dingy, threadbare Grandet house, pages 21–25, and then outline the father's incredible stinginess, pages 31–36, 82–87. For glimpses of Charles and Eugénie, use parts of pages 46–55, 69–74, and 76–82. Another readable Balzac title is *Père Goriot,* while Eliot's *Silas Marner* depicts a miser redeemed by a child's influence.

BARNES, ERIC

The Man Who Lived Twice

1956. Scribner.

Edward Sheldon had background, looks, charm, and wealth plus a great zest for living and a gift for friendship. During his years at Harvard he was thrilled by the great actress, Sarah Bernhardt, and from this devotion developed an interest in the professional stage. In 1907, just after graduation, his first play, *Salvation Nell,* starring Minnie Maddern Fiske, was a smash hit. Other successes followed; *The High Road* and *Romance,* written for Doris Keane, the great love of his life, enjoyed tremendous popularity. In his early thirties, he was stricken by a virulent, incurable form of progressive arthritis and soon was completely unable to move. Within ten years he was entirely blind, and before his death fifteen years later, he was threatened with the loss of his speech and hearing. During these twenty-five years, however, Ned Sheldon became a living legend and a powerful influence in the American theater. Telegrams and letters went out from his bedside to give comfort, hope, and encouragement to his many friends. Actors and writers, doctors and scientists, poets and statesmen came to his New York penthouse apartment to discuss literature, politics, the theater, and problems of morality. He listened while Thornton Wilder read aloud the first version of *Our Town* and saw quickly the passages that needed revision. Robert Sherwood visited him to discuss the scenes of *Abe Lincoln in Illinois,* and Ruth Draper, Helen Howe, and Cornelia Otis Skinner tried out their monologues on him. Although he collaborated on innumerable productions, he insisted on remaining remote from the successes and adulation. His love for people, and a desire to help them achieve their best, made Mr. Sheldon a rare and inspiring figure.

Beautifully written, this book appeals to the teen-ager because of the romance of the theater and the gallantry of Sheldon's fight to rise above his handicap.

A book talk could include a brief outline of Sheldon's life plus several incidents which reveal his personality, such as his impeccable dress when bedridden, page 143; Heifetz' private concert for him, pages 181–82; his way with children, pages 196–200. *Gertrude Lawrence as Mrs. A* by Aldrich and *Act One** by Hart are also appropriate titles to suggest to those who love the theater.

BARTHOLOMEW, CAROL

My Heart Has Seventeen Rooms

1959. Macmillan.

When her youngest child began to chatter in Hindi, Carol Bartholomew realized how well her family had become a part of the local scene. They had come to Nangal because Bart, her engineer husband, was working on the new Bhakra Dam. Carol was happy to take advantage of the unaccustomed luxury of numerous servants and spend her days as a volunteer worker in the local

13

hospital. Her initial dismay over primitive, unsanitary conditions, unfamiliar customs, and caste prejudices soon gave way to an understanding concern for the needs of the people. The seventeen rooms of the little hospital became an important part of her life. When Dr. Gurbux Babbar, the Chief Medical Officer, realized that this was no casual, temporary interest, Carol's responsibilities were quickly enlarged. By the time she left India, she was playing a major role as an operating-room assistant and a general adviser. She consistently refused to take the view that individual effort was useless because the task was so enormous. Her narrative resembles a series of letters touching upon various aspects of Indian life—some of it tragic, some of it dramatic, some of it humorous, all of it interesting. The horrors of poverty and disease are not glossed over, but the people emerge as loving, gracious, and courteous when met with the same attitude on the part of foreigners. This is a warmly human and richly informative account of the family's two-and-a-half-year stay in India seen through Carol's sympathetic and perceptive eyes.

The hospital episodes and descriptions of family life in a foreign land appeal to nursing enthusiasts as well as to girls who enjoyed the Santha Rama Rau books.

Many of Carol's experiences in the hospital wards would be suitable for book talks. The post office escapade, pages 60–61, and the old peddler's techniques, pages 34–36, give interesting slants on the people of India. Simply written, this is a good introduction to more mature books, such as *Dr. Ida** by Wilson, *Anna and the King of Siam** by Landon, *Bridge to the Sun** by Terasaki, and *The Kingdom Within* by Caulfield.

BERNSTEIN, LEONARD

The Joy of Music

1959. Simon & Schuster.

The dynamic young pianist, conductor, and composer, Leonard Bernstein, has presented us with several fascinating, imaginary conversations about music and the expanded and annotated scripts of seven "Omnibus" television programs. The conversations are timely, amusing, and informative and provide a lively discussion of Beethoven, American symphony, and Gershwin. The first chapters could be used very successfully for group readings by music clubs or classes, and could stimulate further discussion among 14 music-minded young people. The style varies from the profound to the pert, and the text is copiously illustrated with bars of music. The first imaginary conversation, which takes place somewhere in New Mexico, will serve as a sample of the method of presentation. The participants are a sixteen-year-old younger brother, who is also a licensed pilot; a British lyric poet; and the author (all identified by initials). A comparison by L. P. of the beautiful hills and the music of Beethoven leads into a discussion of this composer's work and how he measures up to all the elements of music: melody, harmony, rhythm, counterpoint, and orchestration. The conclusion is reached that Beethoven broke all the rules and turned out pieces of breathtaking rightness.

For the thousands of young people who enjoyed the television programs, this is a delightful repeat, and even for those who do not have a musical background or ability there is much appeal.

No chapters lend themselves in the usual way for book talks. *Leonard Bernstein: The Man, His Work, and His World* by Briggs may also be suggested along with a sampling of related recordings.

BISHOP, JIM
The Day Lincoln Was Shot
1955. Harper.

Here is an hour-by-hour account of April 14, 1865, alternating between Lincoln's activities and those in the plot to kill the Chief Executive and members of his Cabinet. The Civil War had just ended, and the President wanted to be lenient with the rebels and assist them in rehabilitating the South. During the day he met with Congressmen, the Cabinet, and the Vice-President; he wanted to be sure that they understood his views. He had had a premonition that he would be assassinated and felt that he might not complete his term in the White House. U.S. Marshal Ward Hill Lamon had begged Lincoln not to go out at night, but the President did not want to disappoint his wife who had planned a theater party. So they went to Ford's Theatre that evening.

On the same day the clever but demented John Wilkes Booth, the leader of the conspirators, was making his feverish, last-minute preparations for the murder. One conspirator was to kill Vice-President Johnson and another, Secretary Seward. Booth himself would shoot the President. The author takes the reader to Ford's Theatre as Booth rehearses each step in the plot. Finally the fatal moment arrived. No attempt was made on Johnson, but 15 several people at the Seward home were badly hurt, and Booth shot Lincoln. The author has permitted the reader to live through Lincoln's last hours and to share the grief of his contemporaries.

Not a difficult book for high school students with an American history background, this has been a favorite title. It is a suspense story told with accuracy and restraint.

The general plan of the book will provide a good introduction to the story. Pages 7–8 picture Lincoln on the last day of his life; pages 18–19 introduce John Wilkes Booth on the same fateful day. Booth's preparations for the assassination at Ford's Theatre, pages 172–74, reveal the details of how the plan was to be carried out. Van Doren's *The Last Days of Lincoln* would be an excellent companion volume; *Abe Lincoln in Illinois** by Sherwood gives a dramatic picture of most of Lincoln's life up to the time he became President.

BJARNHOF, KARL

The Stars Grow Pale

1958. Knopf.

The first-person narrator, a little schoolboy, lived in a small Danish town at the beginning of this century. His parents were simple, poor people. His father was a Swedish immigrant, a brooding and melancholy day laborer who had trouble finding work. His mother was devout and industrious, working at home pasting paper bags to supplement the family income. Both were concerned about the progress of the boy but did not realize that it was his fading eyesight which made him different from the other children. The child was only mildly concerned as he failed to get his eye on the ball when he was playing or accumulated bruises from bumping into obstacles he could not see. An interested schoolteacher let him stand by the board to copy the arithmetic problems, and his quick mind enabled him to memorize and learn easily. He noticed misty circles around the street lamps, but this did not frighten him. When he was finally taken to specialists, it was too late to save his vision. An operation helped to prolong his eyesight for a few years, but the boy had already begun to draw on his inner spirit and create his own world. Because he seldom had companions among his contemporaries, his real friends were adults. Stougard was the man who looked after the vats at the brewery and who shared with the boy his baked

16

potatoes and salt; Valborg was the girl who taught him the notes on the piano and encouraged him to practice; Abeline came to his house to teach him to play the guitar; Baron Wedell, the evangelist, gave him a guitar; Cantor Peterson taught him on the violin; Sofie taught him Braille; the organist gave him instructions on the church organ and discovered he had perfect pitch. But not all the adults were kind. When he finished school and the other pupils were taking their final examination in mathematics, as a joke the teacher asked him to answer the question for which no one else knew the answer, and the boy gave it readily. This teacher had ignored him and told him not to bother to do his lessons, but he had not realized that the boy had been storing in his head everything he heard in class. In spite of this incident the boy was able to face the future with strength and hope because, when he was old enough, he would enter a school which would give him special education.

This sensitive and haunting story of a journey into darkness appeals to mature readers who appreciate poetic and memorable prose. The author himself is blind and an outstanding cellist. Much of this book is autobiographical.

Perhaps it is better to introduce the book to the individual reader rather than to use if for a book talk. However, the father's deep concern for his son's plight is beautifully described in Chapter 9, where he takes the boy out at night to see the woods and the snow and the stars. In Chapter 15 the father buys a splendid Christmas tree and beautiful ornaments so that his son will have in his memory a tree that will go on shining for him year after year when he can no longer see. This book can be followed by *Face to Face** by Mehta and *The Kingdom Within* by Caulfield for other stories of the blind. *An Iceland Fisherman** by Loti is another illustration of the same inner reserve found in *The Stars Grow Pale.*

BOSWORTH, ALLAN R.

The Lovely World of Richi-san

1960. Harper.

Captain Allan Bosworth had been assigned to Tokyo after World War II and was finding it difficult to change his conception of the Japanese and to regard them as friends. He was uncomfortable in their presence and kept wondering what they were thinking behind their calm faces until he met Goto-san, a spare-time street artist, who obviously was enamoured with the author's Jaguar sports car. The American offered him a ride which ended up at the Asano home, where he met the young man's cousins and other assorted relatives. It was pretty Richi-san, who looked about seventeen, that interested Bosworth most because of her fair knowledge of English. Out of this informal meeting came weekly gatherings, and he found himself teaching them conversational English. He also acquired a title, "Papa-san," a respectful and affectionate slang term often applied to the manager of any project. The author's descriptions of the difficulty of English pronunciation for a Japanese are compassionate rather than barbed with ridicule, and his own attempts to master the more complex Japanese language prove equally amusing. It developed that Richi-san was a widow almost twice as old as she looked and that she had one child. Because Captain Bosworth owned a car and the Asanos did not, he was able to show his friends their own country by taking them to places they had never seen; they, in turn, were able to interpret Japan and its culture to him far better than any paid guide would have done. One way to see the lovely countryside was to travel with the Sports Car Club of Japan, a cosmopolitan group consisting mostly of Japanese, American, and British enthusiasts. Richi-san, acting as a guide and interpreter, often accompanied Bosworth. In spite of a late start and unnecessary stops along the way, he won the silver cup for second place in the hundred-mile run to Nikko and Lake Chuzenji. Richi-san felt that this success was achieved because of her prayer to the Buddha. The climb up Mount Fuji, the visit to Hiroshima, a trip to Richi-san's ancestral home for the Festival of the Dead, and the building of a new house—all give intimate and vivid glimpses of family life in Japan.

The author's genuine understanding of people of another culture, and his ability to convey the timeless beauty of that world, have combined to create a personal narrative of appeal to nearly any age group. Readers of Hersey's *Hiroshima* will wonder at the Asanos' apparent lack of bitterness at the bombing and its effects. As Richi-san commented, "Can't be helped, Papa-san. War—it was war."

Almost any chapter could be told, or read in part, to illustrate the flavor, the humor, or the pathos of this book. Chapter 2, "Engrish as it was never spoken Bee-fore," tells how Richi-san analyzed and learned the English language. Chapter 6 gives the touching account of Richi-san's arranged marriage which brought her trouble and heartache. Chapter 9 includes the climb of Fuji and Chapter 14, the visit to Hiroshima. Follow this with *Bridge to the Sun** by Terasaki or *Rain and the Feast of the Stars* by Hatsumi.

BOWEN, CATHERINE D.
Yankee from Olympus
1944. Atlantic-Little.

The very famous Supreme Court Justice, Oliver Wendell Holmes, Jr., was born in 1841. His span of life was to extend far into the next century, for he did not die until March, 1935, at the age of 94—a man of wisdom and love for his country with a world of friends and many honors, beginning with an officer's rank in the Civil War. The first eighty pages of this biography deal with the background and ancestry of this man who was later to make such a mark on American life. Mrs. Bowen has caught the whole spirit of New England—in fact, the America of that era—"Work, money, God." She has pictured Dr. Holmes, the boy's father, and his compatriots, together with their reactions to the events of the time, to history as it developed, and to foreign visitors: Dickens, Jenny Lind, and Edwin Forrest. All this creates a three-dimensional view of the boyhood and early years of Oliver Wendell Holmes, Jr. While his father was writing poems and orations for all occasions, the boy was avidly reading everything that came his way. The years passed and the Civil War was brewing when young Holmes entered Harvard, where there were such teachers as Agassiz, Gray, Darwin, Lowell, and Longfellow. In the spring of his senior year Wendell enlisted for three years, but he was graduated before the Harvard regiment was completed. Wounded three times in the service, he was mustered out as a Lieutenant Colonel shortly before the end of the war. It did not take him long to decide to study law despite his father's "A lawyer can't be a great man." To Wendell, "The law was a door opening into knowledge. It was a window opening out on all mankind." He studied in America and Europe and so devoted himself to the law that his Uncle John had to point out to him that he loved and was beloved by his long-time friend and counselor, Fannie Dixwell. His marriage to her in 1872 brought him great happiness and companionship. The biography moves on through his scholarly years as a law professor at Harvard and then as Chief Justice of Massachusetts. In 1902 he was appointed Justice of the   19

U.S. Supreme Court. Known as the "great dissenter," he was not afraid to disagree with his colleagues on some of the greatest issues of the day. He had a genius for living; the act of learning was a great adventure which he pursued until the day he died.

This book with its excellent index and its scholarly notes and sources is a tremendous reading experience in Americana for the serious, mature student.

The war experiences, pages 149–97, could be used in a book talk. Dr. Holmes's search for his wounded son is a very dramatic story. Wendell's choice of a profession, pages 198–209, is also interesting. His friendship with Fanny and his uncle's pushing him into a proposal, pages 223–26, 242–43, 258–61, are amusing. *The Education of Henry Adams* by Adams and *Adventurous Alliance, The Peabody Sisters of Salem,* and *Three Saints and a Sinner* by Tharp also describe the same locale and some of the same people. *The Doctors Mayo* by Clapesattle shows other young men persistently pursuing their chosen work.

BOWLES, CHESTER

Ambassador's Report

1954. Harper.

In 1951, President Truman appointed Chester Bowles as ambassador to India and Nepal. Accompanied by his wife Steb and his three younger children, Cynthia, Sally, and Sam, he arrived in New Delhi with some very definite ideas about the duties and responsibilities of his diplomatic post. He was very anxious that the people of India should have a true picture of the United States and should understand its ideas about democracy, international affairs, and colonialism. The Bowles family began by living, as nearly as possible, democratic American lives. They turned the huge ambassadorial residence into seven apartments for other staff members and took a smaller house for themselves. The children insisted upon going to Indian schools, and everyone tried to learn some of the languages. Steb showed the servants by her actions that she could do the most menial household tasks. At the Embassy changes were made to lift the morale of the staff and build the interest and enthusiasm of the employees and their families. When the Embassy gave parties, Mr. Bowles, contrary to the practices of ambassadors from several other countries, invited Indians as well as Europeans and served refreshments acceptable to the Indians. His first speech on America's attitudes toward religion, peace, democracy, disarmament, and friendship made a profound impression on the people and opened the way to friendly relationships. In his many long talks with Nehru, he learned much concerning the differences in attitude toward the problems of today's world and the reasons for the Indians holding the opinions they did. He attempted to explain American ideas carefully and conscientiously, and he did not try to cover up the faults and mistakes. He traveled over 60,000 miles through India, visiting hundreds of villages and talking with everyone: students, businessmen, farmers, and workers. He helped to develop and supervise economic and technical assistance programs and acquired at first hand a knowledge of Asian problems. In the work of the Point Four Program in the Indian villages he saw the deep determination of the people to create economic and political freedom through the democratic process. Whether Mr. Bowles is describing Gandhi's policy of nonviolence in India's struggle for independence, giving a vivid close-up portrait of Jawaharlal Nehru, or analyzing the tactics of the Chinese and Russian Communists in Asia, he is perceptive and informative. Such personal experiences as his first impressions upon arriving in India or the colorful trip to Nepal to present his credentials make the book delightful reading. When the United States election brought the inevitable change in diplomatic assignments, the Bowles family reluctantly left the many friends they had made during their eighteen months in India.

This book makes the reader want to pursue many subjects further and add to the fund of information contained herein. Especially appealing are the sketches of the lives of Gandhi and Nehru and such topics as the Marshall Plan, Point Four Program, Indian history, Voice of America, and United States Information Service Libraries. Mature readers who want to understand world affairs find this book very enlightening. It is a good antidote to *The Ugly American** by Lederer.

For a book talk use some of the incidents from Chapter 3, when Mr. Bowles was making changes in the work of the Embassy staff so that they could get to know the Indians better and vice versa. Or explain the work of the specialists in the villages under the Point Four Program in Chapter 14. Amusing and colorful are Mr. Bowles's borrowing of the Italian ambassador's dress clothes in Chapter 4 and the rigorous horseback trip to Nepal in Chapter 17. *At Home in India* by Cynthia Bowles, *Home to India* by Rama Rau, *My Heart Has Seventeen Rooms** by Bartholomew, and *Dr. Ida** by Wilson present other views of India.

BRADBURY, RAY

The Illustrated Man

1958. Doubleday.

One warm afternoon in September the narrator of this story met an unusual human being whose torso was so covered with the most intricate and artistic tattoos that he was called the "Illustrated Man." The stranger explained that years before he had been tattooed by a woman who could see into the future, and each vignette lived a life of its own. At night the illustrations changed and evolved, enacting dozens of separate dramas. The narrator watched the man's body in fascination as eighteen illustrations told their stories. In one tattoo, men from Earth were tramping through the endless rains on Venus, rains which pelted so relentlessly that madness and quick decay followed prolonged exposure. Sun domes with artificial heat and earthlike comforts had been erected, but there were not enough in operation. Would the lost men reach safety and warmth before fungus began to grow on their corpses? Elsewhere, in another illustration, children in various parts of the United States were constructing what looked like make-believe machines from bits of stovepipe and other junk. Their parents thought it was cute to see the little ones so well occupied, but their laughter turned into shrieks of terror when they discovered that beings from another planet were directing the activities in order to conquer Earth. Another episode, called "The Veldt," featured the terrifying prospect of an apparently happy family living in a soundproofed Happylife Home—a house that "clothed and fed and rocked them to sleep and played and sang and was good to them." But the devastating climax came when the pictures on the wall came alive. In the epilogue the narrator's own life was depicted, and when it began to predict his doom at the hands of the Illustrated Man, it was time to escape before the future became the present.

This collection of fantasy and science fiction stories has wise commentaries on our civilization. The stories appeal to the student who wants the unusual, since they stretch far beyond the limitations of ordinary science fiction, piquing, shocking, surprising the mind.

Any one of the episodes can be used as a book talk, or the preliminary pages describing the tattoos could be given as an introduction. Young people can go on to *Seven Science Fiction Novels* by Wells, *Out of the Silent Planet* and *Perelandra* by Lewis, *The Deep Range* by Clarke, and *Earth Is Room Enough* by Asimov.

BRISTOW, GWEN

Celia Garth

1959. Crowell.

Charleston, South Carolina, was bristling with gaiety and excitement on the day in 1779 when blond, brown-eyed Celia Garth arrived to become an apprentice in Mrs. Thorley's dressmaking shop. The American Revolution seemed remote. Every day brought new friends to the attractive twenty-year-old girl, who helped customers select materials and answered their requests in the parlor where they waited for fittings. Eventually Jimmy Rand, a well-to-do young lawyer, began to pay Celia special attention, and with his recommendation she became a seamstress in the luxurious home of enigmatic Mrs. Vivian Lacy. The girl's work so pleased the old lady that she invited Celia to her plantation to supervise the refurbishing of her wardrobe. At this point Jimmy asked Celia to marry him, and she began to plan her wedding. Then suddenly the British moved south, and the war threatened their future. Jimmy left to defend Charleston while Celia accompanied Mrs. Lacy to the city to pack her valuables. The young couple, separated during the long bombardment, faced death many times. The formerly dazzling, white spire of St. Michael's Church, now painted black as a camouflage, became a symbol of defeat when Charleston, inadequately defended, could not withstand the enemy forces. Jimmy was badly wounded and, shortly after he began to recover at the family plantation, he was killed in a raid by Tarleton's men. Stunned by his death, Celia returned to Mrs. Thorley's shop, where she found she could pick up valuable information from the gossip of British officers who accompanied their ladies. Her role as spy for the Revolutionaries brought her into contact with Luke Ansell, Vivian Lacy's son and an important figure in the fight against the British. Their friendship gradually deepened, and they were married before the story ends.

Filled with action, suspense, and romance, this tale of the American Revolution appeals to older girls who liked Elswyth Thane's historical romances.

Celia's first encounter with Vivian Lacy, pages 39–46; the account of the New Year's Ball in Chapter 8; and parts of Chapter 13 are among the many book talk possibilities. Use with *Phantom Fortress* by Lancaster, *Farewell to Valley Forge* and *Sycamore Men* by Taylor, and *Raleigh's Eden* by Fletcher. *Smiling Rebel* by Kane is the story of a Confederate woman spy.

BUCK, PEARL S.

My Several Worlds

1954. Day.

Pearl Buck grew up in a double world—the clean Presbyterian American world of her missionary parents and the living, merry, not-too-clean Chinese world where she shared the thoughts and feelings of her oriental friends and considered the Empress Dowager her own Venerable Ancestor. She spoke the Chinese language as well as English and participated in many of the Chinese customs and holidays. In 1900 the Boxer Rebellion showed her the hatred which the Chinese could feel for white people and gave a prediction of future years when China would lock her gates against foreign intruders. She was educated at home until she was ready for college; then she was sent to a girls' school in Shanghai for a year to accustom her to formal classroom procedure. The germ of Pearl Buck's efforts to spread understanding of other peoples among Americans probably began when she attended Randolph-Macon Woman's College and discovered that neither the students nor the faculty were interested in her experiences in China. After her college training she returned to China to teach high school classes and care for her ailing mother. When she married a young American agriculturist and went to live in North China, she made new friends, found material for stories, and began a serious career as a writer. In 1927, with the help of Chinese friends, she and her family escaped from the Communists. After a brief stay in Japan, where she gained a lasting respect and affection for its friendly people, she returned to China to pursue her writing in earnest. Before long it became apparent that it was impossible to live in China under communism. In 1934 she returned to the United States where, on a farm in Pennsylvania, she and her second husband raised a large family of adopted children. Fame as a Nobel Prize winner in 1938 and the establishment of Welcome House for Asian-American children awaiting adoption are highlights in her life.

Miss Buck's varied roles as writer, teacher, and farmer and her interest in retarded children because of her own little daughter make the book especially interesting to older girls.

Her college years, pages 90–96, contain several incidents which might be developed into a book talk, and pages 141–43 relate an amusing episode concerned with begging in China. Pages 193–96 tell how the author befriended Mrs. Lu, and pages 207–14, how the Chinese woman later returned the favor. Most older girls already will have read *The Good Earth* and may want to follow *My Several Worlds* with *A Bridge for Passing,* in which Miss Buck tells of more recent experiences in Japan. *The House of Exile* by Waln gives the intimate details of the life of an American girl in the home of a very wealthy Chinese family in pre-Communist days. For details of the development of the political situation suggest *Red Star over China* by Snow.

BURGESS, ALAN

The Small Woman

1957. Dutton.

Gladys Aylward, a London parlormaid, was fired with the ambition to be a missionary in China, but when she failed to pass the course that would qualify her for the post, it seemed that there was little hope of achieving her goal. Then one day she learned that Mrs. Jeannie Lawson, an elderly missionary in China, was looking for a younger woman to carry on her work. Gladys wrote to the woman, was accepted, and on October 18, 1930, was on her way to China via the Trans-Siberian Railroad. Her journey was complicated by a war between Russia and China, but by making a wide detour she reached Tientsin, China, and learned that Mrs. Lawson was at a mission station in Shansi Province, in northwest China. Traveling by mule through the mountains, Gladys reached the small, walled town of Yangcheng that was to be her home for many years. While operating the Inn of the Eight Happinesses, a stopping place for mule caravans, the two women used simple Bible stories and homey illustrations to tell the travelers about Christianity. After Mrs. Lawson's death the powerful Mandarin of Yangcheng asked Gladys to serve as his official foot inspector, and thus she was able to tour the mountain villages and talk to many people who might be converted to Christianity. The following years were filled with satisfaction, strange adventures, and hard work; moreover, Gladys acquired a number of children abandoned by their families. When the Japanese invaded Yangcheng in 1938, she and her friends took to the mountains, where she was constantly on the move helping to relieve the suffering of the people. She met and fell in love with Colonel Linnan of Generalissimo Chiang Kai-shek's intelligence service. As she moved about the countryside, she gathered and was able to report important information about Japanese positions and troop movements. Finally the Japanese put a price on her head, and she **25** decided, after much soul-searching, to leave Shansi Province, taking with her the orphans at the mission. Worn out by hardship and privation and separated from Colonel Linnan by the events of the war, Gladys suffered a physical collapse that necessitated her return to England for treatment. After nearly twenty years of work, she left China feeling that she had been richly rewarded in her efforts to serve God and man.

This inspiring story of courage and devotion appeals to many girls.

For book talks tell of Gladys' determination to be a missionary and relate incidents such as her experiences on the Trans-Siberian Railroad, pages 26–40; her first meetings with the Mandarin, pages 76–79; her stopping the convicts' riot, pages 87–94; her relief work after the Japanese bombing, pages 121–28, or her incredible trek through the mountains on foot, and later by train, to Sian with nearly one hundred children, pages 198–247. Use this book with *Keys of the Kingdom** by Cronin and *Nor Scrip, Nor Shoes* by McGoey. Pearl Buck, whose parents were also missionaries in China, gives fine insight into the Chinese life and character in her autobiography, *My Several Worlds.**

BURKE, CLARA HEINTZ, and COMANDINI, ADELE

Doctor Hap

1961. Coward-McCann.

"You will go on a long journey by water to a far land, where you will meet and marry the man of your dreams." The fortune-teller was a member of the Ladies' Aid at a church bazaar in Los Angeles, and to Clara Heintz's sisters this was an amusing prediction. But in 1907 circumstances combined to take nineteen-year-old Clara as traveling companion to Archdeaconess Carter all the way to St. Johns-in-the-Wilderness, a primitive Alaskan mission above the Arctic Circle. From ship, train, and river boat the young woman became acquainted with the country, the sourdoughs, the wildlife, the towns, the prices, and the customs. Untrained to do "anything," Clara was scorned by Archdeacon Stuck who met them at the end of a five weeks' journey and who liked efficient people. But Clara, who had been unaware of her own talents and abilities, soon found that she had made their living quarters attractive, was teaching in the school, had organized a choir, and had learned to cook. Ignorance, superstition, and liquor sold to the Indians by unprincipled white men brought trou-

26

ble and added to the difficulties of the mission work, but the girl enjoyed her work and did not want to leave when her first year was completed. If Clara had not asked for permission to stay for a second year, she probably would never have met Dr. Grafton Burke. The young people were drawn to one another immediately and in a short time decided to marry. Dr. Burke intended to dedicate his life to working among the natives of Alaska, but Mrs. Heintz objected to Clara's remaining there. However, the Bishop and the Archdeacon spoke in the young couple's behalf, and Mama reluctantly withdrew her objections, sending a trunk full of impractical clothing for her daughter's trousseau. Clara and Hap set up housekeeping at the Fort Yukon Mission. In time Dr. Burke had himself appointed justice of the peace so that he could enforce the law. Even though the battle between the couple's youthful idealism and the ruthless, experienced white lawbreakers was uneven at times, "Dr. Hap" did begin to build a fine modern hospital, and the Burkes tried to help the people to establish happy, healthy Christian homes. They knew the heartbreak of separation when their children were sent to California to be educated while they stayed in their Alaskan post. Dr. Burke lived to be only fifty-four, but in the last years of his life he became an ordained minister so that he could attend to souls as well as to bodies.

This is a fast-moving story of devotion and sacrifice which appeals particularly to older girls.

Incidents for book talks include sewing up a woodcutter's scalp, pages 68–71; the story of Clara's broken tooth, pages 112–17; Clara's experience with the drunken trapper, pages 150–55; and Big Belle and the cuckoo clocks, pages 160–64. Use this book as a follow-up for *Mrs. Mike* by Freedman. Also suggest *Ice Palace* by Ferber and *Northern Nurse* by Merrick. For accounts of other courageous missionaries use *The Small Woman** by Burgess, *Bamboo Hospital* by Read, and *Dr. Ida** by Wilson. *Two in the Far North* by Murie mentions the wonderful work of the Burkes at Fort Yukon. On one of their expeditions the Muries were guests at the mission.

CARRIGHAR, SALLY

Moonlight at Midday
1958. Knopf.
"Outside the windows were limitless miles of snow-covered ice— a motionless, silent sea, white and sparkling under the Northern   27

sky, which as usual blazed with stars. Inside, we were eating reindeer steaks, and the room was warm and comforting with the
companionship that binds arctic-dwellers together." Sally Carrighar had come to Alaska to study and write about the animals
of the seashore. Unalakleet (Oo-nulla-klik) offered the greatest
promise of wildlife so she rented an apartment in the trader's
store building. When she began to get acquainted with the people of the village, she was at once impressed by their tranquillity
and the absence of tension and pressure. They were concerned
only with births and deaths; setting up new households; the
problems of food, shelter, and fires for warmth; dancing and
storytelling and other creative activities. One of her new friends
said to her, "You are the first white person who ever stayed here
that didn't come to teach us, or preach to us, or to sell us things."
As their companion in whaling and trapping, Sally had a chance
to know them intimately and to share their daily experiences.
The Eskimos' attitude toward sex is explained frankly but in-
offensively. These people, who are more sensitive, more easily
discouraged, more susceptible to disease, more unselfish, less
adaptable to routine and competition, cannot be thrust into
American cities without careful training. Sally suggests several
sources of income which would enable the Eskimos to remain in
their villages and improve their standard of living. She believes
that the federal government's present plan for the Eskimos will
mean their extermination. In the last part of the book the author
tells what life is like for permanent white residents of Alaskan
cities. Because buildings perched on Alaska's permafrost behave
unpredictably, doors which fit in the morning may not open or
close by evening. Storage of food at fifty degrees below zero is a
problem as the loss of heat, even temporarily, could be disastrous.

Mature readers with a curiosity about the world and its people
enjoy this book very much and show real concern for the future
of the Eskimo.

Incidents for book talks include Sally's first day in Unalakleet,
pages 27–37; the dangers of shooting seal from a kayak, pages 85–
86; and men adrift on ice floes, pages 87–91. Chapter 14 provides
many good anecdotes to tell about "normal living" in Nome. *Wild
Voice of the North* and *Icebound Summer* by Carrighar and
Hearth in the Snow by Buchan are other stories of life in Alaska.
The Howl of the Malemute by Sara Machetanz, who with her
husband spent a more recent winter in Unalakleet, tells of their
attempt to demonstrate on film the raising and training of a dog
team. Margaret Murie, who went to Alaska at the age of nine

and grew up there to marry a young naturalist with the U.S. Fish and Wildlife Service, has told of their experiences in the wilderness of Alaska in her book, *Two in the Far North.*

CATHER, WILLA
Death Comes for the Archbishop
1927. Knopf.
This episodic tale of the 1850's in the United States desert country concerns two dedicated French priests with missionary zeal for spreading the influence of the Catholic church. Life in the Southwest at this time was primitive and travel across the vast wastelands arduous, but the Indians and Mexicans were in need of spiritual guidance and comfort. Father Latour and Father Vaillant represent the two sides of the early Church's effort to propagate the faith. Bishop Latour, sophisticated, cultured, contemplative, had a desire to perpetuate the power and beauty of the Church as a force in the growing Southwest. Eventually his lifetime dream of a beautiful golden church came true—a cathedral that melted fittingly into the hills and desert landscape. On the other hand, Father Vaillant, a priest of the people, devoted himself to the comfort of individuals and to getting money and material needs for the church. He loved all people and they responded. He never minded asking for gifts for the church or the school they had established. This was how he had acquired two handsome, cream-colored mules, Contento and Angelica, for himself and Father Latour.

The various episodes that compose the story reveal the people. An exciting incident occurred when word came that Father Vaillant lay ill of black measles in a distant village. Father Latour and his guide Jacinto became lost in a snowstorm, had to take refuge in a secret mysterious Indian cave, and lost their mules. When they finally reached Father Vaillant, he was recovering without their ministrations. Character vignettes of Don Antonio who helped provide the money for the Santa Fe Cathedral and of Father Latour and his continual gathering of seeds, herbs, and plants to grow around the house of the priests and the church illuminate the story. Father Vaillant's interview with Gregory XVI and his obtaining the Papal blessing for his valises full of sundry items is a charming touch. So brilliant is the characterization that the Archbishop's death is a moving literary experience.

Mature young people, regardless of their religious affiliation, are interested in this story of the early growth of the United States 29 and the courage and accomplishments of the early Southwestern priests.

The time the two priests stopped at Buck Scales' shack for the night and were warned by his wife that their lives were in danger makes a good story to tell, pages 64–77. Readers impressed by the religious theme could try *Amedeo* by Barclay, *The Nun's Story** by Hulme, and *Keys of the Kingdom** by Cronin, while the historical theme can be continued in *Ramona* by Jackson and *The Oregon Trail* by Parkman.

CATHER, WILLA

My Antonia

1918. Houghton.

When Virginia-born Jim Burden was ten, he saw Bohemia-born Antonia for the first time as they traveled by train across the prairie to their new Nebraska homes—she with her immigrant family and he, newly orphaned, to live with his grandparents. The two families became friends, and Jim helped Antonia learn English. After her father's tragic death, she went into the fields to work, carrying a heavy share of the farm responsibilities. When Jim's grandparents retired to Black Hawk, they found Antonia a job as a hired girl with their neighbors, the Harlings, whose house became a happy center for the young people. Antonia baked treats tirelessly, played their games, and was well loved. Other daughters of foreign-born families came to town to earn money to help their parents. Jim often saw them at the dance pavilion where they met the village boys. He liked them better than the town girls, whose parents did not allow them to go to the pavilion, for the immigrant girls were vigorous and loved a good time. Antonia fell in love with a young passenger conductor who promised to marry her. When she went to join him in Denver, he deserted her and she returned home pregnant and unmarried. She went to work again in the fields and took loving care of her little daughter. Jim, after graduating from college, went East to law school, and twenty years passed before he returned as a successful lawyer. He found that Antonia had married a fine farmer and her large family welcomed him as a dear and familiar friend. Antonia's wonderful love of life and her warmhearted personality were unchanged.

My Antonia is a simple narrative of life on the Nebraska prairies. In the city Antonia found heartbreak and tragedy, but

30

when she returned to the land, her life had meaning and she was at peace. A compelling story of the hardy pioneer people who developed America, the book is not difficult, but the reader needs to be mature enough to appreciate the circumstances and characters. Good readers among senior high school girls enjoy the story.

While recommendation to individual girls may be preferable to class use, book talks can be developed from such incidents as the rattlesnake Jim killed, pages 43–50; the wolves and the wedding party, pages 56–60; or Mr. Shimerdas' dramatic death, pages 92–118. As follow-ups use *O Pioneers!* by Cather, *Winter Wheat* by Walker, *Giants in the Earth** by Rölvaag, and *A Sea of Grass* by Richter.

CERAM, C. W.

Gods, Graves, and Scholars

1951. Knopf.

On the forenoon of an August day A.D. 79 there were signs that Mount Vesuvius was about to erupt and that it would be a disaster of unparalleled dimensions. The sun darkened and smoke filled the sky. As the top of the mountain exploded, volcanic cinder and ash sifted down. Amid crashes and terrifying flashes of light, people ran about screaming and animals fell dead. In the city of Herculaneum an avalanche of mud buried the entire city. At Pompeii there was only a light fall of ash, but the people were choked by sulphur fumes. When the sun came out twenty-eight hours later, Pompeii and Herculaneum had ceased to exist. Almost seventeen hundred years passed before the dead cities were resurrected from oblivion. In 1748, excavations were started at the instigation of Maria Amalia Christine, the Queen of Naples, who was intrigued by the wealth of statuary in the palace gardens.

During the first year of World War I, Lord Carnarvon and Howard Carter began the most important of all the Egyptian excavations. The discovery of the tomb of Tutankhamen was their prize and it was an undertaking that was to take years, for it was not until 1926 that the body of the young Pharaoh was uncovered. One hundred and forty-three pieces of jewelry were discovered inside the mummy's bindings. The rooms of the tomb contained golden couches, statues, alabaster vases, and various shrines. Robbers had invaded some of the rooms but had never reached the royal tomb. This discovery was one of the most exciting and widely publicized in archaeological history.

31

The story of Champollion and the reading of the Rosetta Stone, the decipherment of the inscriptions on the monument of Darius the Great, Leonard Woolley's famous excavations at Ur, and John Lloyd Stephens' discovery of the ruins of a great Mayan city are other fascinating stories vividly told in this book, which has been arranged by cultural area rather than by chronological order.

Mature readers will go on from *Gods, Graves, and Scholars* to more detailed accounts of these various archaeological discoveries. This volume shows the human side of many personalities who have made significant contributions to scholarship.

An exciting and dramatic event to tell is Howard Carter's discovery of the antechamber in the tomb of Tutankhamen, pages 180–87. An amusing story is the purchase by John Lloyd Stephens of the old city of Copán from Don José Maria, pages 346–51. The exploration of the Sacred Well of Chichén Itzá, pages 379–90, is fascinating. *Lost Worlds* by White tells many of the same stories in a simpler but equally interesting manner and can be used with less mature readers. *The Ancient Sun Kingdoms of the Americas* by Von Hagen and *Lost Cities, The Lost Pharaohs*, and *The Bull of Minos* by Cottrell also make good reading. Other stories of archaeological expeditions are *They Wrote on Clay* by Chiera and *Nefertiti Lived Here* by Chubb. Two modern stories of early cultures are colorfully told by Heyerdahl in *Kon-Tiki* and *Aku-Aku*.*

CHASE, MARY ELLEN

Windswept

1941. Macmillan.

The house called Windswept was as permanent, impregnable, and undisturbed by wind, storm, waves, or cold as the rocky Maine headland on which it stood. The people who came to live there seemed to partake of its serenity, and even tragedy could not perturb them for long. On Advent Sunday in 1880, fourteen-year-old John Marston came into the possession of land on which Windswept was to stand. His father, Philip Marston, was buried that day—the victim of a freak shooting accident. Opposed by his stern and possessive grandmother, but aided and encouraged by his father's business partner, James Lassiter, John built the house of his father's dreams. Jan Pisek, a young Bohemian immigrant befriended by Philip, became caretaker of Windswept and John spent many vacations there. The lovable but meticulous housekeeper Mrs. Haskell and, later, Jan's good-natured sister Philomena gave the home a strength and solidity which became part of its charm. When John married Eileen Lassiter, they made their home there. Philip and Ann, their children, loved Windswept, too, and were miserable when they were taken abroad or to New York for the winter. Although the author gives little detail about their lives and skips many years, what she does tell is so skillfully done that the reader feels no break in the story and can picture the wonderful characters clearly.

Sensitive young adults who are good readers enjoy this family chronicle which pivots around a homestead.

The complications of plot and the long span of years make recommendation to individuals preferable to book talks. Similar titles include *The Human Comedy* by Saroyan, *Rain on the Wind** by Macken, and *The John Wood Case** by Suckow.

CHUTE, B. J.

Greenwillow

1956. Dutton.

"Long ago, centuries perhaps, the village of Greenwillow had been stood in the corner and forgotten." This enchanting village seems to exist beyond the boundaries of time and space. It is a place of simple people and ordinary events, where life moves with the rhythm of the seasons. An interesting fact about the village is that it has a church with two pastors, two front doors, and two ways of walking before the Lord. For years Reverend Lapp has preached rousing sermons of hellfire and damnation. Now he is joined by Reverend Birdsong who believes that hell is problematical and that "gladness of heart is the life of man." Reverend Lapp's greatest concern, however, is not his clerical rival, but the Briggs family. For generations the oldest son has been cursed with a call to wander and has left the care and concern of his family to others. Amos Briggs is the current wanderer and he comes home only on occasion, but always stays long enough to assure the delightful addition of another young Briggs. Home responsibilities are shouldered by Gideon, his eldest son, who is determined that he will not marry and leave a wife and family behind when he hears the inevitable call to wander. Reverend Lapp believes that the call comes from the devil and must be exorcised. Reverend Birdsong is concerned with the love that develops between Gideon and Dorrie, a village orphan, who is innocent and good. Even Dorrie's delectable baked goods and 33 loving ways are unable to change Gideon's acceptance of a fate of lonely bachelor wandering. In the end Gideon does hear the call, but it is not to leave; rather, he is to return to the land which he loves. By this time Reverend Birdsong's work is done, and he leaves with the curious feeling that when he turns his back, the village will be gone. His beloved Dorrie and Gideon are to be wed, and even Reverend Lapp seems to have mellowed.

There are humor and gentleness in this story of Greenwillow. The people with their joys and sorrows, their problems and their pleasures, come alive in a pastoral setting. Girls particularly respond to this charming tale of fantasy.

An introduction of the characters and an indication of Gideon's fate are sufficient for a book talk. A dramatic and tellable incident occurs when young Micah goes out at night to confront the devil in the hope of preventing Gideon's departure, pages 187–99. Follow with *A City of Bells* and *Pilgrim's Inn* by Goudge, *Portrait of Jennie** by Nathan, and *Brigadoon* by Lerner and Loewe.

COLLINS, WILKIE

The Moonstone [1878]

Harper.

When the Moonstone, an enormous yellow diamond, had been stolen from the forehead of the Moon-God in a Brahmin shrine, a curse had been placed on those who possessed it. Years later the sacred jewel came into the hands of a British officer, John Herncastle, during a battle with the Indians. He took the gem to England, and at his death it was left to his niece, Rachel Verinder. Despite precautions to guard the house, the Moonstone disappeared the first night Rachel had it. In order to help recover the stone, several persons closely connected with the family were asked to write what they knew about the diamond and the events surrounding its disappearance. Mr. Betteredge, the steward of the household, is the first narrator. Although a bit wordy, he gives a good picture of each person present on the fateful night. Lady Verinder is the mistress of the house and a favorite of the old man. Rachel is her daughter and seems determined to obstruct the police investigation. Franklin Blake, the young cousin who delivered the diamond to Rachel on her birthday, is in love with her. Godfrey Ablewhite has also come to help celebrate the birthday and asks Rachel to marry him. Rosanna Spearman, the second maid, has a prison record and so comes under suspicion. Miss

Clark, a poor relative of the Verinders and a self-righteous do-gooder, throws more light on the mystery as the second narrator. Mr. Matthew Bruff, the Verinder family lawyer and the third storyteller, prevents what would have been an unfortunate marriage between Rachel and Godfrey. He is warned that within a year the Moonstone will reappear, and this time the Indians who are trying to regain it will not fail. Franklin Blake picks up the narrative at this point. He decides that his future happiness depends upon the solution of the diamond's mysterious disappearance. He finally unravels the mystery and also wins the love of Rachel.

Because of the involved plot, this book appeals to young people of mature reading ability who enjoy interesting character delineation and an unusual technique for creating suspense.

A brief outline of events leading up to the stone's disappearance will "sell" the book to readers. *The Woman in White* by Collins and *The Nine Tailors* by Sayers are good companion titles.

CONRAD, JOSEPH

Lord Jim [1900]

Doubleday.

We all dream of being heroes, but in a real-life crisis how would we act? Jim, too, had had his heroic imaginings but until his early twenties, when he became chief mate on the *Patna*, there had been no real opportunity to test or prove his courage. The old tramp steamer was forging her way across the Indian Ocean with eight hundred Mecca-bound pilgrims aboard, when one night a collision with something submerged tore a hole in the ship. The captain, convinced that the *Patna* would sink and knowing that there were not enough lifeboats for all the passengers, ordered the officers to lower a boat so that they could get safely away before the approaching storm struck. Jim scorned their cowardice and was determined to go down with the ship, but suddenly and impulsively he jumped overboard to join the officers. The boat was sighted by another ship the next day, and the men were brought into port where they reported the sinking of the *Patna*. Later they learned that their ship had been picked up by a French gunboat and towed into Aden. After the painful inquiry which followed, Jim and the other officers had their certificates canceled and could never work on a ship again. At this point Captain Marlow, narrator of the story, became interested **35** in Jim and found work for him with a ship chandler. After about six months some reference to the *Patna* made him leave the job and move on, even though no one knew his connection with the ship. This happened again and again until finally Marlow helped locate a place for Jim in Patusan, a remote spot in the Celebes. It was two years before Marlow could stop to see him, but he found him well established, with the love and respect of the natives, a house of his own, and a part-white girl named Jewel as his wife. He was watched over and protected by a faithful servant and his devoted wife, but neither of them could save him from his fate.

A fine character novel, *Lord Jim* requires that the reader bring understanding and intelligence for a full appreciation of the story. Mature readers will meditate on the moral involvement and eagerly read of Jim's pursuit of a compensating action.

For a book talk use pages 10–31, 83–111, a description of the scene on the ship when Jim makes his fateful decision. *Away All Boats* by Dodson has many examples of courage, while *The Red Badge of Courage** by Crane tells of another young man and his reaction to a crisis.

COUSTEAU, JACQUES-YVES, and DUGAN, JAMES

Captain Cousteau's Underwater Treasury

1959. Harper.

Vivid moments of high adventure have been selected for this collection of more than fifty stories of the experiences of divers, submariners, and underwater scientists. Tom Eadie, winner of a Congressional Medal of Honor, tells the story of Fred Michels and his own role in bringing up the bodies from the *S-4,* a submarine sunk in a winter collision off Provincetown, Massachusetts. Eadie's rescue of Michels, who had been pinned in the wreckage, is a tense, dramatic story which ends happily when Michels is transferred to the Naval Hospital in a decompression chamber. "California Gold Divers," by Richard Anderson, is a breezy account of diving for gold in the American and Yuba rivers in the area of California's Mother Lode. William Lalor, Jr., one of the crew of the *Nautilus,* the first United States nuclear-powered submarine, reports the exciting moment when the *Nautilus* reached the North Pole. Traveling in comparative comfort and with great ease, the submarine accomplished two goals long sought by those who sail the seas: the opening of a route for rapid voyages between the Atlantic and the Pacific oceans and the reaching of the

North Pole by ship. "Trapped!" tells the submarine experience of Sidney Hart, a Royal Navy stoker in World War II. The *Truant*, on duty in the Adriatic, ran aground on the bottom of an enemy harbor after she had torpedoed a ship at anchor. With an enemy destroyer directly above her, she lay still until the captain decided to try to gun her out of the mud. Miraculously the motors hummed and worked the sub free; the keel scraped on the bottom as she crept out sternwise. During World War II Peter Keeble was Fleet Salvage Officer in the Mediterranean area. Called on to clear the Italian port of Massawa on the Red Sea, Keeble, who had been underwater only once before, did the diving. "Top Secret Dive" is the dramatic story of the diving operation to recover a secret device from a sunken German submarine. Moving among dead bodies, at a depth of 230 feet, Keeble accomplished his mission and miraculously returned safely.

From Darwin and Dumas to Rachel Carson and Jules Verne, these are narratives with humor, suspense, or beautiful descriptions of the wonderland beneath the sea. Whether the reader accompanies William Beebe in the bathysphere to observe marine life or explores the sunken *Andrea Doria* with Ramsey Parkes as he takes photographs, he discovers fascinating facts about the ocean and its contents. Boys especially like this book.

Almost any of the stories could be used for a book talk. "Trapped!," page 187; "Raising the *Leonardo da Vinci*," page 289; and "The Consular Agent," page 298, are outstanding. Many of these stories are excerpts from books worth reading in their entirety. *I Like Diving* by Eadie, *Undersea Patrol* by Young, *The Edge of the Sea* by Carson, *Submarine!* by Beach, *Ordeal by Water* by Keeble, *Lady with a Spear* by Clark, and *Half Mile Down* by Beebe are a few.

COVELLO, LEONARD, and D'AGOSTINO, GUIDO
The Heart Is the Teacher
1958. McGraw-Hill.
"This kid is a tough one, Mr. Covello, but we'll straighten him out," were the words of a boy who a few months earlier had been on the verge of killing his brother's murderers. However, Nat had talked with his principal, Leonard Covello, and his English teacher, Austin Works, and the two men had straightened *him* out. For forty-five years Mr. Covello worked as a teacher, adviser, and principal with boys in the poorest sections of New York City. 37

He understood their problems because he had faced similar ones in his own adolescence. He had come to East Harlem in New York City from Italy when he was nine years of age. The noisy, crowded tenement where the family lived and their inability to speak English made life difficult. They did not succumb to homesickness, however, because they soon found in this new land an element of hopefulness which had been lacking in the old country. Leonard found that teachers played an important role in his life, but he also turned frequently for sympathy, encouragement, and understanding to Mary Accurso, a neighbor girl who recognized his problems as an immigrant. When he graduated from high school, he was awarded a Pulitzer scholarship for study at Columbia. He was interested in teaching, and Mary shared his enthusiasm. As soon as he had a steady income, he and Mary were married, but their happiness was brief since she died a year later. After experience in intelligence work in World War I and a brief sojourn in the business world, Mr. Covello returned to teaching because he thought it was so important. He felt that teachers must be interested in and work with pupils beyond the classroom, and he devoted his life to the boys others regarded as incorrigible delinquents. He found in Rose, Mary's sister, the same enthusiasm and interest in his work which his first wife had had. After a time they were married, and Rose decided to go back to college and become a teacher also. Later, when she found that she could help her husband more in his many projects if she were not tied to a job, she gave up her own career. Through affection and guidance Mr. Covello has proved that wild, rebellious boys can be turned into useful and productive citizens. He feels that the best schools are those deeply rooted in their communities and that the pupils must find a place for themselves and feel a responsibility to their neighborhood and to the world at large.

Young people particularly interested in teaching or other professions concerned with youth are deeply impressed by this man's life and work. His enthusiasm is catching.

Almost every chapter is a warm human-interest story of a life Leonard Covello touched, some boy who was directed to a useful career. Nat's story on pages 185–87 or Lupino's on pages 198–202 are two examples. Other biographies of dedicated teachers who have achieved success in unusual situations are *The Thread That Runs So True* by Stuart and *Miracle in the Mountains** by Kane. *Good Morning, Miss Dove* by Patton and *Good-bye, Mr. Chips* by Hilton are novels about teachers.

CRANE, STEPHEN

The Red Badge of Courage [1895]

(Appleton) Meredith.

Fascinated by the glamor and excitement of uniforms and combat, a young farm boy, Henry Fleming, eagerly enlisted as a Union private during the Civil War. He found himself in a raw, new regiment, eventually bored by inaction but frightened by the conversations about fighting. The men bragged at first about the heroic deeds they would do, but as time passed and they saw no action, they became less and less certain of their glorious conduct under battle stress. Restlessness, loneliness, and apprehension passed in waves over Henry. How would he react to the command to charge? When the first call to march came, everyone was hilarious, but gradually their enthusiasm dulled as their feet began to hurt and they grew tired and hungry. Suddenly the hours of waiting were over and they were fighting. The battle was fierce at first; panic struck the men as the enemy pushed them back. Gradually one man after another took to his heels and Henry, too, turned to run away. He lost his gun but he kept going and soon lost touch with his regiment. Overcome by remorse and the shame of cowardice, he envied the wounds of combatants whom he joined behind the battle zone. Ironically he achieved his "red badge of courage" when another retreating soldier hit him over the head with his rifle in a moment of panic. After finding his direction and reassembling his courage, Henry rejoined his outfit. All round them there were pockets of firing; then the battle broke out again in earnest. Dog-tired and battle weary, the men were inclined to hide behind trees and let the enemy hunt them. Suddenly a hatred of the victorious enemy welled up in Henry, and from then on he fought like a wild cat, gaining the epithet "war devil." Remorse faded as he retrieved the regimental flag from the dying color sergeant and helped rally the men. With a new sense of assurance he faced the future as a man who has "been to touch the great death, and found that, after all, it was but the great death."

A living, readable story of the effect of war on a sensitive mind, this classic has literary excellence plus sound psychological insights. Both boys and girls are deeply moved by the book. It has the perpetual reality of youth with its resilience and resourcefulness. The mother's parting advice, pages 9–11, could have been given in any century, and the boy's progression to self-understanding is unbelievably realistic.

Young people who have seen the movie version need little encouragement to read the book, but a talk can be based upon Henry's reaction to his friend's death, pages 107–15, or on the regimental charge, Chapter 19. Other possibilities are the occasion of Henry's going to war, pages 6–9, and the flight before enemy guns, pages 65–72. *April Morning** by Fast is a similar story. Books about personal courage, such as *Death Be Not Proud** by Gunther and *Marching On* by Boyd, might be suggested for further reading. Foote's *With Sherman to the Sea* tells of a thirteen-year-old drummer boy's experiences in the Civil War. *The Bridge at Andau** by Michener and *Boy on the Rooftop* by Szabo are accounts of teen-age freedom fighters in Hungary.

CRONIN, A. J.

Keys of the Kingdom

1941. Little.

This story of Father Francis Chisholm, a dedicated Catholic priest, begins when he was about nine years of age. He lost his parents as the indirect result of religious persecution and was taken in by his warmhearted Aunt Polly and her husband. They sent him to Holywell to be educated, and when he was a young man, he decided to devote his life to his religion. Francis' seminary days were spent at San Moralis in Spain, and his first appointment after ordination was to the colliery village of Shalesley where, at last, he had a chance to fight for human souls. Here he clashed with Father Kezer, his superior, over providing recreational facilities for the young people of the parish. His second curacy brought him to a familiar city parish in Tynecastle where, with the help of boyhood friends, he unmasked the hoax of Charlotte Neily, a hysterical miraclemonger. From this post he moved in 1902 to his real lifework—a vicariate in China where he found, not the flourishing mission he had been promised, but instead the remnants of a crumbling church with no congregation. Realizing that the people needed medical aid, he opened a small dispensary and gradually made friends and won real converts to the Church. The story of Father Chisholm's years in China is a dramatic one. When he saved the life of Mr. Chia's son, the grateful parent gave him valuable property where he could build a school for the orphan children he was collecting. Three nuns—the haughty Maria-Veronica, Clotilde, and Martha —came out to help educate and care for these children. Famine

40

and civil war tested the courage of Father Chisholm and his co-workers, and at one time he and his Protestant missionary friends were captured and tortured by bandits before making a daring escape. Finally replaced by two younger priests, he came home, weary but indomitable, to spend his remaining years in his native Scotland.

Senior high school boys and girls, regardless of their religious affiliation, read this novel of dedication to a purpose with enjoyment.

For book talks use the incident at the beginning of Part III, "The Unsuccessful Curate," when Father Chisholm manages to establish a recreation center in a mining town, or his discovery, Section IV, Part II, of a small Catholic church established in 1625 in a remote Chinese village and sustained by the leadership of devoted Chinese priests to the present time. The destruction of the gun, pages 257–71, or the capture and torture by the bandits, pages 296–315, provide exciting action but are not typical of the whole book. An account of Father Chisholm's early days in China, pages 149–60, gives a good idea of the general theme. *The Small Woman** by Burgess is a true story of missionary life in China with equally dramatic events and similar evidences of self-sacrifice and devotion. Another account of a missionary is Del Rey's *Her Name Is Mercy,* which is particularly useful with Catholic girls. Other fiction stories featuring priests are *The Little World of Don Camillo* by Guareschi and *The Father Brown Omnibus* by Chesterton.

CROSS, WILBUR
Challengers of the Deep
1959. Sloane.
The complicated atomic submarine of today had its beginnings as far back in history as the reign of Alexander the Great, who went below the surface of the sea in a barrel equipped with glass ports. In this book Mr. Cross traces the development of the underwater craft from that time to the present. Great losses of life and many tragic failures were the price of eventual success. Officers in the Continental Army, in their desperation to strike back at the British fleet lying in New York Harbor, decided to gamble on an unlikely-looking contraption developed in 1775 by David Bushnell, a student at Yale College. Built to accommodate a single operator and a charge of gunpowder, the wooden submarine

Turtle resembled a large egg which could be propelled underwater. By submerging beneath the wooden hull of an enemy ship, the submariner could fasten a screw to the vessel, activate a time-bomb torpedo attached to the screw, and then escape to safety before the gunpowder exploded. Thus the first wartime submarine attack was made by the *Turtle* against the British on Staten Island on September 6, 1776. Little interest was manifested in submarines, however, for the next hundred years. By 1904 experimentation had resumed, and scarcely a year passed by without a serious accident or loss of life in submarines. The United States had good luck up to 1915, but then disaster seemed to accumulate. In 1920 the *S-5* plunged to the bottom in 183 feet of water off the Delaware Capes on a shakedown cruise. The commander knew that the *S-5* was 231 feet long and that if he could raise the stern, it could project above the surface. The odds against success were 1,000 to 1, but the race against time was successful and many of the crew were saved. The dramatic and tragic account of the *S-4* tells why America was aroused to make improvements in design which make today's submarines almost foolproof. When the *S-4* was rammed by a surface ship and went down, a salvage crew was quickly on the job. The sub's control room had been flooded, and the only sound of life came from the torpedo room. Weather conditions made the rescue difficult, and when one of the divers became fouled in the wreckage, precious time was lost. The men in the sub died before they could be rescued. Sir Hubert Wilkins' attempt to explore the underwater arctic regions in 1931 as well as battle stories of United States World War II submarines are included. An important chapter recounts the persistent struggle of Admiral Rickover to develop the atomic submarine. The historic and exciting trips of the *Nautilus* and the *Skate* in 1958 under the polar ice are also a part of the absorbing story of man's efforts to travel below the surface of the sea.

Boys from eighth grade up, interested in war stories or adventure, enjoy this well-told history and want to go on to others.

Material for book talks is abundant. Chapter 7 has the story of the disabled *S-5;* Chapters 8 and 9 cover the more tragic account of the *S-4;* and Chapter 11 contains the story of the *Squalus.* For follow-ups use *Submarine!* and *Around the World Submerged* by Beach, *Men under the Sea* by Ellsberg, *Surface at the Pole* by Calvert, and Nautilus *90 North** by Anderson, or such scientific books as *Seven Miles Down* by Piccard and *2000 Fathoms Down* by Houot.

CUTOLO, SALVATORE R.

Bellevue Is My Home

1956. Doubleday.

July 28, 1945, began as an uneventful Saturday, but ended as a catastrophic milestone in New York City history. Betty Lou Oliver went to work as usual in the world's tallest structure, the Empire State Building, and assumed her accustomed post as operator in one of the high-speed elevators which make activity in the skyscraper possible. Poor visibility disappointed tourists who had come to New York to take pictures from the building's observation platform. Suddenly, without warning, a B-25 bomber hurtled out of the fog and crashed into the seventy-eighth and seventy-ninth floors, slicing cables and sending Betty plunging eighty floors to the subbasement. When she regained consciousness, the young woman found herself in Bellevue Hospital, where she began a painful and courageous struggle back to health. Whether flooded with patients from such a disaster or admitting a sick vagrant from the Bowery, Bellevue's facilities are ready to demonstrate that it is one of the finest municipal hospitals in the world. Covering five square city blocks and capable of housing more than 2,500 patients, it consists of not one but fifteen buildings. Despite its popular association with mental cases, Bellevue is more than a center for psychiatric rehabilitation. Dr. Cutolo explains that there is sterilized equipment kept on hand that can be arranged in and around a taxi in case of an emergency birth occurring while the patient is on the way to the hospital; that in the emergency ward, if there are more doctors than nurses available, the doctors turn in and do what must be done; that when an emergency call comes, the hospital has a speed-with-caution rule that applies even to the ambulances. Seven bells rung three times in a row is a disaster signal, and the whole hospital girds itself for action. During big celebrations Bellevue always has an emergency unit on hand just in case. As is to be expected in a large city, the emergencies may be bullets, burns, jump victims, accidents, attempted suicides, near-murder victims, coronaries, alcoholics, psychotics, and the like. This hospital is the largest medical teaching center in the world, attracting students and doctors from everywhere, as Vienna, Paris, and Edinburgh once did. Dr. Cutolo, who has virtually made it his home for more than thirty years, has guided the institution's development and seen methods and facilities improve with the growth of medical research. As the story of the hospital unfolds, bits of Dr. Cutolo's private life appear: his father's death during a fifteen-minute nap, a brief respite before he saw his office patients; the death of his first wife after a kidney-stone operation when no one in Bellevue could do anything to save her; his pride in his son who became an Air Force lieutenant; his "testing" and holding-off from marrying his second wife for fear she could not live with the type of working doctor he was.

This book interests embryo nurses and doctors and any curious-minded boy or girl who wishes to know how medical and psychiatric treatments are administered inside and outside great hospitals.

There are many stories that can be told. The Betty Oliver case, pages 121–26; the 1947 smallpox outbreak, Chapter 13; and a brief description of facilities, pages 58–60, are a few suggestions. For further reading about doctors or hospitals use *Bamboo Hospital* by Read, *The Doctors Mayo* by Clapesattle, *Over My Dead Body** by Opie, and *The Man Next to Me* by Barker.

DAVIS, BURKE

To Appomattox

1959. (Rinehart) Holt.

By the first of April, 1865, the Union Army under Grant threatened to encircle the Confederate capital and cut off the last railroad connections. Food was scarce, and horses and mules as well as humans were on scanty rations. Warehouses converted into makeshift hospitals were crowded with the wounded, and so many soldiers had deserted that in the trenches men were twenty feet apart. Jefferson Davis knew the end was near and sent his wife and family to North Carolina. In describing the first nine days in April, the author moves from one participant or observer to another to present a vivid picture of the closing days of the Civil War through the eyes of officers, gunners, infantrymen, and civilians. By April 2 the Union forces had swept toward Petersburg, and General Lee warned President Davis and his associates to evacuate. The next day Richmond was burning, and local rowdies were pillaging army stores and warehouses. As the Union troops entered the city, they offered protection to the southern women who remained and began putting out the fires. On April 4, President Lincoln reached Richmond by boat, talked with southern leaders, and responded to the cheers of the freed slaves. Retreats, skirmishes, and desertions plagued the dwindling Confederate troops, but Lee was determined not to surrender. Eventually defeat seemed inevitable despite the willingness of many southern soldiers to fight, and Lee agreed to meet Grant on April 9 at the Appomattox Court House to discuss terms of surrender.

The day-by-day method of presentation and the use of actual accounts make this a particularly gripping book for boys interested in the Civil War period.

It is preferable to recommend the title to mature readers individually than to use it for a book talk. *This Hallowed Ground* by Catton, *The Gray Captain** by Wheelwright, and *The Blue and the Gray* by Commager are a few suggestions for further reading.

DICKENS, CHARLES

Great Expectations [1850]

Dodd.

Philip Pirrip, known as Pip, was orphaned when he was a small child and grudgingly "brought up by hand" by his older sister and her husband. They lived in a small English village in the marsh country, only twenty miles from the sea where a prison ship was anchored. One Christmas Eve when Pip was visiting the cemetery, he was accosted by a rough-looking stranger who demanded that the boy bring him food and a file to cut the iron chain which bound his leg. Pip obliged, and the escaped convict promised Pip that some day he would reward him for his help. Some time later Pip was sent on an errand to Satis House, the gloomy mansion of the odd Miss Havisham. Here he found an old white-haired lady in a darkened house where all the clocks had been stopped on the day her bridegroom failed to appear for the wedding ceremony. The only ray of sunshine in the gloomy place was lovely Estelle—cool and haughty. Miss Havisham had adopted the little girl, hoping that eventually she would break the hearts of many men as a kind of repayment for the old lady's own suffering. Pip was invited to come to the house regularly, and Estelle began early to make the opposite sex unhappy, for she enjoyed teasing her shy playmate. At fourteen Pip was apprenticed to his brother-in-law Joe and spent four years learning the trade of blacksmith. One day Mr. Jaggers, a lawyer from London whom Pip had seen at Miss Havisham's, came to tell Pip that he was to inherit a handsome sum of money and must prepare himself by becoming a gentleman. He was to go to London where arrangements had been made for a relative of Miss Havisham to tutor him. Although the benefactor's name was not revealed, Pip thought that it must be the old lady herself, but **45** later he discovered that it was the old convict, Magwitch, whom he had befriended. Magwitch, after regaining his freedom, had worked very hard to get the money to make Pip a gentleman and had risked great dangers to return to England and enjoy the realization of his dream. Although Pip felt only abhorrence and repugnance toward the old man and was determined to get him out of the country and end their relationship, he recognized the great debt he owed him. To complicate matters, Pip discovered that Magwitch was Estelle's unknown father. Pip made elaborate plans to smuggle the old convict to France, but the plan failed and his benefactor was taken to prison, tried, and condemned to die. Before he was executed, he died in prison and his fortune was forfeited to the Crown, leaving Pip penniless again.

Young people who are good readers and like long, adventurous, romantic novels enjoy this book.

A good book talk could consist of the introduction of the main characters and the chapter describing Miss Havisham's unhappy situation. This story can be a good introduction to Dickens and can be followed by *Oliver Twist* and *David Copperfield*. *Wuthering Heights* by Brontë is also a good follow-up.

DITMARS, RAYMOND L.

Thrills of a Naturalist's Quest

1932. Macmillan.

Whether he was hunting fer-de-lances in Honduras, collecting copperheads in Massachusetts, stalking rare frogs in the lowlands of the Savannah River, or transporting king cobras or pythons by public conveyance, Raymond Ditmars had an exciting adventure and has told about it with suspense and humor. Even as a small boy he was interested in reptiles and collected them. As time went on, this became a serious hobby. His sympathetic parents allowed him to keep his specimens at home, and with his modest earnings from the museum where he went to work after graduation, he began to fill the cages in a spareroom. Field trips and association with other naturalists spurred him on. A human-interest story about him appeared in a newspaper and brought numerous requests for information on how to care for snakes, especially sick ones. Associating with other herpetologists, Raymond traded specimens until his collection rivaled that of the Central Park Zoo. His large and varied assortment, which eventually was the basis of the collection at the Bronx Zoo, brought

him a job there. Appointed curator of reptiles in 1899, and later head of the department of mammals, he was able to devote full time to his real interest. In building the collection he traveled a great deal, and in addition he studied the habits of his charges and wrote several books on snakes. A pioneer in collecting venom for use in preparing snake-bite serums, he helped determine potencies and developed techniques for counteracting snake bites which have been accepted throughout the world. Working with a large collection of animals at a time when display techniques were still unperfected, Dr. Ditmars made experiments to discover which reptiles could be kept together safely, what kind of food and shelter certain rare specimens required, and how careful animal keepers should be in handling their charges.

Boys and girls with an interest in biology enjoy the gripping episodes told in simple, nontechnical language, as well as the picture of a great zoo during its development.

There are many incidents worth recounting: the time Dr. Ditmars helped get the old skin off a boa when he was visiting the zoo during his lunch hour, pages 32–39; the story of getting a python for his collection, pages 65–67; finding special food for a rare reptile in Rio, pages 78–84; the hilarious account of the pink snake and the lizard with two tails lost in the Plaza Hotel, pages 87–91. Follow-up titles would be *Strange Animals I Have Known* by Ditmars, *My Zoo Family* by Martini, *The World of Amphibians and Reptiles* by Mertens, *Zoo in My Luggage* by Durrell, *Snakes Alive, and How They Live* by Pope, and *Ant Hill Odyssey* by Mann.

DOOLEY, THOMAS A.

Deliver Us from Evil

1956. Farrar.

Operations "Passage to Freedom" and "Cockroach" were American attempts begun late in 1954 to evacuate refugees from Communist-controlled North Vietnam to the safety of Saigon in the south. Instrumental in helping these unfortunate and bewildered people reach freedom was a young Navy doctor, Lieutenant Thomas A. Dooley, in charge of temporary refugee camps near Haiphong. According to the Geneva agreement, the Communists would take control of the area by May, 1955, but citizens desiring to leave their homes could do so before that time. The difficulties and reprisals thrown in their way were clear violations of the treaty terms and multiplied the problems of an already staggering task. During the evacuation period, Dr. Dooley helped 47 process 600,000 homeless people—men, women, and children whose desire for religious freedom and a chance for a new life outweighed the strong bonds of land and family ties. With a knowledge of both French and Vietnamese, Dooley set up camps for the fleeing people, providing food, water, and medical care. Battling against the Communist propagandists who claimed that Americans were monsters, Dooley emphasized in his work that only because of the U.S. Navy was he able to minister to their dire needs. In describing the abject miseries of the hungry, sick travelers, the author mentions the terrible tortures inflicted by the revengeful Communist Vietminh leaders. The near miracles he performed in treating maimed children as well as mutilated teen-agers and adults went far in establishing him as a symbol of American good will. Red tape, official channels, and protocol were thrown aside as he pushed through his program of assistance. American companies responded generously to his pleas for drugs, medicines, vitamins, and soap. When these were given to the people, the words, "Dai La My-Quoc Vien-Tro (This is American aid)" were said. When the evacuation period ended and Dooley's work was completed, he was decorated by the South Vietnam President as one "beloved by a whole nation."

Both boys and girls interested in medicine and stories of courageous lives are attracted to this simply written account of a young doctor working under extreme hardships. His own losing but heroic battle against cancer adds a certain ironic note to this diary of his brilliant performance in Indo-China.

Base book talks on the background of the division of Vietnam, page 58; the problems of camp life, pages 65–77; and the work of Madame Ngai and her remarkable orphanage, pages 156–72. Similar medical titles include *Doctor Hap** by Burke, *Prophet in the Wilderness** by Hagedorn, *The Night They Burned the Mountain* and *The Edge of Tomorrow* by Dooley. Novels relating to American successes and failures abroad include *The Ugly American** by Lederer and *A Bell for Adano** by Hersey.

DOSTOEVSKY, FYODOR

Crime and Punishment; translated by Constance Garnett [1866]

Macmillan.

The story opens with the poor student Raskolnikov, clad in rags, entering the street from his garret and making his way to his pawnbroker's apartment—a place he has evidently had under surveillance for months. He is determined to commit murder. Loathing himself and his plot, he is impelled to proceed with his carefully thought-out plan and kills not only the old pawnbroker but her gentle half-sister Lizaveta who happens by at the wrong moment. He has time only to take the woman's purse and to stuff his pockets with jewelry when he is terrified by a sound at the door and flees, narrowly missing other men who have come to the apartment. He is apparently not suspected at first by the police, but his queer actions and obsessive desire for information about the crime make even his friends begin to question his connection with the murders. The rest of the story involves the punishment for the crime. Raskolnikov endeavors to lead a normal life even though guilt and fear obsess him. One night he comes upon the scene of an accident and sees that Marmeladov, a man he had known slightly, has been run over by horses and a carriage. He accompanies the injured man home and gives the man's wife twenty roubles which his mother had given him. This is the occasion for his first meeting with Sonia, Marmeladov's daughter, who had become a prostitute in order to help support the family. Raskolnikov's mother and sister had spoiled him, sacrificing in order to give him money. His sister had even agreed to a distasteful marriage which would mean increased financial assistance to her brother, but Raskolnikov is able to talk her out of this arrangement when she and their mother come to St. Petersburg and he introduces her to one of his own friends. During this time he surmises that the police suspect him, and he feels the net closing around him. He severs his connections with his family and friends, finally concluding that he faces two alternatives: suicide or confession. He decides to confess to Sonia and she persuades him to go to the police. When he is sentenced to eight years of hard labor in Siberia, the devoted Sonia follows him there to help him in his regeneration and to marry him when he is released.

This long, involved novel with several subplots is only for the mature reader. It is an interesting psychological study of a sensitive person driven to crime and suffering mental and physical aftereffects.

A book talk summarizing the first chapters, including the preparations for the crime but omitting the actual murders, might be presented to an advanced group. Discussion groups would be a far more interesting use, since the moral values involved are sure to produce differences of opinion. Otherwise recommend the novel to individuals in the library. This book could follow the 49 reading of *Anna Karenina** by Tolstoi. Other stories of crime and punishment are *An American Tragedy* by Dreiser, *Romola* by Eliot, and *The Marble Faun* by Hawthorne. *Les Misérables* by Hugo might also be suggested.

DUMAS, ALEXANDRE

The Three Musketeers [1844]

Dodd.

When D'Artagnan was eighteen years of age, his father gave him a horse, fifteen crowns, a letter of introduction to M. de Treville, commander of the King's Musketeers, plus some good advice, and sent him to make his fortune at the court of Louis XIII of France. Before he had been in Paris long, he had managed to offend three of the King's Musketeers, and duels were arranged. When he met the first, Athos, he learned that his other two challengers, Aramis and Porthos, were Athos' seconds. Just as the duel was about to begin, five guardsmen from Cardinal Richelieu happened along, and a free-for-all took place from which the Musketeers and D'Artagnan came away victorious. As a result the four became bosom friends although D'Artagnan could not become a Musketeer until there was a vacancy. The intrigue which furnishes the action of the story was the result of Cardinal Richelieu's having been spurned by Anne of Austria, wife of Louis XIII. Humiliated, the Cardinal tried to discredit Anne with the King and thus get his revenge. The Duke of Buckingham, the most powerful man in England, loved Anne, and Richelieu wanted to prove that Anne returned his love. One of the Queen's ladies had arranged a meeting between the Duke and the Queen, and at that time Anne had given her admirer twelve diamond aiguillettes, a present to her from the King. The Cardinal seemed to have spies everywhere, and when he learned of the Queen's gift to Buckingham, he commissioned an accomplice in England, the Countess de Winter, to steal two of the aiguillettes and bring them back to him. He had the King plan a celebration and persuaded him to ask the Queen to wear the aiguillettes. The manner in which D'Artagnan became embroiled in the conspiracy and saved the day for the Queen is suspenseful and exciting. Although D'Artagnan is the heroic protagonist of the main plot and the three Musketeers have a part in it, each of these gallant gentlemen has the lead in an interesting subplot.

Good readers, especially boys, who like an exciting, well-told story with historical background enjoy this book very much. The loose morals of the period make having a mistress an accepted practice, which even as young a man as D'Artagnan took for granted.

A summary of the first part of the story is sufficient to interest potential readers. This story is continued in *Twenty Years After* and *The Vicomte de Bragelonne*. *Under the Red Robe* by Weyman, *The Count of Monte Cristo* and *The Man in the Iron Mask* by Dumas, and *The White Company* by Doyle are also good follow-ups. *The Moneyman* by Costain and *Désirée* by Selinko are stories of French life at court in different periods of history.

EDMONDS, WALTER
Drums along the Mohawk
1936. Little.

To the settlers of the German Flats along the Mohawk River, the Continental Congress and the Continental Army seemed far away and indifferent to their pleas for ammunition and supplies and their fear of Indian raids. Farmers, not soldiers, the men took up arms to protect their families, not to fight the war in a remote campaign with the regular army. In spite of the impending danger, Gilbert Martin persuaded Magdelana Borst to marry him, and with their possessions and new cow they moved to the Deerfield settlement in the Mohawk Valley. Like many young families of that area Magdelana and her husband took pleasure in their humble cabin and their developing farm. Gilbert was reluctant to go to military muster, and yet his pride in his equipment prodded him into attendance. Scouts had kept a close watch of the surrounding territory so that they could give a warning if the Indians came. Through the day-to-day activities of the Deerfield settlers the reader follows the course of the war, experiencing the innumerable raids of the Destructives, the burning of the cabins and crops, the assaults on the fort which sheltered them. The tough, fatherly German colonial leader Herkimer, the self-seeking Butler and Johnson, the inordinately proud "White Indian" Joseph Brant—all play their roles along with the fictional characters. At last the successful march of the militia commanded by Marinus Willet led to Butler's death and the rout of his army. If it had not been for the tough independence of the settlers, and their hatred for the arrogant British and the Indians, this territory might have been lost to the American colonies. **51**

This is an adult novel which gives a vivid picture of one segment of the American Revolution. There are brutalities toward captives, torture, scalping, abuse of women, and reprisals of the militia. These are harsh moments and frank scenes, but this is an authentic picture of frontier life and fighting from 1776 to 1783. Recommend this book only to mature readers; they like it very much.

One incident for telling is Adam Helmer's race to warn the settlers at Andrustown of the coming of the Indians, pages 376–82. John Brick's *The King's Rangers* gives a sympathetic account of Butler's Rangers and the loyalists in the Mohawk Valley during the Revolution. Other realistic pictures of the war are *Rabble in Arms* and *Arundel* by Roberts, and *Sycamore Men* by Taylor.

ELLIS, WILLIAM D.

The Bounty Lands

1952. World.

Tom Woodbridge was only nineteen when he decided to leave the farm he operated for Elnathan Shuldane near Concord, Massachusetts, and go west. His only inheritance was a fading, creased document—a Bounty Land warrant for one hundred acres in the Northwest Territory—which had been his father's payment for service in the Continental Army. Because the government land survey was not completed, and some of the ex-soldiers were anxious to cash their warrants, many unscrupulous men like Shuldane bought hundreds of these Bounty Land warrants for less acreage than the amount specified by the documents. Tom refused to accept less acreage for his warrant and headed west with the document and two Bedford pigs rescued from Shuldane's dinner table—precious possessions that were the result of twenty years of careful breeding. In Mesopotamia, Shuldane's tract west of Fort Pitt, Tom started off on the wrong foot with his neighbors. Angered because he could not have the first land he chose, he hotheadedly made an offer and traded his warrant for only twenty acres located six miles from the other settlers. His refusal to request the aid of the other men in building his cabin or to help build the blockhouse resulted in mutual enmity. The atmosphere changed when Tom burned down his own partly finished cabin as a warning signal to the villagers of an Indian raid. Thanks to his sacrifice, the settlers reached safety in the blockhouse and were more than willing to help rebuild the Woodbridge cabin. In the meantime, Shuldane had sent his daughter Veronica, whom Tom had known in the East, and his lawyer Blair to look over affairs in Mesopotamia. When circumstances forced Tom and Veronica to spend the night at his cabin, public opinion compelled them to marry. Shuldane was infuriated at this, and when the government required him to return a thousand acres of land because of an incorrect survey, he included Tom's land. This left Tom as a squatter, but his Bounty warrant was returned to him. He continued to raise Bedford hogs and joined the government surveying crew, sending Veronica to live in the village while he was away. Months of hard work and a bit of clever maneuvering resulted in Tom's possession of 140 acres. During his absence Veronica had gone back east for the birth of their daughter. When she returned home, she and Tom worked together in a variety of difficult situations to build up their rare strain of pigs, virtually unknown in that part of the country.

This richly detailed novel of frontier life in early nineteenth-century America appeals to mature young adults who are willing to follow an involved story line. The feeling for the period and the reality of the characters reward the conscientious reader. The love interest attracts older girls, while boys enjoy the action and suspense of the Indian raids.

The complex plot may make recommendation to individual students preferable to book talk presentation. However, the occasion of Tom's warning the settlement of an Indian raid by burning his own newly built cabin might be used, pages 44–60. American historical novels of similar depth include *Drums along the Mohawk** by Edmonds, *The Yankee from Tennessee** by Gerson, and *Jonathan Blair: Bounty Lands Lawyer* by Ellis.

FAST, HOWARD

April Morning
1961. Crown.

Woven into this fictional account of the opening of the American Revolution is the picture of a father and son who have not understood each other and the story of the boy's first encounter with war. The action takes place in Lexington, Massachusetts, within a twenty-four-hour period beginning on April 18, 1775. Adam, who was just fifteen, had been scolded by his father so often that he felt a good word had never been said to him by the older man. Adam's chief confidante was his grandmother, who   **53** understood both his dour father Moses and the restless teen-ager. That night the sound of racing hoofs roused the village. All the men and boys of the town gathered at the Common to hear what news the rider carried. He reported that the British Army had marched out of Boston, undoubtedly headed for Concord and its supply of ammunition. The order was given for the militia to assemble, and more volunteers were solicited. Adam signed up, and his father did not object because he believed that the British could be talked out of fighting. Moses was the best debater for miles around and just the one, he thought, to get the British to back down. But he never had a chance to use his persuasive powers; the British opened fire almost upon arrival and Moses was one of the casualties. The other militia men, including Adam, turned and scattered as they ran. The boy hid in a neighbor's smokehouse and cried himself to sleep. He was awakened by the voices of two British soldiers talking about burning the building. As soon as they moved away, Adam escaped. He fell across a stone wall into the arms of an old man, Solomon Chandler, who calmed him, telling him that he had left his boyhood behind and become a man since morning. Adams and Chandler, with other colonials, gathered near Mill Brook fork to hide in ambush and intercept the British on their way back. Chandler took command of the small company and deployed the men all along both sides of the road. As the redcoats passed, the colonials shot with deadly accuracy, and officers and men fell in the suddenly disorganized British columns. Then the colonials leaped to their feet and ran to other vantage points from which they could continue to snipe. That night a sad and much wiser boy returned home to shoulder the responsibilities of a family and to help in the defense of his country.

Because this is a historical novel and, in addition, portrays feelings about war in general, it has an important message to all teen-agers. This account is told with an economy of words and moves at such a rapid pace that younger teen-agers read it as a war-adventure story. Older readers comprehend the more subtle feelings about war itself.

A book talk can be built around the night rider and the signing of the muster role, pages 54–69. Pages 103–5 describe an exciting scene as Adam hides in the shed and listens to some British soldiers. A natural book to use with this is *The Red Badge of Courage** by Crane. *William Diamond's Drum* by Tourtellot and *With Sherman to the Sea* by Foote are other stories of boys in

times of war.

FERMI, LAURA

Atoms in the Family

1954. Univ. of Chicago Pr.

On December 2, 1942, a cryptic message: "The Italian navigator has reached the New World," announced the beginning of the Atomic Age. Enrico Fermi, winner of the Nobel Prize and the Congressional Medal for Merit, was the leader of the research team that had brought about the first man-made self-sustaining chain reaction—the great experimental step which led to the atom bomb. At the age of seventeen this brilliant young Italian scientist had applied for a fellowship at a little-known institution for outstanding students of science and letters in Pisa in his native country. Later in Rome he pioneered with experiments in atom-smashing on a small scale. The author first met Fermi in Rome and learned that he was not only an outstanding physicist but a first-rate mountain climber and a brilliant conversationalist. They were married four years later. Fermi's teaching continued apace with his studies, and as the leader of a series of experiments in radioactivity he won the Nobel Prize in 1938. Mussolini had decreed a set of anti-Semitic laws which deprived Jews of full citizenship, passports, and other rights. Fearful for his Jewish wife and their two children, Enrico Fermi took his family with him to Stockholm for the Nobel Prize ceremonies and then continued on to the United States. He soon became immersed in the atomic experiments at Columbia University and later in the Manhattan Project at the University of Chicago and at the Los Alamos laboratories. Through Laura Fermi's perceptive eyes we see the great physicists: Niels Bohr, Edward Teller, and Harold Urey. There are accounts of Bruno Pontecorvo, who defected to the Soviets, and of Klaus Fuchs, the master spy. The homely details of life in New Mexico make Enrico and his colleagues stand out as real people.

There are humor and affection in this sympathetic and devoted account. Readers with an interest in atomic science are fascinated by the descriptions of early experiments and work with cyclotrons, while older girls enjoy the intimate view of a great scientist as seen by his wife.

Amusing and dramatic incidents may be used to introduce the book. The day the news came that Fermi had won the Nobel Prize, Chapter 13; the first glimpse of American shores and reactions to a new home, Chapter 15; the success of the atomic pile, Chapter 19; life at Los Alamos, Chapter 20 and 22—are all suitable for a book talk. For other personal views of scientists, suggest *Madame Curie* by Curie, *Prophet in the Wilderness** by Hagedorn, and *Einstein* by Michelmore.

FITCH, JOHN, and NOLAN, WILLIAM F.

Adventure on Wheels

1959. Putnam.

As a native of Indianapolis who attended the Big Race from earliest childhood, John Fitch was naturally interested in speed, cars, and design. While in the R.A.F. during World War II, he studied architecture at nearby Cambridge, but car racing was in his blood. After the war he tried several careers including selling sports cars. The sports car race at Bridgehampton tempted him, and he decided to enter in a borrowed MG-TC, although he had no previous experience in race driving. His judgment was appalling, and he drove with no idea how to shift down smoothly for greater power, but with beginner's luck he took fifth place. The exhilaration carried him on into a proposal of marriage, and the girl accepted. This was the beginning of a completely new life for John Fitch—ten years of participation in such races as Le Mans, Mille Miglia, the Mexican Road Race, the Alpine Rally, and the Targa Florio. Each race is minutely described from its beginning, through trouble with a slipping clutch, failing brakes, oil leaks, and near crashes, to the final victory or defeat. Here also are the years of work and experiment that go into the inception and refinement of a racing car, and the hours of testing and uncertainty before the actual race begins. Fitch's experiences as technical adviser for the film *The Racers* show the same care for detail evident in his other endeavors. In addition to the racing story, there is a running commentary on his marriage, his three sons, and his philosophy that there is a supranational fraternity of airmen.

Boys interested in speed, excitement, and cars find this book a rewarding reading experience. Fitch emphasizes the wisdom of safe driving and for a number of years has been associated with a scientifically engineered track on which experts test various materials and constructions to ensure safety.

Chapter 16, "The Racers," and Chapter 18, the disaster at Le Mans, may be used for book talks. *Omnibus of Speed* edited by Beaumont, *Nuvolari* by Lurani, *Gentlemen, Start Your Engines* by Shaw, *Famous Auto Races and Rallies,* by Lessner, and *Cars at Speed* by Daley have the same appeal.

FORESTER, CECIL S.

The Good Shepherd
1955. Little.

An Allied convoy of thirty-seven smoky, poky merchant ships of all sizes and types, guarded by four destroyers, was crossing the Atlantic to England with an American naval commander, George Krause, in charge. It was imperative for the men, women, and children waiting in Europe that these ships reach their destination, or the expectant ones would be "hungry, cold and diseased." Suddenly called to the bridge by a report of radar contact ahead, Krause remained there for the next forty-eight hours with no time for sleep and little for food. From Wednesday, Forenoon Watch, to Friday, Morning Watch, the attention and action never shift from Commander Krause, as he tries to save his convoy from an encircling U-boat wolf pack. Though untried in battle, his wisdom, his decision, his courage, his integrity, and his complete devotion to duty carry him through. Ships burning, exploding, or sinking; men being lost or rescued; depth charges and guns seeking the enemy; torpedoes tracking—all combine to build ever mounting suspense. When the maneuvering and bloodshed are finished, the "good shepherd" has "fought the good fight and finished the course." Exhausted, yet almost with reluctance, he hands over his convoy when the relief escort from England reaches him.

This is a wonderful World War II sea novel, but, more important, it is a character study of great power. Commander Krause will long remain in the memory of each reader as a man whose personal life was completely submerged in his devotion to duty. Older boys who are good readers and who enjoy combat stories like this very much.

The killing of the first sub can be used for a book talk; see either pages 39–95 or 79–95. Recommend *Away All Boats* by Dodson, *The Caine Mutiny* by Wouk, *The Long Haul* by Rayner, *Submarine!* by Beach, *Undersea Patrol* by Young, and *Battle Submerged* by Cope as good Navy stories. Forester has written many other good seafaring tales.

FORESTER, CECIL S.

The Last Nine Days of the Bismarck
1959. Little.

When Prime Minister Winston Churchill gave orders to the British Navy to sink the German battleship *Bismarck,* he spoke for his nation with the comment that "the eyes of the whole world are upon us." Early in 1941, before the United States was precipitated into World War II by the Pearl Harbor attack, the British were fighting a desperate battle on several fronts, and their convoys crossing the Atlantic were taking heavy losses inflicted by German submarines. Now another deadly weapon, a ship larger and faster than any other then afloat and commanded by the clever, devoted Admiral Lutjens, was to be released into the Atlantic. The chance to eliminate this formidable opponent, the *Bismarck,* resulted from intelligence reports which indicated she was sailing north out of the Baltic. Poor weather and lack of instruments developed later in the war made exact plotting of the ship's route uncertain. The British battleship *Hood,* in port for repairs, was ordered into action with civilian workmen still aboard. Instructions from the Admiralty for intercepting the *Bismarck's* course were lucky, for several routes had been possible. The two mighty ships met in the Denmark Strait, and the encounter proved disastrous. Newspaper sellers in London soon displayed the headline *"Hood* Sunk." The loss was a staggering blow to British morale as well as an admission that the Third Reich ruled the Atlantic. The days which followed, filled with a frantic search for the *Bismarck* and culminating in her destruction, constituted one of the most important and suspenseful episodes of the war.

Many teen-age boys are drawn to this compact volume with its tense, dramatic style and gripping picture of the men on both sides of the conflict during the last days of a famous ship. Although conversations are fictional, the writing conveys the excitement of battle by its economy of description.

A mention of the return of the *Bismarck* to action and its threat to British shipping, pages 3–12, is sufficient introduction to a class, many of whom know the film version of the story. *The Good Shepherd** by Forester and *Submarine!* by Beach are follow-ups with naval themes, while Shirer's *The Rise and Fall of the Third Reich** is a detailed resource title for the mature reader.

FRANK, PAT

Alas, Babylon

1959. Lippincott.

Randy Bragg was an attractive, thirty-two-year-old bachelor and lawyer who lived on a small fruit ranch in Florida. His brother Mark, married and the father of two children, was an Air Force

Colonel with the Strategic Air Command in Omaha. He had agreed to alert Randy when the Russians were about to make an all-out attack on the United States, and to send his family to Florida for shelter. The code was "Alas, Babylon." The attack occurred on schedule, and with it came destruction and chaos. Because Randy had been forewarned, he had been able to purchase supplies which, although haphazardly bought, made him the best prepared of anyone in Fort Repose. He had had time to warn Malachai, his Negro neighbor; Lib McGovern, his girl; and his good friend, Dr. Dan Gunn. Destruction and horror followed the attack, and the shortage of food and supplies changed charming, affable people into greedy, grasping animals overnight. The only surviving member of the federal government automatically became acting President and declared martial law. Each day conditions grew worse. Randy, as the only Army Reserve officer in the area, had to take command at Fort Repose to protect the community from itself and from invading outlaws. With volunteer help he succeeded in routing the highwaymen who were looting and killing. The effort to survive called forth everyone's ingenuity, cooperation, and endurance.

The tense excitement and the impact of a nuclear attack on American civilization are made so realistic that the reader feels this could happen here. Older boys and girls are attracted to this book because it provides such a vivid picture of the horror of modern warfare and the obvious need for continuing efforts for peace.

Introduce the characters and the situation so that the group appreciates what has happened and what preparations Randy has been able to make. This is usually enough to sell the book to many readers. *On the Beach* by Shute, *Hiroshima* by Hersey, *Earth Abides* by Stewart, and *The Flowers of Hiroshima** by Morris are excellent follow-up titles.

FROST, ROBERT

Complete Poems of Robert Frost
1949. Holt.
Woods at evening, a crumbling wall, a lonely boy in the country, snow, birch trees, wandering tramps, a prize chicken, fear of storms, trees, a sugar orchard—all these and many, many more ideas, pictures, people, and stories come and go in the simplest way through Robert Frost's poetry. The stark simplicity of the language, the almost continuous evocation of the New England   59

landscape, and the molding of the rhyme and rhythm to the need of the tale or the occasion—these things make the intention, the picture, the drama, real. For those who have heard Frost's voice, always, ever, that slow, resonant, undramatic emphasis will pervade their reading. In at least one of the twenty-five subdivisions of this delightful book almost anyone can find lines which mean something special to him. The lyrics in *A Boy's Will* represent the poet's youthful growth and follow the seasons in nature. From the familiar "The Pasture" to the wistful "Reluctance," the reader moves through the images of winter, spring, summer, and autumn. *Mountain Interval* contains the well-known "The Road Not Taken," where the first-person speaker characterizes himself as one who wastes energy regretting the choice he has made. It also includes "Birches" with its philosophic insight, "Earth's the right place for love: I don't know where it's likely to go better." In *New Hampshire* we find the popular "Stopping by the Woods on a Snowy Evening." In the last stanza the speaker notes that the woods are "lovely, dark and deep." He says that he must leave the scene and be getting along, and the lines have interesting implications. Does the speaker have the urge to escape into the peacefulness of death, or is he committed to life with all its complexities? "A Considerable Speck" in *Time Out* turns out to be a microscopic mite with intelligence, which causes the poet to rejoice when on any sheet of paper he finds the "least display of mind."

Young adults find Frost's poems easy and enjoyable to read because they deal with realistic and homely subjects. He is an original writer but follows conventional forms. His poems have meaning and feeling; they begin in delight and end in wisdom.

The best way to introduce these poems is to read several of them aloud. *Complete Poems* would be a good follow-up for Frost's *You Come Too,* favorite poems for younger readers and a fine introduction to the poet's work. *In the Clearing* is a collection of some of his most recent writing. Other popular collections of poetry are *Collected Poems* by Coffin, *Final Harvest* by Dickinson, and *Collected Lyrics* by Millay.

FULLER, IOLA

The Loon Feather

1940. Harcourt.

Though her famous father Tecumseh died when Oneta was quite small, she had acquired all the pride, dignity, and leadership qualities of that great Indian warrior. From her beautiful mother Naneda she had inherited grace, sensitivity, and serenity. These qualities were enhanced by the culture, education, and refinement which she added from her stepfather, Pierre Debans, an aristocratic Frenchman employed by the American Fur Company. When Oneta's mother died shortly after her second marriage, she left Paul, a baby son, for Oneta to help raise. With the aid of Marthe, an Ojibway devoted to Tecumseh, Oneta hoped to teach her brother the Indian ways, customs, and manners which were part of his heritage. But the family moved in with Grand'mere, Pierre's energetic mother, and Oneta was sent off to Quebec to be educated by the Ursuline nuns. For twelve years she was gone from her beloved Mackinac. When she finally returned, she was happy to find Paul developing the best traits of his Indian forebears and not agreeing in every case with his white father. Oneta had no social life since the women at the fort considered her beneath them, and as a result she began to teach at the Mission. There she met Dr. Reynolds, a young doctor who had been on the ship as she was returning home. He came to care for the sick children, and when Paul's leg was shattered, he visited the boy at home every day for months. Otherwise Oneta saw the doctor only as an escort for one of the belles at the fort. Although Pierre had married an Indian, he considered them ignorant, filthy, and inferior, his wife and Oneta being exceptions. This attitude made trouble for the fur company as time went on. Oneta thought a great deal of her stepfather in spite of his faults, and although Paul refused to follow in his father's footsteps and with Baptiste established a fish-shipping business, she was glad to see him make peace with Pierre and win his admiration and respect. When the Indians were provoked to uprising by Pierre's attitude, it was Oneta as Tecumseh's daughter, bearing her father's headdress and deerskin coat, who persuaded them to join Black Hawk and unite with the other tribes rather than seek vengeance on a few. When Dr. Reynolds asked Oneta to marry him, old Marthe's prophecy, made at her birth, came true, "You will bring to your people a man who is greater than a warrior."

The story has a rich historical background told with deep feeling and colorful incidents and is a fair picture of the Indian world matched against the white. The Indians are treated not as noble primitives or bloodthirsty savages, but as human beings beset with the normal problems of any race. Thus this becomes one of the outstanding novels for racial understanding. Girls who are sensitive to an introspective story enjoy this book.

Because of the need to give the background of the story in some detail this makes a long book talk, and the librarian may prefer to introduce it to individuals. However, such incidents as the account of Rosanne and Jacques' wedding, pages 345–52, or the dramatic plea for peace as Oneta speaks to her people, pages 382–96, may be used. Oneta's statement concerning her mixed marriage is an appropriate quote to close a book talk, "Out of the happiness of those years has come a rich deepening of the truth. I felt that day that when there is a likeness of spirit, two people are of one kind. And if there is not that likeness the two are divided by something even greater than the accident of race." *The Shining Trail* by the author, *Laughing Boy* by La Farge, and *Blood Brother** by Arnold as well as *Ramona* by Jackson are also mature stories of American Indians. A story of conflict between the traditions of the Indians and life in the modern white man's world may be found in *When the Legends Die* by Borland.

GALLICO, PAUL

The Snow Goose

1941. Knopf.

In the spring of 1930, Philip Rhayader bought an abandoned lighthouse and the marshland around it along the Essex coast of England. An aura of mystery hung over the young hunchbacked painter who lived there alone, capturing on canvas the birds he loved. Year after year the wild creatures flew back to his bird sanctuary—a haven from other men's cruelty. It was his reputation for kindness which drew young Fritha to Philip's isolated home to seek aid for a wounded snow goose. Thus began a friendship between these two who loved wild creatures. The snow goose, which they named the Lost Princess, came and went with the seasons until finally she returned to stay. Similarly, as Fritha grew into young womanhood, she became more and more aware of the need to be with Philip. In 1940, when British troops were trapped at Dunkirk, Philip set sail alone in his small boat to help with the evacuation. Amid the heavy bombardment, the snow goose hovered overhead, heartening the scores of soldiers rescued by Philip's action. Only when the enemy ended his heroic service, did the bird fly back to England, circling the lighthouse as if to signal Fritha that her beloved Philip was never to return. Even the lighthouse itself experienced the ravages of war so that in the end "only the frightless gulls wheeled and soared and mewed their plaint over the place where it had been."

The poetic language and the intensity of feeling and mood create a gem of poignant beauty which leaves few readers, boys or girls, unmoved. The sad, triumphant sacrifice of a man giving himself for his friends and his country stands as a brilliant argument against the madness of war.

Fritha's first visit to the lighthouse, pages 15–22, is an excellent introductory episode. The haunting quality of the love theme is reminiscent of *Green Mansions** by Hudson, *Tryst* by Thane, *An Iceland Fisherman** by Loti, or *None Shall Know* by Albrand.

GALSWORTHY, JOHN

The Forsyte Saga

1922. Scribner.

The Forsyte Saga includes three novels about the Forsyte family: *The Man of Property, In Chancery,* and *To Let.* The reader is first introduced to the Forsytes at old Jolyon's home in the late 1880's. The family was celebrating the engagement of Miss June, old Jolyon's granddaughter, to the architect, Philip Bosinney. Present were three generations of Forsytes looking askance at the stranger about to become a member of the family. This is also the reader's first glimpse of the "man of property"—Soames Forsyte. He was having trouble with his lovely wife, Irene, who retained little love for this self-important man. In an effort to please her, Soames decided to build a country place and hired young Bosinney as the architect. The two men quarreled several times over the plans and cost of the house, but Soames finally gave in and spent the additional money Bosinney needed. All males were attracted to Irene, and the young architect was no exception. In this instance Irene returned his love. She refused to move into the new house and asked Soames to release her. When he refused, she left him only to come back a few days later when Bosinney was killed in an accident. At this point the first book ends. Irene left Soames again and, taking her maiden name, settled into an apartment and gave music lessons to make a living. Old Jolyon bought Soames's new home and in this way became friendly with Irene, who made his last days happy with her gentleness and charm. Soames, the leading character in the second volume, continued to watch his fortune grow, but his desire to have a family was frustrated. He decided to marry a French girl, Annette, while Irene married young Jolyon who was now a widower. The last volume opens in the year 1920 in a world to which time and war had brought many changes. Soames and Annette had a 63 daughter named Fleur, and Jolyon and Irene had a son, Jon. When the children were grown up, they met accidentally and fell in love, unaware of the former relationship between Irene and Soames. Eventually young Jon learned the details of his mother's earlier marriage; he gave up Fleur and left England for America, where he was joined by his mother. Fleur, thwarted in her love for Jon, married someone else. One by one the old Forsytes had died, and when Timothy, the last of them, passed on, Soames felt lonely and old as he realized that the Forsyte Age was finished.

In presenting the vast canvas of the Forsyte family with all the characters of three generations so well delineated, Galsworthy has given us a feeling of being a part of this great English upper-middle-class family and of having some understanding of the shades of relationship therein. The first book of the trilogy, the one which originally bore the Forsyte title, is the best and most enthralling. As an exposition of English manners and mores from Victorian times to post World War I, the *Saga* appeals to mature young people who like social history.

While there are a number of interesting accounts of family gatherings to use as book talks, the best way to introduce this classic is by describing the central members of the family tree. For similar family stories suggest *Windswept** by Chase, *The Valley of Decision* by Davenport, *H. M. Pulham, Esquire* by Marquand, and the Jalna stories by De la Roche.

GANN, ERNEST

Fate Is the Hunter

1961. Simon & Schuster.

The night was sinister. Both pilots were uneasy and troubled, but neither knew why. There was overcast above and below, yet the weather was fine. They were flying a new plane with a light load of passengers. As they neared New York, the tower gave them a good weather report and clearance to land. When the pilot was figuring their arrival time in New York on the slide rule, he noticed that they were flying fifty feet too high—sloppy flying— and easily adjusted the throttles and stabilizer wheel to bring the plane to exactly 5,000 feet. At this moment he decided that his seat was somewhat too far back and bent down to ease it forward a notch. As he straightened up, the copilot gave a horrified gasp which drew the pilot's attention to the windshield. The sight of a green wing-tip light and two flickering tongues of engine-exhaust flame just ahead froze his hands on the control wheel. It was too late for any reaction. The plane passed so close that they felt as though they could reach out and touch it. Then suddenly it was gone, and they were safe. The pilot contacted the tower in New York and got the report that there was no traffic. From where had the outlaw come? What had made the pilot bring the plane down fifty feet at the right moment so that with such a small margin he missed a collision? The author and pilot, Ernest Gann, asked similar questions many times during his flying career. He believes that pilots' lives are an unending war with fate, and because they take up their profession knowing this full well, the story of their experiences is an inspiring one. Mr. Gann began his career as a barnstorming pilot, went through the rigorous training for commercial airline pilots, flew passenger and cargo planes, and took part in World War II and the Korean War. After experiencing many narrow escapes while friends perished in similar circumstances, he decided to quit flying before *his* luck ran out. He speaks with real affection and admiration for the veteran pilots who trained him. One of his instructors, Captain Ross, considered Gann a professional challenge, and eventually the younger man could set a plane down on a dime and handle it in flight under any conditions. Whether he describes being caught in an ice storm; flying blind to land a burning, disabled plane in Newfoundland; flying over unexplored territory in the Andes without oxygen; or fighting to keep an ailing plane in the air on a flight between California and Honolulu, he keeps the story taut with suspense.

The vivid, dramatic presentation of these very personal reminiscences draws the reader into the cockpit and allows him to share vicariously the author's feelings and actions, the secrets as well as the beauties of flight. Occasional crudities are part of the tension of the moment, and any mature reader who appreciates a well-told story responds with admiration, whether or not he brought to it a previous interest in flying.

Book talk possibilities include Gann's first attempts at landing, Chapter 2, and the search for and eventual rescue of sick and injured men in a plane down somewhere in eastern Canada, Chapters 11 and 12. Chapter 10 contains the story of a flight from Greenland to Iceland, when visibility was only forty feet and there was no radio contact to bring the plane to the field. Other authors who have described the vastness and beauty of the skies are Saint Exupéry in *Wind, Sand and Stars** and *Night Flight* and Murchie in *Song of the Sky.* Also suggest *Under My Wings* by Rowe, *The Spirit of St. Louis** by Charles Lindbergh, and *Listen! the Wind* and *North to the Orient* by Anne Lindbergh.

GERSON, NOEL B.

The Yankee from Tennessee

1960. Doubleday.

When Abraham Lincoln died in the little boardinghouse across the street from Ford's Theatre, a man became President who was destined to be nearly obscured by a nation's devotion to his illustrious predecessor. Born into the poorest of families in Raleigh, North Carolina, Andrew Johnson was apprenticed to a tailor at the age of ten. In 1827, carried along by the westward movement, he established a tailor shop in the small town of Greeneville, Tennessee. With the help of his wife Eliza, Andrew learned to read and write and built up a thriving business. When local politicians attempted to limit the franchise to residents with a certain financial standing, Andrew's temper flared, and he fought back by running for the post of alderman. He was elected by an overwhelming majority. His reputation for honest politics and forthrightness grew, and gradually he progressed through the ranks to Mayor of Greeneville and Governor of Tennessee to become a U.S. Senator in 1857. His efforts to keep Tennessee in the Union during the Civil War ended in failure and nearly cost him his life at the hands of outraged Confederates. Eventually, because of his popularity in the North, his stand on a controlled elimination of slavery, and a compassionate view of rebel leaders which appealed to Lincoln, he became Vice-President in 1865—a Southern Democrat serving with a Republican. Upon Lincoln's death, the Democrat Johnson found himself faced with a Republican-controlled Congress. Feuds with the Radicals over various Reconstruction measures, his willingness to submit to an impeachment trial in 1868 rather than to jeopardize the powers of the Presidency, and his final vindication were blazing events in a tumultuous career. In 1875, six years after he left the White House, Johnson was reelected to the U.S. Senate for a brief, victorious term. To the end he upheld the humanitarian beliefs of Lincoln and shared the passion to preserve the Union demonstrated by the man for whom he was named—Andrew Jackson.

This is a powerful book giving an excellent picture of the times and of a great man who is unfortunately little known today. A book for older students with an interest in American history, this biographical novel often creates a desire to read more

66

about Johnson, Lincoln, Stanton, and the other personalities of the day. Boys enjoy the tension of the political and military battles, while girls warm to the picture of Johnson's family.

Book talks could highlight his struggle for an education, pages 47–55; the problems facing him as President, pages 322–30; and the impeachment trial which he precipitated, pages 346–57. Books covering the same period include *The Day Lincoln Was Shot** by Bishop and *To Appomattox** by Davis, while Kennedy's *Profiles in Courage** presents other men who risked political suicide for their beliefs. *Many a Voyage* by Erdman is the fictionized biography of Edmund Ross whose vote acquitted President Johnson at the impeachment trial.

GIBSON, WILLIAM

The Miracle Worker

1957. Knopf.

The "miracle worker" in this script of the television play is Annie Sullivan, a young, poverty-stricken, once nearly blind student from Perkins Institute in Boston who agreed to become a tutor to a blind, deaf, mute, six-year-old girl, Helen Keller. Through Helen Annie created a miracle—a miracle achieved through infinite patience and an obstinate determination to reach into the dark, fear-filled recesses of a little girl's mind and replace darkness with light. Annie realized at once that language was the key that could unlock Helen's mind so that the child could comprehend what was going on around her. But how did one teach the meaning of words to a little girl who knew no sound—a child who had been pampered, protected, and pitied by her family until her temper tantrums and willfulness ruled the home? In the face of family opposition Annie firmly followed a plan of training. By removing Helen from the smothering and uncritical devotion of her family into isolation for two weeks, Annie trained the child to become dependent on her. She patiently spelled words in the palm of Helen's hand, but the child was unable to associate the word and the object. Greatly discouraged, Annie was almost ready to give up when the miracle was wrought—holding Helen's hand under the pump, she saw the child's face transformed with joy when she realized that the word "water" being spelled in her hand was the cool liquid she felt. Quickly she recognized other objects and asked the name of everything she touched, so that in a short time she developed an amazing vocabulary.

67

The play may be difficult for slow or immature readers, but older students accustomed to stage directions find it a rewarding experience.

Helen's initial encounter with Annie, pages 37–39; the episode in which another child aids the teaching process, pages 89–92; or Annie's conversation with Mrs. Keller, pages 73–78, furnish ample book talk material. This can be used with *The Story of My Life* by Keller, *Anne Sullivan Macy* by Braddy, or *Helen Keller* by Brooks. *My Left Foot* by Brown, *Face to Face** by Mehta, *Over My Dead Body** by Opie, and *Make a Joyful Sound* by Waite are other stories of people who overcame their handicaps.

GODDEN, RUMER

An Episode of Sparrows

1955. Viking.

To the residents of Mortimer Square, a once aristocratic section of London, the children from nearby Catford Street were like a flock of noisy, cheeping sparrows. Lonely Lovejoy Mason, not yet eleven, was one of these suspect children. One day she snatched a stray packet of seeds from the hands of little Sparkey, the newsboy. Although she had some difficulty in spelling out "cornflowers," the picture of the blue flowers made her yearn to plant the tiny specks. There was no place for growing things among the asphalt and cobblestones of the street, but she found a small spot in the rubble of a bombed-out area and cleared a plot for a garden. Money stolen from the church candlebox helped buy gardening equipment, and a net lifted from a baby carriage protected the seedlings. Sparkey, however, wreaked his revenge when a gang of boys led by Tip Malone drove Lovejoy from this garden attempt and trampled the cornflowers. Touched by Lovejoy's heartbreak Tip later helped her locate a new site in an old graveyard behind a partially demolished church. Soil was the requisite here, and the best soil, of course, was in the carefully tended gardens in Mortimer Square. Quantities of earth began to vanish mysteriously from the gardens to provide nourishment for their flowers. Disaster followed when the children were caught and taken to the police station. Lovejoy was placed in a girls' home, and Tip decided to enter naval training, but a surprise ending gives the young people a chance for happiness.

Older girls respond to this delicate story of a child's search for happiness.

Book talks could be based on the destruction of the first garden, pages 91–97, and, if needed, the apprehension of the children, pages 171–77. Similar books with plots centering around youngsters include *Greenwillow** by Chute, *The Family Nobody Wanted* by Doss, *A City of Bells* by Goudge, *Cheaper by the Dozen* by Gilbreth, *Old Herbaceous* by Arkell, and *The Family* by Federova.

GOODWYN, FRANK

The Black Bull

1958. Doubleday.

One of the big herds on the Candelaria Ranch in south Texas was being moved into the corrals near the ranch house. Two *vaqueros*, friends, were riding near each other. Pedro presented the handsome young cowhand Robelín with a fawn he had found, suggesting that he give it to Josefa whom Robelín admired greatly. Both men knew that the mother of the fawn would mourn for her lost offspring, but both felt that the gift was important. Deep in thought, the fawn in his arms, Robelín rode on alone, but when the bereaved doe appeared at the side of the cattle drive, he guiltily released the baby. That night at the dance Josefa seemed to be paying much attention to another cowhand, Eugenio. Pedro urged Robelín to propose to Josefa before he lost her. Robelín loved his liberty and even Josefa would not be able to hold him in the settlement near the ranch house for more than a few days at a time. But, unwilling to lose her to Eugenio, Robelín proposed and was readily accepted. The next day the herd had to be sorted for market. During this work a magnificent, big, black bull managed to jump from the loading chute and escape back to the range. Robelín and Eugenio were sent after him. The animal soon showed how formidable and clever it was by tricking the men as they trailed him and goring Robelín's horse. That night the bull disappeared, and it was several days before Robelín was free to find his trail again. The pursuit stretched over many miles and many days. Robelín stopped at neighboring ranches for a meal occasionally, but usually he ate and slept by his own lonely campfire. One day he caught up with the bull. Not until he had his rope securely on the animal's horns did he realize how foolhardy he had been. No man should be alone when he has roped a vicious animal. At first Robelín did not know what to do with the bull, but as they traveled along a rope's length apart, the cowboy discovered a way to subdue the

animal. With its four feet tied, Robelín sat down to rest and decide what to do next. He began to talk to the bull; he admired its
size, its speed, and its power. How sad that it was destined to
hang on a hook in a packing house! The bull and Robelín had
much in common; they were both about to give up their liberty.
Suddenly the cowhand decided that the bull should go free, and
that decision brings the story to a fast and devastating end.

This simple, well-told tale has the qualities of a classic in its
field. Good readers like the interesting assortment of characters,
especially don Agustín who composed the ballad about the black
bull.

The episode concerning the fawn which Pedro gave to Robelín
to use as a gift for Josefa, sets the theme of the story, pages 17–22;
the story of the aristocratic Spanish don who composed the ballad, pages 182–98 and 219–22, makes good telling. *I'll Tell You a
Tale* by Dobie is a group of short stories which are rich in the
folklore of the Old West.

GRZIMEK, BERNHARD, and GRZIMEK, MICHAEL
Serengeti Shall Not Die
1961. Dutton.

The threat of extermination hangs over the wild beasts of Africa.
Because of wanton killing by big-game hunters and by poachers,
it is possible that lions, elephants, zebras, rhinoceroses, giraffes,
and the like will be seen in the future only in circuses and zoos.
Even the large game preserves such as the Serengeti National
Park in Tanganyika are not a guarantee of protection. The British government had proposed cutting the Serengeti to provide
more land for the Masai tribesmen. Dr. Bernard Grzimek (pro-
nounced *jĭ mĕk*) and his son, Michael, convinced that the proposed
boundaries would deprive the wild animals of much of their graz-
ing land and leave them unprotected during their migrations along
established routes outside the new borders, vowed that "one small
part of the continent at least should retain its original splendour,"
that "Serengeti shall not die." They decided that a census of the
wildlife population and a study of migration paths were imperative. Since this area of 4,500 square miles offered only one poor
road, the Grzimeks bought and learned to fly a Piper Cub,
painted with zebra stripes for easy identification from the air. During the year of their investigations they made some surprising
discoveries which upset previous assumptions about the Serengeti
animals. The experiences recorded here show them counting

heads and marking herds by several ingenious methods which included a "miracle gun." Throughout the book are sensitively written, often amusing vignettes about animal behavior and the Masai tribesmen. A chapter on the shocking misdeeds of poachers and the accounts of dwindling herds point up the need for immediate action.

This book has great appeal for boys from the ninth grade up. Though young Michael Grzimek was killed in a plane crash at the close of their work, the account is far from melancholy. The close relationship evident in the father-son team is especially fine. The mishaps they encountered heighten the feeling of adventure and danger associated with living among wild animals. Unusually good colored and black-and-white photographs add appeal.

For book talks use Chapter 4 on the Serengeti lions, the description of the miracle guns in Chapter 10, or the section on wart hogs, pages 86–88. An accident while catching zebras, pages 146–51, is also tellable. Moorehead's *No Room in the Ark* is a less exciting, more adult picture of African game conditions today. Adamson's books, *Born Free** and *Living Free,* plus *Seal Morning* by Farre and *Living Treasure* by Sanderson are other animal stories. Durrell's *Three Tickets to Adventure* and *The Drunken Forest* tell of the author's experiences capturing wild creatures for zoos.

GUNTHER, JOHN
Death Be Not Proud
1949. Harper.

For fifteen months Johnny Gunther fought gallantly against the progressive devastation of a brain tumor. Numerous operations and repeated attempts to allay the cancer were for him merely annoyances, interruptions in his studies at the Deerfield Academy. With a brilliant, inquiring mind he began to look at his illness as a scientific curiosity—something to investigate along with the theory of relativity. Courageously he pursued his mathematical interests, studied for the Harvard entrance examinations, and prepared for the future. The Gunthers, fortified and encouraged by doctors, teachers, and friends, watched the inevitable course of the incurable disease. The miracle for which they prayed did not occur. Alert to the end, Johnny died at the age of seventeen.

Rather than a sentimental account of personal grief, Gunther presents a case history of heroism in a boy with faults as well as great abilities. While the biography is largely a medical document, there are strength and warmth in the joint struggle in which Johnny and his parents engaged. A few teen-agers may be upset by the medical details, but those mature readers who like stories about the handicapped claim this as a favorite.

Book talks could be based upon the initial operation as described in the Foreword, pages 4–5, or on the discovery of the disease, pages 25–29, but it would be unwise to belabor the story by too much description. Other books about the handicapped include *Over My Dead Body** by Opie, *Wish I Might* by Smith, and *Miracle at Carville** by Martin.

HAGEDORN, HERMANN
Prophet in the Wilderness
1958. Macmillan.

An exciting and stimulating career as a talented organist and a brilliant theologian teaching in a great university brought deep satisfaction and joy to Albert Schweitzer. But when he was twenty-one, he paused to reflect on his reason for being and his choice of a profession. He made the decision that at the age of thirty he would relinquish his university position and devote the remainder of his life to service to others. A chance perusal of a missionary magazine pointed out the great need for trained medical help in French Equatorial Africa. Thus he started over again in pursuit of a career in medicine and found a coworker and devoted companion in Helene Bresslau who became his wife. On Easter Sunday in 1913, Dr. Schweitzer and his wife embarked for Africa, where they were to spend the next fifty years in dedicated service to the people of Lambaréné. Using funds obtained from friends, and from organ recitals and royalties from his writings, he built a jungle hospital—a crude medical station where the work was done by the people of the area with Schweitzer as their foreman. By normal standards the equipment was shockingly inadequate; to the needy it was a haven of help. The news spread about operations, treatment, and provision for families who brought their sick ones miles to the doctor. Despite shortages caused by the World Wars the work has progressed steadily and been recognized as a genuine effort in practical brotherhood. Dr. Schweitzer's unique and controversial "reverence for life" philosophy, his unorthodox views of Christianity, and his definitive biography of

Bach were milestones in an amazing career. The chief goal of his life was realized—to help those in pain even though it meant giving up a brilliant career in a European setting. Despite critics who claim that he treats his patients as children, and a recent movement to evict him from the newly independent state of Gabon, he remains a humanitarian of giant stature.

In *Memoirs of Childhood and Youth* (Macmillan, 1949), Albert Schweitzer says, "Sometimes our light goes out but is blown again into flame by an encounter with another human being. Each of us owes the deepest thanks to those who have rekindled that inner light." An encounter with Albert Schweitzer inspires the reader in this very manner. High school students also find encouragement from this story of a man who has lived in three worlds and made a great contribution in each career.

A dramatic incident to tell is Dr. Schweitzer's realization, at the age of twenty-one, that his personal happiness was not sufficient and that he must share his life with others, pages 53–54. Follow this with the story of his choosing the French Congo for his career of direct service, pages 74–75. Anderson's *The World of Albert Schweitzer* is an admirable pictorial supplement, while Franck's *Days with Albert Schweitzer* provides a recent view of life at Lambaréné written by an American dentist. *Albert Schweitzer: Genius of the Jungle* by Gollomb is an excellent account of the earlier years of his three careers. The Thomas A. Dooley books, such as *Deliver Us from Evil,** tell of similar humanitarian efforts in southeast Asia. *The Nun's Story** by Hulme and *White Witch Doctor* by Stinetorf are other stories of medical missionaries in Africa.

HAGEDORN, HERMANN

The Roosevelt Family of Sagamore Hill

1954. Macmillan.

The family life of one of America's most colorful presidents, Theodore Roosevelt, is revealed in this account of vacations and holidays spent at Sagamore Hill near Oyster Bay, New York, during the years from 1887 to the close of the First World War. Against a background of politics and public concern for people and their problems, the reader becomes involved in the daily activities of a vigorous American family. Edith and Theodore Roosevelt surrounded their six children with affection and discipline and showed a keen interest in their growth and development. Swimming, tennis, hikes, camping out, and romps were all

73

part of the daily routine. Through the years, even as their father grew older, he was always the pivot around which life at Sagamore Hill revolved. The greatest change in the lives of this tightly knit family occurred swiftly and without warning. At a public reception at the 1901 Pan American Exposition in Buffalo, President McKinley was assassinated, and Vice-President Roosevelt was called to Buffalo to be sworn in as President. Within a few weeks the family had taken up residence at the White House. Mrs. Roosevelt brought dignity and charm to the social life in Washington. With grace and humor she was able to keep a check on her husband's reckless exuberance. Alice's coming-out party, the escapades of the White House Gang, pets in all quarters, roller skating in the halls—all made the Roosevelts a colorful and beloved family for the nation to watch. Summers were still spent at Sagamore Hill where national and world figures came: the Russians and the Japanese to negotiate a peace, members of the Cabinet, former Rough Riders, old friends and people with problems and requests. The simple life of America's first citizen often astonished them. A candle lighted their way to bed, and the President himself often brought them an extra blanket if the night was chilly. The United States was stepping more confidently and importantly into international affairs, and the President's personality, home, and family helped to impress foreign dignitaries very favorably with the American way of life.

This is a story of happy parenthood—of a man and his wife, of the house they loved, and of the six children they brought up in it. To have parents who were loving, strong, and understanding, setting high goals and expecting the best, but ready to help when they fell short, meant that the Roosevelt children grew up in a family worthy of imitation and respect. Both boys and girls mature enough to appreciate this fine family enjoy the book very much.

There are many incidents to be used in a book talk to stimulate interest. The children's adventures in the White House, pages 146–48; the President dodging the Secret Service men, pages 153–55; the poem about the strenuous life of the President at Sagamore, page 174; or camping out with the boys, pages 178–80, are possibilities. Suggest, as other family stories, *Hyphenated Family* by Hagedorn, in which the author writes of his own family and a completely different way of life; *Windswept** by Chase; or *Life with Father* by Day. *The Good Years** by Lord fills in the background of the 1900's, while *Sunrise at Campobello** by Schary tells of the family life of later Roosevelts.

HANNUM, ALBERTA

Spin a Silver Dollar

1945. Viking.

Bill and Sallie Lippincott, newly graduated from the University of Chicago in 1938, spent the summer in the National Park Service at Canyon de Chelley and fell in love with the Southwest. Acting on impulse, they bought Wide Ruin on the Navaho Reservation. Renovating the old trading post to make a comfortable home and a place of business was not easy, especially with unreliable Indian labor, but at last the ancient walls sheltered attractive living quarters. The trading post was remodeled with business going on as usual, and Bill and Sallie began to learn about the habits and customs of their colorful Indian customers. Each was a story in himself. There was Little Woman, the oldest woman of all the clans, wrinkled and thin but very much alive and interested in all that went on at the post. Then there was Joe Toddy, who loved a good time and bright, gaudy shirts and who served as a general handyman around the store. Most intriguing of all was Jimmy, the small son of Joe Toddy. Sallie noticed one day that he was drawing on stone as his ancestors had done. Thereafter she provided him with paper, crayons, pencils, and paints, and Bill made a place in the back of the store where the little boy could work undisturbed. Frequently they were surprised and pleased to find a finished drawing shyly slipped near them. As Jimmy's skill grew, his individual style and his color sense developed. The fundamentals of rhythm and balance seemed to come to him naturally. Gradually a market for his paintings was created, but he remained the shy, taciturn, observant lad of the early days. Sallie and Bill also recognized the ancient artistry of the Navahos in rugmaking and insisted that in their weaving they use traditional patterns and native dyes instead of the patterns and garish colors which caught the tourist's eye. Slowly their reputation for fine rugs began to spread across the country.

This is a beautiful book: beautiful because of the pictures of the Navaho artist; beautiful because of the sympathetic appreciation of his talent by the Lippincotts; and beautiful because of the author's skill in putting all these people into a book. Boys and girls interested in the Indians of the Southwest or their art enjoy this book. It is also important for the picture of the development of an adolescent.

Many anecdotes might be used to introduce the book, but some of the best are: Little Woman's ride in the car, pages 16–17; Bill's difficulty in setting up a bookkeeping system, pages 46–47; Little Woman's gift of a hand-woven rug, page 56; Joe Toddy's visit to Colorado Springs, pages 69–70; and the sing to cure Ben Navaho's snake bite, pages 148–57. The large reproductions of Jimmy's paintings, with the signature "Beatien Yazz," which have appeared in the magazine, *Arizona Highways*, add to a book talk. The sequel, *Paint the Wind*, tells of Jimmy's Marine service during World War II, his interest in oriental painting, his return to the reservation, and his love story. Mature readers might also be introduced to *Laughing Boy* by La Farge and *Our Son Pablo* by Gordon.

HANSBERRY, LORRAINE

A Raisin in the Sun
1959. Random.

A shabby, cramped flat in Chicago's Southside is home for the Negro Younger family: Walter Lee, his pregnant wife Ruth, their young son Travis, Walter's sister Beneatha, and their mother Lena. At thirty-five, Walter rebels against his lack of money and his chauffeur's job. He longs to advance in the world, to take his wife and son out of their crowded, bug-infested apartment. In a large life-insurance settlement that comes to his recently widowed mother, he sees a chance to realize his dreams by joining in a rather dubious business partnership. For Walter, money is the antidote to despair. His sister Beneatha desperately hopes to become a doctor, and although her mother is sympathetic toward this ambition, she is disheartened by the girl's growing atheism and idealistic views. Lena's desire to leave the squalor of tenement life prompts her to reject Walter's business deal and make a down payment on a house in a white neighborhood. When Walter is entrusted with the balance of the check, he is victimized by his associate. Crushed by remorse, Walter finally realizes that money alone cannot cure his situation and redeems himself by assuming his responsibilities as head of the family. The entire group can see a brightening future in the new surroundings despite the threat of discrimination.

More than just a plea for integration, this play reveals how a family can be revitalized, not by a sudden financial windfall, but by mutual love and understanding. Older high school students can associate readily with Beneatha's moods and the realistically portrayed tensions of family life.

Lena's announcement of her purchase of the house and Walter's reaction, pages 81–87, or her response to his loss of the money, pages 113–18, could be used in book talks, but the references to Ruth's abortion attempt might make informal recommendations to individual students preferable to class use. The racial tensions in *Cry, the Beloved Country** by Paton and *To Kill a Mockingbird** by Lee interest readers who want similar books.

HARDY, THOMAS
The Mayor of Casterbridge [1886]
St. Martins.

Under the influence of too much rum, Michael Henchard, an itinerant hay-trusser, traded his wife Susan and his little girl for five guineas to a sailor, Richard Newson. The latter was a kindly man and was good to his newly acquired family. Simple soul that Susan was, she stayed with Newson as his wife perfectly content until a friend, to whom she confided her secret, ridiculed her for accepting such a situation. A time of sadness and doubt followed, and Susan told Newson that she thought she could no longer stay with him. Finally, to give her a way out, the sailor husband devised a plot so that Susan would believe he had been lost at sea. Then with her daughter Elizabeth Jane, now grown, she set out in search of Henchard who had prospered in the eighteen years which had passed. He had settled in Casterbridge where he had become a prosperous merchant and mayor of the town. Desirous of atoning for his sin against her, Michael arranged with Susan to court her as the Widow Newson and marry her. This would save his face as the community did not know of his early marriage to her. Life was serene for the family until Michael became jealous of his young manager, Donald Farfrae, who had become a real asset to his grain business. Their relationship went from bad to worse, and finally Henchard asked Farfrae to leave and stop seeing Elizabeth. About this time Susan died. Several events occurred which disturbed the relationship between Henchard and Elizabeth, and she asked his permission to leave as she had found a position as housekeeper-companion to a lady she had met in the park. Henchard was quite upset when he found that she was living with his former mistress, Lucetta. Donald Farfrae's falling in love with Lucetta was the last straw. Elizabeth's future seemed to be marred by unhappiness, but at the end of the story the situation brightens.

This story is easier to read than some of Hardy's other novels and thus is a good introduction to the author.

To promote interest mention Henchard's villainous act, Chapter 1, and then indicate his dilemma when Susan confronts him eighteen years later, Chapter 11. Hardy's *Under the Greenwood Tree* and *Far from the Madding Crowd* are set in the same locale, while Hugo's *Les Misérables* presents another picture of a man fleeing from his past.

HART, MOSS

Act One

1959. Random.

At the age of seven Moss Hart fell in love with the theater and lived for Thursday and Saturday afternoons when he could attend vaudeville acts and stock-company productions with his Aunt Kate. Born to poverty and drabness in the Bronx, he dreamed of the magic world of the theater and determined to become a part of what he pictured as a glamorous and satisfying way of life. His desire and determination were fed by his avid reading of theatrical news and by his Aunt Kate's vivid description of the plays that she, the only Broadway-theater-going member of the family, was fortunate enough to see. Hart's young life was hard because he had to leave school and go to work to supplement the meager family income. He hoped for a job in a theatrical office but had to settle for work in the storage vault of a large wholesale furrier. This work added to the family income but did little to satisfy his desire to become an actor. His preoccupation with the theater and his disgust at his narrow existence estranged his family and left him lonely and miserable. Finally, through a fortunate coincidence, he became office boy for Augustus Pitou Theatrical Enterprises which booked shows all over the United States. It was not Broadway, but at least he could meet actors and listen to their exciting chatter. He also got free passes to stage productions and could take his aunt, who by then could no longer afford even the gallery. While working for Mr. Pitou, Hart wrote anonymously his first play, *The Beloved Bandit*. Pitou produced this but it failed miserably, and Hart lost his job. For the next six years he directed little-theater groups during the winter and spent his summers as social director for adult camps. He was also writing plays and trying to perfect his craftsmanship as a writer. His efforts at serious drama were rejected by the producers, and it was not until he turned to satirical comedy in *Once in a Lifetime* that he attracted notice. A well-known producer liked the play and suggested that Hart collaborate with George S. Kaufman in readying it for production. This was the beginning of the famous partnership that created so many Broadway hits.

Hart makes us familiar with the inner workings of the modern theater—its struggles of writing, rewriting, and production. He reveals the kindliness and interest that most great theater personalities show to their coworkers. His story appeals to mature, sensitive teen-agers who like a warm, human story of a boy who made good and to those interested in the development of the theater.

For book talks use Hart's first sight of Broadway described on pages 3–5; his manner of getting the office-boy job with Pitou, pages 27–41; his description of a camp social director's duties, pages 138–49; his use of costumes to hide his lack of proper clothes at the Half Moon Country Club, pages 199–203; or the decision to leave the Brooklyn apartment after his first success, pages 438–41. This book might be followed by such Kaufman-Hart plays as *You Can't Take It with You, The Man Who Came to Dinner,* and *The American Way.* Other biographies of people connected with the stage are *Dance to the Piper* and *And Promenade Home* by De Mille, *The Man Who Lived Twice** by Barnes, and *Gertrude Lawrence as Mrs. A* by Aldrich.

HEMINGWAY, ERNEST
The Old Man and the Sea
1952. Scribner.

It is the month of September, "the month when the great fish comes" in the Gulf Stream. Suddenly Santiago feels a tug on his line. The old man has been fishing for eighty-four days without a nibble; perhaps now his luck has changed. Perhaps at long last he will prove to his young friend Manolin that he is a fisherman to be admired. As the huge fish begins to tow his boat, however, the old man realizes that this is to be no ordinary catch; his very life is being challenged by an unseen, unbelievably powerful creature. To release the line would mean safety and defeat; to pursue might bring death or a dream realized. Careful manipulation of the taut line by bleeding, cramped hands; conservation of waning strength; and mental discipline absorb his waking hours and invade his brief snatches of sleep as the solitary battle continues for three exhausting days. Finally he kills the monstrous fish and fastens it to the side of his skiff before he heads for home. He is thinking how much the victory means to him when his prize is attacked by sharks, which leave him only a pitiful skeleton as a trophy by the time he reaches his little harbor. The searing pain, exhaustion, and bitter disappointment fade, however, when young Manolin and the villagers are awed by his accomplishment, and the boy reaffirms their partnership.

Here is a profound character study of youth and old age and a vivid description of the mysterious glories of the sea, overlaid with the futility and poignancy of the old man's desperate battle for recognition. Whether read simply as a rousing fish story or as a tale symbolizing the human struggle against the impersonal elements of life, this slim novel represents an almost epic treatment of the nobility of courage. Boys rather than girls ask for this book.

Book talks could be developed from Santiago's first encounter with the fish, pages 45–50; from his philosophizing, pages 82–83; or from the episode, pages 96–100, when the fish suddenly arches above the water. Interested readers might consider reading Ruark's *The Old Man and the Boy* and Melville's *Moby Dick*. Other stories of incredible courage are *We Die Alone** by Howarth and *Endurance** by Lansing.

HÉMON, LOUIS

Maria Chapdelaine

1921. Macmillan.

Maria was the daughter of a French Canadian named Samuel Chapdelaine, whose passion was clearing land. Five times since his boyhood he had left a comfortable farm to wrest a new one from the wilderness. Now the Chapdelaines lived more than a dozen miles away from Peribonka on the other side of the river above Honfleur in southern Quebec. Maria had just returned from a visit to relatives, and she and her father stayed overnight in Peribonka. The young men at church the next morning looked approvingly at her and discussed the location of the home and the difficulties of reaching it for the purpose of courting. Yet Maria was not without suitors. François Paradis, whose father had been an old neighbor, renewed his acquaintance with the family in the spring on his way to buy furs from the Indians. Eutrope Gagnon, a neighboring farmer, and Lorenzo Surprenant, who had emigrated to the United States and told glowingly of the easier life there, also wanted to marry Maria. In July François came back just in time to join the family on Ste. Anne's day when they went blueberrying. François told Maria of his expected income for the coming year and promised to return in the spring if she would wait for him. Maria knew he was the only man for her. Winter came early that year and it was a bad one. Just before Christmas Maria asked her mother if a person who said a thousand Aves on the day before Christmas would have his wish granted. With her mother's assurance that the act of devotion very seldom failed, Maria said the thousand Aves to ensure François' return in the spring. On New Year's night Eutrope came to call and brought bad news. François had asked for time off from work beginning the middle of December and including New Year's so that he could go to see Maria. For some reason the train was not running; he had set off on snowshoes and became lost in a blizzard. A numbness descended upon Maria which even the high masses her family arranged for François failed to ease. Lorenzo Surprenant tried his best to persuade Maria to give up the hard frontier life and return to the United States with him. Eutrope also tried to persuade her to become his wife but she told him to wait. In April Madame Chapdelaine was stricken with an unknown illness, and her great suffering took Maria's attentions away from her own grief. When the mother died, Maria's father began to recall his wife's courage and cheerfulness during their many years of hardship. Maria realized that she could do no less than her mother had done—stay with her own people and help to conquer the wilderness.

This is a quiet story of kindly day-by-day living, of cutting trees and wrenching their stumps from the ground, of daily prayer and meals of pea soup, pork, and potatoes. It appeals to sensitive and serious girls.

For a book talk use the family outing for blueberries when François and Maria silently make their vows, Chapter V; or the visit to church and at the Larouche home in Peribonka in Chapter I. For follow-ups use *Shadows on the Rock* by Cather, *An Iceland Fisherman** by Loti, and *Giants in the Earth** by Rölvaag.

HERSEY, JOHN
A Bell for Adano
1944. Knopf.
When the bell had been wrenched from its place of honor on the town hall by Mussolini and shipped away to be made into a

cannon, the spirit of the people of Adano had gone with it. The bell had regulated the business of the town and the personal affairs of its citizens; it had recalled their proud history and had cheered them with the comforting sound of its centuries-old voice. Now the silence was disturbed only by the insignificant tinkle of church bells; the heart of Adano was missing. When this Italian town fell into American hands following the flight of the Fascist forces near the end of World War II, the new senior civil affairs officer was confronted with the bell problem early in his career. Anxious to establish a democratic government and to bring the town back to normalcy, Major Victor Joppolo conferred with a committee of local dignitaries about community needs. Although lack of food won out as the most immediate problem, replacement of the bell ran a close second. Joppolo, an Italian-American who could speak the language and share a sense of the heritage of the people, was a keen observer of human nature. Disheartened fishermen resumed their trade, so vital to the local economy, when the Major broke tradition by leaving his office and visiting the stubborn old leader on his fishboat. Fair dealing with criminals, sensible decisions about flour requirements, the countermanding of the General's order prohibiting the movement of mule carts, and a special effort to attend church services endeared him to the local citizenry. Joppolo brought out the best in the people because he represented all they had hoped an American would be. A delicate friendship with Tina, a fisherman's daughter, merely heightened the Major's longing for his wife and depressed him when he came to realize that his role in Tina's life was merely one of trying to locate her missing sweetheart. After much maneuvering, the Major obtained a historic bell from a United States ship named for a heroic Italian-American of World War I, and had it hoisted to the place of honor on the town hall. His fine work, however, came to an abrupt end when he was relieved of duty for countermanding the General's order concerning the mule carts.

More than just a picture of how an occupying army should treat the defeated, this frequently humorous and earthy novel underlines the need for empathy and imaginative action in international relations. Language is sometimes coarse but never deliberately sensational. It is popular with older boys devoted to war stories or with those who enjoyed Lederer's The Ugly American.*

For book talks, compare fat Craxi who pleads priority for food with rich, old Cacopardo who eloquently pleads the case for the bell, pages 17–23. Share the Major's short talk to his officials, some of them held-over Fascists, as he gives them his concept of democracy, page 45. Suggest *The Teahouse of the August Moon* by Patrick (play) or Sneider (novel) and *The King from Ashtabula* by Sneider as amusing and somewhat satirical presentations of American occupation forces.

HERSEY, JOHN
A Single Pebble
1956. Knopf.

A young American engineer was assigned to investigate the possibility of building a dam to harness the energy of the Yangtze River. In order to decide upon the site he traveled the treacherous river on an ancient junk hauled by human laborers, straining like beasts of burden along century-old paths. He admired the steely, ruthless junk owner and his young wife, Su-ling, who nursed the engineer during a sudden illness. Through the legends, poetry, and stories she recited, the young American began to appreciate the tradition and pride of the Chinese people. The head tracker, who directed and encouraged the men hauling the boats over the rapids and through the gorges, was called Old Pebble. His appearance belied his name, however. The engineer was fascinated by this young, powerful, confident worker whose life goal was to direct the junk through the dangerous waters. On the other hand, Old Pebble was resentful of the American's intrusion, and frightened by his desire to change the river so that it would no longer need the skillful piloting which was the young workman's main talent. Old Pebble's death in a frightening accident affected the American profoundly, and he began to understand that Western technology might not be the only answer to man's misery.

The conflict between the old and the new appeals particularly to mature high school boys who enjoyed Hilton's *Lost Horizon.**

The delicacy of the narrative and the dreamlike mingling of old and modern viewpoints, however, are difficult to transmit in a book talk. A brief summary such as given above could attract interested readers. Otherwise introduce this book to individuals. Other books dealing with old China and its way of life are Buck's *My Several Worlds** as well as her *The Good Earth,* Burgess' *The Small Woman,** and Cronin's *Keys of the Kingdom.** The philosophical theme can be continued in *The Bridge of San Luis Rey* by Wilder and *The Old Man and the Sea** by Hemingway.

HEYERDAHL, THOR

Aku-Aku

1958. Rand McNally.

"I had no *aku-aku*. Nor did I know what an *aku-aku* was, so I could hardly have used one if I had had it." So opens this intriguing true-adventure story of archaeological research on Easter Island—a lonely Polynesian Island in the middle of the South Pacific, now used by the Chilean navy for sheep raising. To Easter Island came Thor Heyerdahl, of *Kon-Tiki* fame, with his archaeological expedition and his family. He had long dreamed of attempting to solve the mystery of the huge hand-carved statues that resemble nothing anywhere else in the world. How these vast figures, ranging in height from 30 feet to 90 feet, were transported for miles to the platforms where they were to stand and then crowned by a huge topknot of another color of stone, weighing several tons, had the scientists baffled. Eventually it became evident that three different groups of people had occupied the island at various times. The first group built as the early South Americans had. Their statues, which Heyerdahl's party brought to light for the first time, were not like the famous ones which had been produced by the second group of inhabitants known as the "long ears." The third group was the one from which the present residents were descended. One member of the second group had survived and intermarried with the conquerors, however, and his descendants were still among the people of the island. The oldest of these was the mayor of the village. When he was asked by the author to demonstrate how the statues had been carved, transported, set up, and topped by the gigantic cylinder of red stone, he proceeded to amaze the scientists by doing just that. Many more astonishing facts came to light as the natives became convinced—despite his protests—that Señor Kon-Tiki, as they called Heyerdahl, had very strong supernatural powers. Even Father Sebastian, who had lived on the island for many years, had not known that the natives still kept ancient stone carvings and wooden inscribed tablets of immense historical value in secret family caves. Each cave was guarded by at least one *aku-aku* or spirit, but after a secret ceremony to placate the *aku-akus*, Heyerdahl was able to visit several of the caves. He also explored the caves originally used as hideouts

84

from enemies, reached by long tunnels through which only a thin man could wriggle with his hands over his head.

Heyerdahl's story appeals to adventure-minded teen-agers, even to those with limited reading ability.

Many passages are suitable for telling or reading, especially Heyerdahl's perilous and exciting midnight trips. One of the most spine-tingling is told in Chapter III, when he and a native decide to explore a tunnel which Father Sebastian described as the worst he had ever entered. The sensation that there was no escape, because the contour seemed to change, leaves the reader gasping for air. Another dramatic story, told in Chapter V, is the mayor's bargain to raise the biggest statue; while the most amusing is the incident in Chapter X of the strike of the men on the island of Rapa Ita. The legend of the death of the "long ears," pages 123–28, also provides book talk material. Use as follow-ups *Gods, Graves, and Scholars** by Ceram and *Book of the Seven Seas* by Freuchen. Metraux's *Easter Island* will appeal to those who want more archaeological facts about the Stone Age civilization in the Pacific. *Caves of Adventure* by Tazieff and *Caves of Mystery* by Douglas provide additional thrills for speleologists.

HILTON, JAMES

Lost Horizon

1933. Morrow.

A fantastic experience faced four people as they entered an airplane which was to evacuate them from the revolution-torn Indian city of Baskul in 1931. Hugh Conway and his young associate Captain Charles Mallinson were both members of the British Consular Service and faced reassignment now that their posts had been abandoned. Miss Roberta Brinklow looked forward to another missionary field where she could continue her work for the Eastern Mission, while Henry Barnard, the only American in the group, appeared to be on his way to further financial speculations. Soon after their flight to safety began, however, the group realized that their armed pilot was flying an unknown route. A brief refueling stop in the mountains and more hazardous hours in the air brought them to a jolting landing somewhere on the high, desolate Tibetan plateau. The pilot's death and the rigors of the windy, cold region seemed to spell extinction until a caravan bearing a distinguished-looking Chinese gentleman came along and led the quartet to an almost inaccessible retreat, **85** the lamasery of Shangri-La. Here they found central heat, plumbing, fine rooms, and excellent food as well as a magnificent library and art collection. Although they were promised that porters would later take them out of the retreat, Conway had a feeling that they were not destined to leave. Eventually Conway met the High Lama who told him an incredible story of Father Perrault, a Capuchin friar lost in the mountains in 1734. He had found sanctuary in a lamasery and adopted the Buddhist faith. His life was prolonged by some drugs he perfected and by the marvelous air. Later, tribesmen helped him build Shangri-La. Conway realized that the High Lama was Father Perrault, now 250 years old. The kidnaping of their plane had been deliberate; the High Lama, fearing civilization might be destroyed, wanted more people as a nucleus for a new world. Conway alone was allowed to learn the secret of Shangri-La—a slowing of the aging processes which extended productive life almost indefinitely, so that the residents could pursue knowledge and skills for centuries, uninterrupted by senility. Once an inhabitant's life had been prolonged, however, he must remain in Shangri-La or suffer rapid decay. Escape was always possible, but the perilous journey to the outer world could lead only to death. When the porters did come and Mallinson insisted on leaving, Conway was reluctant to go but felt that he must protect his friend. The two men and a fragile girl, Lo-tsen, left the peace of Shangri-La, and from this point the story is hazy. What happened to them is not known.

This is a story of drama, of quiet beauty, of satire, and of humor. Readers who enjoy the fantasy of Paul Gallico and Robert Nathan read *Lost Horizon* with interest and pleasure.

Book talk possibilities include the arrival of the party at the monastery, pages 53–64; a passage from the meeting between the High Lama and Conway, pages 153–92; or the secret of longevity, pages 140–41. As follow-ups use *Green Mansions** by Hudson, *Tryst* by Thane, *Gulliver's Travels* by Swift, and *The Angel Who Pawned Her Harp* by Terrot.

HODNETT, EDWARD

Poems To Read Aloud

1957. Norton.

The *Revenge* was lying in the Azores with five other English ships, repairing their gear and nursing the crews through sickness, when word came that fifty-three Spanish ships of war were drawing near. While the five other ships slipped away, the *Re-*

venge remained behind to take on the patients and try to make her escape later. She was overtaken by the Spanish ships and put up a gallant fight before she sank. Her story, immortalized by Tennyson in "The *Revenge*," was chosen for this collection along with a great variety of narrative poems ranging from "The Deacon's Masterpiece" by Holmes to "Casey at the Bat" by Thayer. In the introduction the editor says that the poems were chosen for readability, literary excellence, and variety. Many of the poets included have written a great number of poems which might have been selected, and it is suggested that the reader explore the complete works of these authors and discover these for himself. Lyric poems have also been included, and these range from "Meeting at Night" by Browning to such familiar lines as "The Lake Isle of Innisfree" by Yeats. The whimsey of Lewis Carroll and Ogden Nash, the philosophical approach of John Donne, and the pathos of A. E. Housman are among the dozens of moods represented. John Donne's "A Hymn to God the Father" was chosen as an example of how a poem should be read, and the editor gives some very helpful suggestions. He also thinks that listening to poetry recordings will help a reader improve his reading ability so that the experience of the listener will be as delightful as that of the reader. Reading aloud is the best way to understand a poem. Young adults accustomed to singing the latest hit tunes or taking part in guitar-accompanied folk sings may be unaware that they are reciting poetry in public. Reading verse aloud as a hobby may not be practiced widely outside Greenwich Village or academic circles, but the art of poetry recitation can be developed with this collection, selected for that purpose. The alphabetical-by-poet arrangement produces no subject grouping, but facilitates quick location while creating interesting juxtapositions of style and content. Christopher Marlowe shares a page with Don Marquis, and Edith Sitwell faces Sir Philip Sidney. An index of titles and first lines speeds location of favorite poems not known by writer.

This book appeals to anyone who likes poetry. A poetry club could be organized, using this collection as an introduction to many types of verse and supplementing it with recordings or guest poet appearances.

For a book talk the librarian might read a variety of poems by old and new authors: "The Listeners" by De la Mare, "A Late Lark" by Henley, "Flannan Isle" by Gibson, "The Ladies of St. James's" by Dobson, and "Bears" by Guiterman. Suggest *Complete Poems** by Frost, *Final Harvest* by Dickinson, *Collected* 87

Lyrics by Millay, *A Book of Americans* by Bénet, and *Times Three* by McGinley as other books of poetry which young people enjoy.

HOLT, RACKHAM

George Washington Carver

1943. Doubleday.

Henry Ford, Thomas Edison, and Franklin D. Roosevelt counted him among their friends. Honorary degrees, tributes, and laudatory speeches were bestowed upon him liberally and deservedly. His books and technical articles were milestones in the fields of experimental science and mycology. He was a man of honor and intellect who happened to be a Negro. Born of slave parents in Diamond Grove, Missouri, in 1864, the orphaned George grew up with the Carvers, white owners of his mother, and knew the discontent and uncertainty of the Reconstruction era. His people had been freed, but their freedom was not enriched by education and the opportunity to advance socially. After a boyhood of living with various families and picking up a piecemeal education, George attended Simpson College in Indianola, Iowa, in 1890, and then enrolled in the Iowa Agricultural College in Ames in 1891. By diligent application and the development of a natural gift for working with plants, he graduated in 1894 and stayed on as an assistant botanist. An artistic streak had revealed itself years before, and a painting of his won honorable mention at the Chicago World's Fair of 1893, but experimental science was his major interest. In 1896 he joined the staff of the Tuskegee Institute in Alabama and began working to help his people help themselves. Tuskegee, founded by Booker T. Washington in 1881, was a pioneer school for Negroes and was to be Carver's home for nearly fifty years. The extent of his research—often unorthodox but always thorough and precise—produced untold scientific advances and proved that a dark skin did not equal a slow mind. Lucrative patents, fine clothes, payment for research, awards and honors, an increase in salary—none of these things interested Professor Carver. His hope was to be a worthy representative of his people and to open up the possibilities of utilizing natural products. That they could be used he demonstrated; their ultimate development he left to others. With cotton slowly debilitating the soil and the economy of the South, Carver introduced the revolutionary idea of rotating crops and planting the cowpea, otherwise known as soybean, to help revitalize the land.

Traveling classrooms in wagons brought the people visual proof of how to use plants and plant products to improve diet, land, and living conditions; how to make cheap but effective paints, dyes, and building materials at home from products available around the farm. When cotton began to lose its position as the king crop, the peanut helped support the economy. Shampoo, plastics, paper, ink, coffee, shaving cream—three hundred products could be derived from the plant the gentle botanist had been working with for years. Synthetics from sweet potatoes, dehydration of foods, and other ideas advanced by Carver years before became important factors during World War II. Until his death in 1943 at the age of eighty-three, prejudice, misunderstanding, and criticism haunted him, but his interpretation of nature to the world remains a lasting tribute.

A laudatory, often sentimental biography, this presentation of Carver nevertheless transmits much of a unique man's spirit and accomplishments. The language is simple enough to appeal to the slowest readers, while the impact of his scientific discoveries will intrigue the mature young adult.

A "natural" for the student who enjoyed Washington's *Up from Slavery*, this biography can be introduced by mentioning George's narrow escape from death in infancy, pages 1–4; the day after Christmas in 1892 when the boys at school outfitted him and sent him to Cedar Rapids to display four of his pictures, pages 86–87; some of the products derived from the cowpea and peanut, page 228; and by contrasting his humble origin with his eventual fame. Books about other outstanding Negroes include *My Lord, What a Morning** by Anderson, *Victory over Myself* by Patterson, *It's Good To Be Alive* by Campanella, *Angel Mo' and Her Son, Roland Hayes* by Helm, *The Honey-Pod Tree* by Walker, and *Doctor Dan* by Buckler.

HOWARTH, DAVID
D-Day: The Sixth of June, 1944
1959. McGraw-Hill.

On June 6, 1944, more than 100,000 English and American troops, supported by 5,333 ships and landing craft and 9,210 aircraft, made the largest landing ever attempted in enemy territory. It was an assault on the Normandy coast in an effort to establish a second front and force the Germans to surrender. The D-Day invasion of the continent had been planned for months as a combined sea-air-land operation to surprise and conquer the

German forces. The greatest danger was the weather, and the generals made and discarded many plans before the critical hour arrived. At last, General Eisenhower made the decision to proceed. The author tells the story through the experiences of about thirty men who took part in the invasion. During the night, parachutists and gliders carrying demolition teams, engineers, and fighting men landed in France with orders to blow up bridges or secure them, capture gun emplacements and pillboxes, and in other ways prepare the ground for the main infantry landing. Visibility was poor, and many pilots had inadequate training for this mission. Thus the men were scattered when they came down, and it was up to the few who were on target to carry out the assignment often without the necessary equipment. With daylight the landings on the beaches began, frequently with serious errors. One group came ashore a mile farther south than planned, but the infantrymen used their common sense and initiative and headed for their objectives as soon as they had oriented themselves. Despite the blunder, only twelve men were killed and a hundred wounded. This was a contrast to Omaha Beach where nearly everything went wrong. The air bombardment missed its targets; the amphibious tanks were lost at sea; the demolition task force lost nearly half its number almost at once; and the beach was in a state of chaos when the infantry arrived. German emplacements were pouring lead onto the beach and landing craft. Survivors assumed that the invasion had failed, but seven hours later their position improved. Meanwhile, on the British beaches the landings were also going ahead often under very tough conditions. Some of the British units had been more carefully prepared and meticulously briefed than the American units, with the result that fewer men were lost in their initial assault.

At times the reader may wonder how the attack ever succeeded when the obstacles were so immense, and then he knows that with such raw courage, doggedness, and heroism it could not have failed. Boys read this vivid account of the individual exploits of the invasion forces with great interest and excitement.

For one book talk possibility consider the capture of the Merville battery by the British 9th Parachute Division, pages 40–50. The heroic, decisive leadership of General Theodore Roosevelt, Jr., produces a smile as well as a feeling of pride, pages 102–3. George Mabry, who was smaller than other men, proved his worth by leading the advance on one section of Utah Beach, pages 110–16. Other excellent accounts of D-Day are *Invasion: '44* by Turner, *The Longest Day* by Ryan, and *The Far Shore* by

Ellsberg. Howarth's other books of the war might also be suggested: *We Die Alone,** Sledge Patrol,* and *Across to Norway.*

HOWARTH, DAVID
We Die Alone
1955. Macmillan.

On the 29th of March, 1943, a fishing boat with twelve men on board made landfall on the northern coast of German-occupied Norway. Four of the men were Norwegian soldiers and trained saboteurs. On board were eight tons of explosives, food, equipment, and weapons. Within a day of their arrival, however, all of the plans and supplies had been blown to pieces and the adventures, tragedies, and self-sacrifice which followed became a matter of chance and of courage. When the men realized that they had been betrayed, they blew up their boat, escaping in a small dinghy. The Germans opened fire, and Jan Baalsrud was the only one to escape. A manhunt began, and the enemy searched relentlessly for him in the fjords and villages. Jan became a symbol to his countrymen who felt that somehow he must escape, that the Germans must be ridiculed and humiliated. Wounded and weary, he sought shelter and care and was never rejected by the sturdy people who faced death at the Germans' hands if they were caught aiding him. Jan's flight to the Swedish border involved weeks of perilous adventure. At one point he skied through a group of sleepy German soldiers on their way to breakfast; he caused an avalanche and, after a fall of three hundred feet, was buried in the snow. He dug himself out, but injured, frozen, and finally snow-blind he wandered helplessly. After several days he bumped into a house and there met Marius. Jan was so badly frozen that gangrene attacked his feet and he became a helpless invalid. He had to be moved on a stretcher or sledge, and at one point spent three weeks in a sleeping bag in the open on a high plateau, covered by four feet of snow during a blizzard. Finally a breathtaking journey in the midst of a herd of reindeer driven by two Lapps brought him to the Swedish border and freedom.

The high adventure and overpowering drama of this true story appeal especially to boys.

Almost any chapter makes exciting reading and telling. The avalanche, pages 85–97; the deserted hut episode, pages 115–32; Chapter 11, in which Marius and his friends risk their lives to take Jan up to the plateau—are all good incidents for book

talks. Other World War II escapes are *A Man Escaped* by Devigny, *The Colditz Story* by Reid, *The Wooden Horse** by Williams, and *The Long Walk* by Rawicz.

HUDSON, WILLIAM

Green Mansions

1916. Dodd.

A birdlike voice echoed throughout the tropical forest, but the
lush foliage concealed the source of the melody, too lilting to be
human and yet too cleverly evasive to be a birdsong. It was a
sound which brought a man back again and again to a secluded
part of a Venezuelan forest, shunned by superstitious Indians as
an evil wood. It was the singing of Rima, a girl more bird than
human, which was to haunt the man's dreams forever. Abel,
forced to flee for his life from political enemies in Venezuela,
had taken refuge in the interior with a tribe of Indians. One day
he had come upon a section of forest which resembled a park,
and there he had heard Rima for the first time. When he finally
chanced upon the slim girl with the long dark hair who seemed
able to communicate with the animals, he realized that it was she
whom the tribesmen feared as the evil daughter of Didi. Rima,
through an intimate knowledge of her forest companions, saved
Abel from the effects of a snake's poison and nursed him back to
health in the hut of old Nuflo, her adopted grandfather. After
this, Abel realized he loved the girl, but she was more concerned
with finding her own unknown people. Willing to do anything
for Rima, Abel set out with her and Nuflo to locate her former
home. At the conclusion of a long, fruitless journey, the two men
returned to find Nuflo's hut destroyed and the girl, who had returned ahead of them, gone. Only a blackened, smoldering tree
remained as a memorial to Rima, who had been trapped and
sacrificed by the Indians in the flaming pyre. Abel, obsessed by
Rima's beauty, eventually realized that only after his own death
could he recapture her perfection, but meanwhile he must make
himself worthy of her.

This tale is not easy reading but it appeals to mature lovers of
fantasy. Use it with readers who enjoyed *The Enchanted* by
Coatsworth or *Tryst* by Thane.

A brief description of Abel and his first encounter with Rima
might be enough for a book talk to classes. The poetical qualities of the story may make introduction only to individual readers preferable. The unrequited love theme is repeated in *Por-*

*trait of Jennie** by Nathan; another unusual story in which the young man survives a tragic love is *Laughing Boy* by La Farge. This is also only for mature readers and one which the librarian should read before recommending.

HULME, KATHRYN

The Nun's Story
1956. Little.

This is the story of the metamorphosis of Gabrielle Van der Mal of Belgium into Sister Luke in a renowned nursing order and her seventeen years of struggle with conformity and obedience. The author creates a very real picture of this young nun, with excellent descriptions of the daily disciplines of convent life. At the end of Gabrielle's stay at the mother house, she took her vows and was sent to the School of Tropical Medicines where she enjoyed working under her instructor, Dr. Goovaerts. Her next assignment was to a sanitorium for mental diseases, where she was nearly killed when she went alone to the cell of a violent patient and where beloved Sister Marie was fatally stabbed in the back while on duty in a ward. When the time came for her final vows, Sister Luke's dream to go to Africa was realized. She spent six satisfying years in Katanga, working with a malaria expert and chief surgeon, Dr. Fortunati. She trained the natives to assist in various hospital routines and shared the dramatic work of Father Vermeuhlen from the leper colony. These years had their share of horrifying experiences. Sister Luke saw three Italians buried alive in quicksand and the remains of her helper, Banza, who had been consumed by man-eating ants. Finally she contracted tuberculosis and became a patient in an African hospital. She eventually recovered and returned to duty. She was asked to take a patient home to Belgium, and there she reentered the mother house for reassignment and a rest. She was working as a nurse in pulmonary surgery in a hospital on the Holland border when the Nazis invaded at the beginning of World War II, and became involved, to the consternation of her superiors, in the work of the underground. She hid a British flier in a hospital room supposedly sealed for fumigation, passed messages, and held conferences with young nursing aides who also were part of the underground. Through all of this, she continued to examine herself, to ask whether she had the right to be a nun when she was disobeying the rules of her order. Eventually she realized that she must renounce her vows and return to the world. Her   93 interest in surgery, medicine, and her patients came before her allegiance to her religious order.

Suggest this to girls of average, or better, reading ability who are interested in nursing, medicine, or a religious vocation.

The first few chapters give a vivid description of a nun's preparation for the novitiate and life in a religious community and could be used as a book talk. There are objections to *The Nun's Story* from some Catholic orders, although others assign it as a book report. Check with local parochial schools before recommending it to Catholic classes or individual readers. Other books of similar interest are *Northern Nurse* by Merrick, *White Witch Doctor* by Stinetorf, *Nun in Red China* by Sister Mary Victoria, and *Her Name Is Mercy* by Del Rey.

HUXLEY, ALDOUS

Brave New World

1932. Harper.

It all started with Ford and his Model T. Under Ford's influence, mass production and consumer happiness were primary goals; human aspirations shifted from truth and beauty to comfort and security. A new society emerged in which all babies were conceived and nurtured scientifically in bottles under state control. By "decanting" the genetically predetermined embryos at various stages of development, nearly complete control of mental and physical characteristics was possible. Some babies became clever Alphas; others grew into capable Betas, stupid Gammas, and on down the stratification to insensate workers. State nurseries, equipped with hypnotic recordings and staffed by psychological manipulators, turned out individuals conditioned to accept their required places in the social framework with no desire to be imaginative or creative. With stability supreme and dissatisfaction eliminated, comfort and happiness became synonymous. Depression was cured by the happiness drug "soma," and complete freedom of sexual expression from childhood made inhibitions unknown. Birth control was universal, and the mere mention of normal birth, parental love, and family life caused acute embarrassment. For fun, the citizens attended the "feelies" —movies with tactile senses—or took part in exhausting orgies accompanied by artificial music. Ford superseded God, and the devout made the sign of a T as in Model T. Suffering, heroism, and the right to struggle for a cause were abolished. Books mentioning an earlier way of life were kept in vaults for rare con-

94

sultation. One citizen, Bernard Marx, was imperfectly conditioned to be an Alpha and experienced annoying dissatisfactions. In order to settle his mind, he and his friend Lenina visited the "uncivilized" area in New Mexico where they were revolted by people living in family groups rather than in antiseptic surroundings. One of the natives, John Savage, fell in love with Lenina and returned to London with them, but the cold, sterile, inhuman way of life forced him into a hermit's existence in the country, where he became a tourist attraction. His great anguish and the ridicule of the citizens eventually caused him to commit suicide rather than endure the insensitivity of the totalitarian, comfort-centered society.

Huxley's concern for the encroachment of standardization and scientific control of humanity bursts forth in this shocking and hideously prophetic glimpse of a possible future world. Here is a bitter, satiric challenge to our society. The forceful writing and important implications of the story make it imperative that the librarian read it before suggesting it to mature young adults.

The frank discussion of sexual promiscuity, included not for sensation but to emphasize the dehumanization of the citizens, makes this a novel for recommendation to individuals rather than for a book talk title. Titles which also present pictures of changed societies include *Nineteen Eighty-four* by Orwell, *Looking Backward* by Bellamy, and Huxley's sequel, *Brave New World Revisited*. The librarian should read all of these before recommending them.

JAMES, HENRY
The Portrait of a Lady [1881]
Modern Library.

Ralph Touchett would probably have asked Isabel Archer to marry him if his health had been better. Although he was an American, he had lived in England most of his life because his father had amassed a fortune in the banking business there and the family home was there. Ralph introduced Isabel to a good friend and neighbor, Lord Warburton, who promptly fell in love with her and proposed marriage. Isabel came from an American family of moderate means; she was a student and a dreamer, whose restless mind was trained and ready for whatever future would greet her. She had been carried off to England by her aunt Mrs. Touchett, Ralph's mother, who for years had lived a strange semiseparated life from her cultured, invalid husband. Now that

95

Isabel had an invitation to travel, she was not willing to settle down; besides, she valued her freedom, even in marriage. Tradition and protocol might well enslave her if she married into the nobility. A well-to-do American friend, Caspar Goodwood, had followed her to England, but he had no better luck with his proposal than Warburton. When Ralph saw that Isabel would not accept either young man, he persuaded his father to leave to Isabel a good part of the inheritance intended for him. Upon the elder Mr. Touchett's death a short time later, Isabel became wealthy. Shortly thereafter she and her aunt left for Italy, seeking culture, pleasure, and the best of the world's treasures. Pursued by all her former admirers, Isabel went her own sweet way, always hunting for the best of everything. Thus she was trapped —by his surface brilliance—into marrying the self-centered, small-souled, money-hungry Gilbert Osmond against whom everyone warned her. The change in Isabel began with her marriage; too late she realized her mistake. Bit by bit she learned the details of Osmond's past life, the reason for her own vast inheritance, and the depth of love each of her two early suitors had had for her. Most of all, she came to appreciate Ralph before he died. Isabel was one who stuck to a bargain no matter how disagreeable it might be, and she returned to Italy after Ralph's funeral to resume her life with Osmond.

This is a psychological character novel of great penetration and a valuable commentary on the foibles of the human race. Older girls appreciate it.

A summary of the beginning of the story, including Isabel's refusal of Lord Warburton, arouses interest. *Vanity Fair** by Thackeray; *The Return of the Native, Tess of the D'Urbervilles,* and *The Mayor of Casterbridge** by Hardy; *The House of Mirth* and *The Age of Innocence* by Wharton; and the novels of Jane Austen are suggested for those who ask for other mature titles.

JENKINS, ELIZABETH

Elizabeth the Great

1959. Coward-McCann.

Princess Elizabeth was only three when her mother, Anne Boleyn, was beheaded and only eight when Catherine Howard, another of her father's wives, met the same end, but the events made her realize the power of a king and the uncertainty of marriage. She vowed then that she would never wed. When her father, Henry VIII, died, the succession arranged was Edward, Mary, Elizabeth, and then a member of Henry's sister Mary's family. For eleven years Elizabeth was surrounded by plots, intrigues, and conspiracies, but she had the good sense to keep clear of all of them and thus, through a very difficult period, managed to keep her head on her shoulders. At twenty-five, with Edward and Mary dead, she ascended the throne. Then began a long contest between Elizabeth and her ministers—they to find a suitable husband for her and she to stall them off without appearing to do so. Tall, slender, and straight, the queen had her father's ability and physical magnetism combined with some of her mother's fascination and a strain of hysteria. When she appointed William Cecil as Secretary of State, they began a lifelong partnership nourished by mutual aims and respect. They saw the future of England bound up with the Reformation; they deplored the ruinous waste of war; and they agreed that the national credit must be reestablished. Elizabeth had an instinct for diplomacy and finance that amounted to genius. On occasion she could act as ruthlessly as her father, yet she was humane and had a real capacity for gratitude. She gave a steadfast loyalty to her friends, but did not hesitate to dispose of those who threatened her position. Generally speaking, she was a good ruler. Near the end of her life, her health failed, her temper was shorter, and her memory not always good, but her sharp mind did not desert her. Her people had loved her from the first, and as the years passed this love grew to adoration.

Senior high school students interested in this dramatic period of history enjoy this frank but excellent biography. The theory that Elizabeth was the mistress of one man or another is discounted by the author for lack of proof.

For a book talk give a short explanation of the marriages of Henry VIII and the resulting heirs to the throne, and then use Chapter 3 as an example of the dangers surrounding Elizabeth before she became queen. This book can be used with *King's Fool* and *My Lady of Cleves* by Barnes, *All the Queen's Men* by Anthony, *Kenilworth* by Scott, *Lady in Waiting* by Sutcliff, and *Elizabeth and Essex* by Strachey.

KANE, HARNETT

Miracle in the Mountains

1956. Doubleday.

"Not to be ministered unto, but to minister" were the words upon which Martha Berry based her rich life. Born into a well-to-do plantation family, she might have enjoyed the pleasures of a Southern belle and been a social leader; instead she chose to do something to improve the lot of the mountain people of Georgia. It started on a Sunday afternoon when she was reading in a little log cabin near her home. Three grimy little boys watched her from the window. At first they were too shy to talk, but finally they were persuaded to tell where they came from—Trapp Holler and Possum Trot. They did not go to school or Sunday School because there were none available. Soon she was holding them spellbound with stories from the Bible, and as the weeks passed, their friends and relatives joined the circle. These people needed to learn to read and write. Thus began Martha Berry's log-cabin school. Out of it grew one of the most unique educational institutions in America. Its campus has over 30,000 acres of woods, fields, mountains, and lakes. Many of the buildings have been put up by the boys themselves, and they have constructed much of the furniture, in addition to carrying an academic program. The girls have learned homemaking, cooking, sewing, and weaving, and have helped to keep the buildings in order. Much of the food used at the school has been raised by Berry students. Martha Berry, small and pretty, was determined to provide a richer life for the Southern highlanders. For almost six decades she was tireless in traveling around the country making friends for the Berry schools and securing financial aid. She was supported in her beliefs and in her work by many: the wealthy and influential like Andrew Carnegie, who offered $25,000 if she could raise an equal amount; President Theodore Roosevelt, who infected others with his enthusiasm for the school; and Mr. and Mrs. Henry Ford who gave generously of their money, interest, and ideas to further the program. Nothing was ever impossible for her and her students to accomplish. At one time a middle-aged couple gave a chapel in memory of their son who had died during his school years. The plans were made to finish it by spring and dedicate it. One day Miss Berry received a letter that the donors would be at the school in the fall for the dedication. Only Martha could imagine the chapel could be finished six months early. When she insisted, it was completed by the boys working almost night and day. No matter how hard they had to work, the boys and girls who graduated from Berry were devoted to the school and to Martha, and the training they received brought many of them public recognition as the years passed. Eventually Martha Berry was honored by many higher institutions of learning and organizations here and abroad.

Any girl interested in social work or teaching enjoys this book. It is a picture of a woman dedicated to helping people to help themselves and accepting only the best efforts of each. By her example Martha Berry encouraged her staff and students to attempt the impossible and succeed. There are warmth, humor, and understanding in the biography.

Almost every chapter has tellable incidents and anecdotes. Martha's first experience in having the boys work for their expenses and her first students, pages 60–67; her meetings with Andrew Carnegie, pages 99–109; one of her prize students, Eugene Gunby, pages 158–64; and finishing the chapel six months early, pages 192–95 are suggested. Life stories of other teachers are *The Heart Is the Teacher** by Covello, *Yours with Love, Kate* by Mason, and *The Thread That Runs So True* by Stuart.

KENNEDY, JOHN F.

Profiles in Courage

1961. Harper.

Right or wrong, all the men whom the author has chosen as examples of courage were convinced that their course of action was the best for the United States. Usually they were vilified for their decisions; sometimes vindication came during their lifetimes. Each chose to sacrifice his political career, if necessary, rather than vote against his principles. These men were: John Quincy Adams, who believed that private interest must not be put in opposition to public good; Daniel Webster, who voted in favor of the Compromise of 1850 in order to preserve the Union and thereby defied the people of his state; Thomas Hart Benton and Sam Houston, both of whom put the preservation of the Union before their constituents' opinions on slavery; Edmund G. Ross, whose vote in 1868 saved President Andrew Johnson from being impeached; Lucius Lamar, a Southerner, who dared to stand with the North after the Civil War when he thought the bill before Congress was for the good of the whole country even though it did not benefit his state at the time; George W. Norris, who deserted his party's stand when he thought it was wrong; and Robert A. Taft, who spoke out against the death sentences given at the Nuremberg trials although most Americans felt them to be just. A Senator experiences tremendous pressures which influence the stand he takes on any issue. He must consider his party's position, the desires of his constituents, conflicting ideas of special-interest groups, the opinions of his colleagues, and his own pride in office. Believing that as a nation we have forgotten courageous acts of the past, Mr. Kennedy wrote this book as a reminder. He says: "A nation which has forgotten the quality of courage which in the past has been brought to public life is not as likely to insist upon or regard that quality in its chosen leaders today. . . ."

This book was popular with both boys and girls even before the author became President. The stories of courageous statesmen appeal to the idealism of young people.

Any of the chapters could be used for a book talk. Chapter 6 on Edmund Ross can be tied in with *Many a Voyage* by Erdman or Gerson's *The Yankee from Tennessee.** Also suggest *Immortal Wife* by Stone, *The Crisis* by Churchill, and *Six Feet Six* by James.

KIPLING, RUDYARD

Kim [1901]

Doubleday.

Kimball O'Hara was a young rascal, and yet the nickname given to him by the people of Lahore was "Little Friend of All the World." The orphan son of a young Irish sergeant stationed in India, he was cared for by an Indian woman after the death of his parents. On his own most of the time, he had picked up the local dialects, acted as faithful messenger for certain fashionable men of the city, and was an intimate of the begging priests. Kim's keen and curious mind was intrigued by an old lama from Tibet whom he chanced to meet in the city. When he learned that the priest was searching for the sacred River of the Arrow, he volunteered to go with him as his pupil. He confessed to the lama that he, too, was making a search—for a Red Bull on a green field. During the journey Kim delivered an important message to the British for the horse trader Mahbub Ali. As he and the lama continued on the trip, meeting a variety of people, Kim exhibited enough worldly wisdom to get food and lodging, often for nothing and sometimes with a donation as well. Finally he found the Red Bull for which he had been searching. It was the emblem on the green flag of his father's former regiment, the Mavericks, making camp along the road. That night Kim was apprehended as he sneaked into the camp area, but the amulet he wore containing his birth certificate and his father's discharge papers proved his connection with the regiment. The men offered to pay for

Kim's education and he was enrolled in school, where he studied for three confining years. During vacations he returned to Mahbub Ali and began his training for the Great Game, as the secret service was called. When he left school, he was allowed to turn his back on his English background and rejoin the lama. Together they moved about India seeking the sacred river, and Kim had several opportunities to aid his colleagues in the Great Game before he finally brought the lama to his rest.

A particularly good picture of India at the beginning of this century, the story appeals to mature readers who enjoy details.

A brief mention of Kim's unique freedom and his adeptness at deception, begging, and spying, Chapter 2, provide an adequate introduction. For views of modern India, suggest *Nectar in a Sieve** by Markandaya and *Amrita* by Jhabvala. *A Passage to India* by Forster and *My Heart Has Seventeen Rooms** by Bartholomew give still other pictures of India. *Broad Highway* by Farnol is the story of another perilous journey and of high adventure.

LANDON, MARGARET
Anna and the King of Siam
1944. Day.
Left penniless by bank failure and her young husband's untimely death, Anna Leonowens had to support her two children and herself. A well-educated woman, she was able to open a school for officers' children in India, but it was not a financial success. After a year she began negotiations for the position of governess to the royal children of Siam. She sent her small daughter to school in England but kept the younger child, Louis, with her when she set out for Siam. The first person she met from the Royal household was the prime minister, or the Kralahome, who was neither courteous nor hospitable. In time, however, Anna's dignity, common sense, and courage commanded his respect. Several weeks later she saw the King, and soon she began to teach the children and such members of his harem as wished to learn. Anna was appalled at the squalor, subservience, and brutality she witnessed. The King had absolute control over the life and death of his subjects and was very short-tempered and vindictive. The atmosphere of the harem was oppressive, and because of her hatred for slavery and any insult to human dignity, Anna could not be silent. Many times she interceded with the King on behalf of 101

unfortunate people, and there were only two she could not save. For five years she struggled with the difficult task of teaching, at the same time trying to instill Western ideals. She also acted as part-time secretary and sometimes as hostess and adviser to the King for social affairs involving representatives of foreign governments. Finally the climate and the uncertainties of life at court broke her health, and she was obliged to return to England. She promised to return if she were able, but the King died and she changed her plans. A very important day came later in her life when she learned that her pupil, Prince Chulalongkorn, upon being crowned King, had abolished slavery forever and declared the people free—free to worship and to speak.

Senior high school girls and some boys enjoy this book.

There are many delightful, amusing, or impressive passages that might be read or told. Pages 24–29 describe Anna's arrival and first day in Bangkok. The description of the palace and her first audience with the King is amusing, pages 55–61; her introduction to the children and women of the harem caused her surprise, pages 95–99; the coming of the red snake was propitious, if frightening, pages 105–7; the freeing of the slave L'Ore was fascinating, pages 163–84. Although *Fanny and the Regent of Siam* was written by Minney, it is almost a sequel. *Windows for the Crown Prince* by Vining tells of another governess-teacher's influence on an heir to a throne.

LANSING, ALFRED

Endurance: Shackleton's Incredible Voyage

1959. McGraw-Hill.

"The order to abandon ship was given at 5 P.M. For most of the men, however, no order was needed because by then everybody knew that the ship was done and that it was time to give up trying to save her." Thus begins the dramatic survival story of twenty-seven men on an Antarctic expedition led by Sir Ernest Shackleton. On August 1, 1914, they had sailed from England on the *Endurance* bound for South Georgia Island, where they took on sled dogs with which they hoped to cross the Antarctic continent overland from west to east. After leaving South Georgia, they threaded their way in and out of ice floes until the ship was finally hemmed in by ice in every direction. A northerly gale compressed the pack around the *Endurance,* and from January until October she was locked in the ice. Just before the pressures

102

began to break her up, the order was given to abandon ship. The dogs, food, three boats, and all useful items were salvaged. The men planned to make their way to Paulet Island, 346 miles to the northwest, where there were stores left by an earlier expedition. They expected to drag two of the boats with them across the ice as they would probably encounter some open water. The journey became so difficult, however, that they abandoned the idea and made camp, hoping the movement of the ice would take them closer to Paulet. In an effort to hasten their approach they moved camp several times, only to discover that they were drifting diagonally and probably would miss the island altogether. Shackleton's courage and tough command kept up their morale in spite of tremendous hardships. As the ice floes began to break up, the men had to move camp frequently, and when their piece of ice was reduced to scarcely fifty yards across, they were forced to take to the boats. Rain, cold, thirst, lack of sleep and food, frostbite, and adverse winds combined to cause them incredible suffering, and only a miracle brought them to Elephant Island. From here Shackleton and a picked crew set off for a whaling station on South Georgia, 870 miles away. In spite of endless miseries they reached the island in seventeen days, completing probably the most remarkable small-boat voyage in history. After landing on the opposite side of the island from the whaling station, Shackleton and two of the crew made the climb over the "impassable" mountain of rugged rocks and glaciers, because they were not strong enough to sail the 130 miles around. Eventually all the men from the expedition were rescued.

This is one of the great adventure stories of our time. It is the triumph over such incredible odds that appeals to the young adult who looks for hero tales in the twentieth century. Each time a miraculous turn of events saves the party, the reader breathes a sigh of relief. The story is harrowing but represents thrilling testimony to the resourcefulness of men and their ability to fight back despair.

Abandoning the *Endurance*, pages 2–8, is a good introduction to the story, while the attack of a sea leopard on page 102, and the opening of an ice crack directly under a tent, pages 144–45, are short, exciting incidents which could be mentioned. *The Impossible Journey of Sir Ernest Shackleton* by Bixby gives a different account of the same expedition. Other tales of polar experiences are *90° South* by Siple, *Antarctic Scout* by Chappell, *Operation Deepfreeze* by Dufek, *Alone* by Byrd, and *The Crossing of Antarctica* by Fuchs.

LEDERER, WILLIAM J., and BURDICK, EUGENE

The Ugly American

1958. Norton.

These vignettes of Americans living in Asian countries show both good and bad representatives. If the balance seems to be uneven, it is done with a purpose, for the authors wrote the book intending to shake its readers' complacency. Although the characters are imaginary, the authors testify that many of the stupid and tragic events typify American ineptness in foreign relations. Ambassador Sears represents the diplomat whose political activities ensure for him the eventual reward of a judgeship. Meanwhile he acts as the U.S. representative in a small Asian country, neither knowing the language nor understanding the people and their problems. The Russian representative, carefully trained for this particular country, capitalizes on Sears's ignorance and mistakes, and wins friends for Russia at American expense. The ugly American himself, introduced late in the book, is an engineer who develops a practical water pump powered by a bicycle. His companion is a Sarkhanese, who is just as unattractive physically as the American. Together the two men set about building the pumps and organizing the men of the countryside to act as salesmen. Helping the local people help themselves provides the key to success. Two other dramatic stories are those of Father Finian in Burma and John Colvin in Sarkhan. In an epilogue the authors explain their purpose and tell where they received their ideas for some of the characters.

This book interests any teen-age boy or girl who is concerned about the relationship of the United States and its world neighbors.

Since each of the chapters is a short story in itself, it is not difficult to adapt one for a book talk. Chapter 10, "The Ragtime Kid"; Chapters 17–18, the story of the ugly American; Chapter 19, the story of the bent backs of Chang 'Dong; and the stories of the two Lucky Lou's in the first two chapters are a few suggestions. In *A Nation of Sheep,* Lederer attempts to answer the numerous inquiries he has received as a result of *The Ugly American. Ambassador's Report** by Bowles and the Thomas A. Dooley's books, such as *Deliver Us from Evil,** show the kind of representatives the United States needs abroad. *Friend to Friend* by Buck and Romulo is another book which points out American mistakes as well as successes overseas. *Rice Roots* and *The Twisted Image* by Goodfriend should also be recommended.

104

LEE, HARPER
To Kill a Mockingbird
1960. Lippincott.

This is an unsentimental account of small-town family life in
Maycomb, Alabama, in the 1930's. It is especially the story of one
family, the Finches. The father, Atticus, is a lawyer and legisla-
tor; the son Jem is ten; and Jean Louise, more commonly known
as Scout, is the tomboy younger sister. When Atticus is at the
office or out of town, Calpurnia, the Negro cook, looks after the
children whose mother is dead. With Scout as narrator a picture
of the town, the people, and a way of life emerges. Most of the
book centers around the adventures of the children and their
friend Dill, who comes to Maycomb during vacations. Many of
their adventures are connected with Boo Radley, a recluse neighbor who has not been outside his home for many years. The children are curious and have many escapades attempting to find out
about this man whom they have never seen. Atticus is involved
in a case of a young Negro, Tom Robinson, who has been accused of raping Mayella Ewell, a girl from the town's most dis-
reputable white family. To the dismay of his neighbors and
friends Atticus, believing that Tom is innocent, decides to defend him. When a group threatens to lynch the Negro, Atticus
attempts to protect him, but it is Scout who actually saves the
day. The children see abuse heaped on themselves and their
father as a result of his stand. Against their father's orders, Jem
and Scout go to the courthouse to watch the trial. Friendly
Negroes let them sit in the colored section, and through Scout's
eyes the reader witnesses the trial. Although Tom is convicted,
the jury did deliberate outside the courtroom and many people
felt that he was innocent. Mayella's father, trying to get even
with Atticus for showing him up as a liar, tries to kill Jem and
Scout, but Boo Radley, who has always watched the children,
saves them.

Mature young people from ninth grade up are enthusiastic
about this book. It has a quiet style, but the picture of Southern
childhood through Scout's eyes is very appealing. The trial is
excellently handled without sensationalism. It is not the charge
of rape which is important, but the fact that prejudice is operating to ruin the life of a human being. This discovery makes a
great impression on Jem, and when he finds it disturbing, Atticus
tries to explain it so that the boy sees the event in its proper
perspective. The manner in which Atticus and Calpurnia handle   105

many difficult events as the children are growing up shows how values can be instilled in the younger generation by patience, understanding, and discipline, coupled with common sense.

Book talks can be based on the occasion when Walter Cunningham comes home to lunch with Scout, pages 25–31, and the incident in which Jem ruins Mrs. Dubose's camellias, pages 108–21. This book could be used as a follow-up for *South Town* by Graham, a story in which a Negro family plays the leading roles. Other stories showing close family relationships are *Mama's Bank Account* by Forbes and *Mary Emma and Company* by Moody, while titles dealing with racial problems are *Cry, the Beloved Country** by Paton and *A Raisin in the Sun** by Hansberry.

LEVIN, IRA

No Time for Sergeants   (Play)

1956. Random.

Will Stockdale, a good-natured hillbilly from Georgia, did not know that Pa had torn up the annoying letters from the draft board until Mr. McKinney, the government man, came around to check up on the situation. With his patriotic duty revealed to him, Will agreed to go along and be inducted. His intentions were "to get along in the draft and not have no trouble," but the ways of the military were incomprehensible to him. He was plagued with practical jokes and insults and forced to establish his prowess as a fighter and the defender of Ben Whitledge, another recruit. Since his new buddy wanted to follow family tradition and transfer into the Infantry—the group "doin' the real fightin' "—Will crashed in upon Sergeant King the first night in camp and stated the case. As a consequence, King tried to punish the ingenuous Will by making him Permanent Latrine Orderly —a post which Will considered a position of honor. When the Captain in charge learned of King's maneuver, he demanded that Will be classified and moved on to another unit unless the Sergeant wanted to assume the newly created post himself. A battery of physical and psychological tests produced hilarious results, and since classification seemed impossible, Sergeant King and Irvin, another inductee, concocted a plot to implicate Will in a brawl and have him dismissed on a disorderly conduct charge. Will, of course, emerged unscathed, and King bore the brunt of the riot. The next morning, when Will's elaborately rigged latrine equipment saluted a pleased visiting Colonel, the future seemed bright for the boys until the bedraggled King wandered in to disgrace them all. Temporarily demoted, the hapless King joined Ben and Will in Gunnery School. Final disaster came when Ben and Will boarded a plane which became lost and flew into the New Mexico atomic testing area just as a bomb was detonated. The pair were assumed missing, received posthumous decorations for bravery, and then appeared unharmed. Their mere presence threatened to disrupt the dignity of the ceremony, and at the end they were transferred to the Infantry.

The humor of Will's blunders, the commentary on prejudice, and the satire on military life combine to produce a readable and unique drama. The earthy dialogue and situations make this a play for recommendation to individual older boys rather than for a book talk title. The play is based on the novel, *No Time for Sergeants,* by Mac Hyman.

The same kind of ingenuous bumbling is repeated in *Anything Can Happen* by Papashvily, *The Education of Hyman Kaplan* by Ross, and *Jest Olga* by Reed. Another humorous story of army life is Hargrove's *See Here, Private Hargrove.*

LEWIS, SINCLAIR

Arrowsmith

1925. Harcourt.

Martin Arrowsmith grew up in Elk Mills in the state of Winnemac. Encouraged by Doctor Vickerson, the village practitioner, he decided on a medical career. Bacteriology interested him most, and he worked closely with Professor Max Gottlieb, who lived for pure scientific research. Martin decided to follow in the great man's footsteps, but he gave up this idea when he met an attractive nurse, Leora Tozer. They began their married life in her hometown, Wheatsylvania, North Dakota. Family troubles and local distrust of the new doctor made life unbearable, and so they moved to a larger town where Martin eventually became head of the Department of Public Health. At this he was a failure. Publication of a scientific paper, however, brought him to the attention again of old Professor Gottlieb, and the young doctor accepted a position with him at McGurk Institute in New York. Working conditions there seemed ideal for both men until they learned that their associates demanded showy results and were less interested in unglamorous, pure research. When a plague broke out on St. Hubert in the West Indies, Martin and Leora hurried there to help fight the epidemic and test his newly developed antitoxin. He worked furiously to curb the disease which 107 spread daily. Leora accidentally smoked a cigarette saturated with germs, and when she died Martin lost interest in his work. As soon as the plague abated, he returned to New York. Later he married wealthy Joyce Lanyon, a young widow whose shallow code was the same as the fashionable scientists at McGurk. When it was evident that she and his new friends refused to understand and accept his work for itself and not for fame and promotion, he left them to carry on independent research in Vermont.

An emotional portrayal of the sham and hypocrisy which can invade medical practice, this novel appeals to mature young adults who identify with a man chafing under the conventional patterns of society.

Book talks can be based upon a general description of Arrowsmith's dreams for the future and his early frustrations, pages 10–15, 35–42, 55–62, 148–52, and 162–69. *The Citadel* and *Shannon's Way* by Cronin deal with similar conflicts between the pressures of society and research, while Camus' *The Plague* depicts another doctor's struggle against an epidemic in a large city. Try *Bellevue Is My Home** by Cutolo, *Prophet in the Wilderness** by Hagedorn, and *Doctor Hap** by Burke for true accounts of dedicated doctors.

LINDBERGH, CHARLES A.

The Spirit of St. Louis

1953. Scribner.

On May 20, 1927, after months of dreams and preparation a young pilot, Charles Lindbergh, took off from Roosevelt Field, New York, and landed some thirty-three hours and 3,600 miles later at Le Bourget Aerodrome, Paris. The year before, when he had been flying the mail from St. Louis to Chicago, he had decided to try for the $25,000 prize offered by Raymond Orteig for the first nonstop flight across the Atlantic. All he needed were backers, money, and a plane. Suddenly two St. Louis businessmen offered to handle the financial end while Lindbergh negotiated for the plane. Other fliers favored a trimotored plane while Lindbergh was set on a single-engined one. He finally found a small manufacturing company in California which promised a specially designed plane in two months. Each man in the shop working on it took a personal interest in the flight, and no pains were too great and no hours too long to insure that everything was perfect and finished on time. Meanwhile other fliers had found backers and planes, all trimotored; these competitors were notable: Commander Byrd, Nungesser and Coli, René Fonck, and Noel Davis. It looked as though these men would be ready before Lindbergh was. Just as he started his test flights, the papers began to report crack-ups of the other planes, and the two French fliers who took off from Paris crashed in the Atlantic. After ample testing Lindbergh flew to St. Louis, making a record flight; then on to New York for some adjustments and repairs and to wait for good flying conditions. Finally, on May 20, he took off in partly foggy weather, fully prepared to turn back if it did not clear. Visibility improved and he turned toward Nova Scotia. As he flew he reminisced, and the reader learns much about the early days of aviation and also about Lindbergh's childhood and youth. When sleep nearly overtook him, he fought it with every method he knew. At the first sight of Ireland he was alarmed, because he had not expected to reach the island for another two hours and he thought he must be very much off course. But he soon identified it and flew on toward Paris, where he was greeted by a tumultuous reception and the American ambassador.

Written in the first person and usually in the present tense, this account makes the reader feel as if he were in the cockpit with the pilot. Touched with the mature philosophy of a thinking scientist, this book is an inspiration to older boys. Its stylistic construction is a work of art.

An early experience of flying the night mail without lights is an exciting incident to tell, pages 5–9. Or use the time Lindbergh had a contract for fireworks when he was barnstorming and had to fly at night, pages 181–87. Other accounts of pioneer pilots may be found in *Wind, Sand and Stars** by Saint Exupéry, *Visibility Unlimited* by Grace, and *Under My Wings* by Rowe.

LLEWELLYN, RICHARD

How Green Was My Valley

1940. Macmillan.

With his shirts and socks wrapped in the little blue cloth that once was his mother's head shawl, Huw Morgan looked about the sturdy little house being engulfed by mining slag and recalled his life there. He had grown up in the small Welsh mining town in the beautiful, peaceful valley, the youngest boy in a family with a strict, religious father and five headstrong, independent brothers. His earliest recollections were of his father and brothers coming home from the mines on Saturday night and giving his mother their earnings. Times were good and the money box in the kitchen was full, but soon trouble began to come to the mines. When the price of coal declined, wages dropped and the miners were restless and unhappy. Huw's brother Davy became a union organizer, and two of his other brothers, Owen and Gwilym, helped him. Their father was opposed to unionizing the mines and felt there were other ways to deal with the owners. Finally, however, the men went on strike and the mines closed down. After six months of watching their families starve, the men agreed to return to work for lower wages. The book deals not only with the labor troubles but with the daily affairs of this warmhearted family. The reader shares their closeness in family gatherings, the gentleness of their teasing, the bitterness of their arguments, and the joy of their celebrations. One by one the brothers and sisters married and established their own homes. Huw was the pet of the family because of an illness brought on by the exposure he endured when he saved his mother's life, and for years he was confined to bed. His questions about the ways of adults were sometimes answered by his favorite sister-in-law, Bronwen, or by the minister, Mr. Gruffydd. It was the minister who gave Huw the faith that he would walk again and carried him up the mountain to see the daffodils. He demanded the best from Huw, and the boy tried hard to live up to his friend's expectations. There was sadness in the family as well as joy. Owen's stubbornness made him reject the girl he loved. She married his brother Gwilym, but her love for Owen drove her out of her mind and brought an early, tragic death. Angharad wanted to marry Mr. Gruffydd, but as a minister he was dependent upon the sincere but meager generosity of his parish, and he knew he would never have much to offer her. She married someone else, but neither was really happy. As time went on, Ivor and Mr. Morgan were killed in mine accidents. Huw went to work in the mines when he finished school but soon left to make his living as a carpenter and cabinetmaker. Year after year the slag piles became larger and larger, encroaching upon the village, and finally, when the family home was threatened, only Huw remained.

This story, with its singing rhythms of Welsh speech, appeals to both boys and girls who are mature readers. It is a book of great beauty, human understanding, and sympathy. In his creation of the Morgan family the author has succeeded in presenting

splendid characters, each with a distinct personality. The joy of the people, their gift for music, and their love for the old ways so fast disappearing provide a unique background.

Incidents which might be used for book talks are Huw's successful efforts to save his mother's life, pages 58–66, and his moving experience with his father just before the older man died in a mine cave-in, pages 490–93. Books of similar interest are *The Stars Look Down* by Cronin and *The Valley of Decision* by Davenport.

LORD, WALTER

The Good Years

1960. Harper.

The "good years" were the fourteen years between the optimistic opening of the twentieth century and the fateful assassination of an Austrian archduke at Sarajevo. It was the time "after plumbing and before taxes." Peace was taken for granted, prosperity was on the upswing, and men were experimenting with ideas as well as with the phenomena of the laboratory. Newspaper headlines proclaimed the marvels of the 1901 Pan-American Exposition in Buffalo, where electric lights were first used for display effects. A few days later the same papers were bordered in black; the Exposition had gained additional fame as the site of President McKinley's assassination. Wealthy dowagers and poor factory girls were seen on Fifth Avenue, not as shoppers but as united marchers in the suffragette movement. The vigor and enthusiasm of "Teddy" Roosevelt and his magnificent family seemed to color the times, so full of promise and hope for a better world. Peary's controversial discovery of the North Pole fed the newspaper hoppers for months, while stories about strange flights by the Wright brothers appeared with increasing frequency. The disastrous earthquake and fire in San Francisco stirred up the compassion of the American people and showed the world the resiliency of a nation under stress. Millionaires heaped up their securities free from taxes, played with the country's financial machinery, and helped quell a panic which the government could not control. It was a time of great extremes— the very rich were trying to outdo one another in costly social functions, while almost two million children of the poor worked a sixty-hour week for forty cents a day. The Boxer Rebellion, Wilson's rise and decline, and the *Titanic* disaster all contributed their part to the excitement of the day. It was a kind of "last fling" of adolescent happiness before the miseries which began in 1914, but it was a period which also glowed with the enthusiasm of youth.

Mature students who enjoy history recounted with dramatic and vivid details enjoy this episodic account. Lord's flair for writing makes the times come alive, brings the past into the present.

Book talk material abounds, but the assassination, pages 41–52, and part of the earthquake description, pages 120–33, are especially effective. For more details about this period suggest *The Big Change* by Allen, *The Roosevelt Family of Sagamore Hill** by Hagedorn, or Lord's *A Night To Remember*. Mature young adults might go on to Tuchman's *The Guns of August** for a concentrated study of the beginnings of World War I and White's *The Making of the President, 1960* for a comparison of changes in political methods.

LOTI, PIERRE
An Iceland Fisherman [1886]
Dutton.

In Brittany there lives a group of people somewhat removed from their countrymen by a tradition of work generations old—a tradition which seams the brow, toughens the body, and scars the soul. Every February the men say farewell to wives or sweethearts and sail for the fishing grounds off Iceland. With the first mists of autumn the fishermen return for a brief resumption of family life. Gaud Mevel had been born in Paimpol and had lived there until she was six. Then her father, who was prosperous, had moved to Paris where they lived while Gaud grew up and until her father retired. Returning to Paimpol, they found the people reluctant to accept Gaud with her fashionable clothes. Her cousin Sylvestre, with whom she had played as a child, was very happy in his engagement to Marie Gaos. He wanted to see Gaud marry his best friend, Yann Gaos, but his brawny companion was tempestuous, impatient of marital ties, proud, stubborn, and by his own confession in love with the sea. Gaud, however, had fallen in love with Yann the first time she had met him on the street in Sylvestre's company. At a wedding a short time later they were partners, and Yann gave every evidence of having fallen in love with her. Afterward he avoided her, although she sometimes saw him with other girls, and neither she nor Sylvestre could understand any reason for his coolness. The next season found Sylvestre in the army, and Yann was at sea when word came of his friend's

112

death in China. Gaud wrote to Yann to tell him, but she did not mention that her own father had died and had left her penniless. Sylvestre's grandmother was destitute without his support; so Gaud moved into her cottage to take care of the old woman. The next winter a misfortune to Grandmother Yvonne drew Yann and Gaud together, and he asked Gaud to marry him. An idyllic but short courtship, a quiet wedding, and a week's honeymoon followed before Yann left for the Iceland fishing grounds. Gaud was left to wait and yearn, for he never returned.

A lyrical saga, this classic catches the moods of nature and the ways of simple people. Here are primitive superstition and sturdy faith, the majestic beauty of sky and sea, fog and gale. Older girls and boys, especially those sensitive to fine writing, appreciate this story.

For girls, describe Gaud's visit to Yann's home when, lovesick, she stays and stays, looking for a glimpse of him, pages 67–77. For boys, tell of Yann's declaration that someday he will marry the sea, pages 3–13. Other romantic stories with a sea background are *Rain on the Wind** by Macken, *Silas Crockett* by Chase, *Moby Dick* by Melville, and *The Cruise of the Cachalot* by Bullen.

MACKEN, WALTER

Rain on the Wind

1950. Macmillan.

In the west of Ireland is Claddagh, a town of sturdy, Viking-blooded fisherfolk. As sure as the tide's out or the mackerel's in, the men take to sea in their currachs, and the women wait their return with mugs of hot tea and chunks of pancake. Mico, son of Micil Mor, was born a true Claddaghman. From boyhood he had the love of the sea and was strong, bronzed by the sun and spray, and destined to be poor but content in his poverty. Mico grew up to be tall and sturdy, but a red, rough birthmark clawed its way down the left side of his face as if to remind his mother of the pain with which she bore him. His brother Tommy was handsome with a brilliant though shallow mind. Their mother's favorite, Tommy wanted to escape poverty and drudgery and become a fine gentleman. Mico wanted only to join his father and grandfather in the fishing boat. As he grew from scamp-size with mischief on his mind to man-size with stirrings of love in his heart, he knew the warmth of friendship with the old schoolmaster; with Gran, slowly losing his physical strength; with his

113

plucky and loyal friend Twacky; and with Peter and Jo, whose keen minds and deep understanding upheld him. Love came to Mico at fourteen on an enchanted summer night when he was visiting his Uncle James and the young people were digging on the beach for the glittering sand eels. The girl's name was Maeve and she discounted his ugly face, but her love was for Coimin, Mico's older friend. Even after Mico returned home and his first love was wed, he kept the magic of that evening alive. Violence came to Mico, too. To the violence of suicide he lost his best friend Peter; to the violence of the sea he lost his beloved Coimin; and the violence within himself brought him close to murdering his brother. Near the end of the story, when Maeve came to Claddagh, Mico had the bittersweet joy of being united with her.

This poetical, moving story of Irish life appeals to the mature young adult who enjoys the development of memorable characters in fiction. Mico's growth from a naughty boy chasing geese to a shy, strong man is unforgettable.

For book talks introduce Mico, the tot in red petticoats, as he wallops the gander and is pursued to the quayside, pages 1–6; show him trapped in the fairy thorn tree surrounded by the beady eyes of a thousand rats, Chapter 4; show him at sea when there's "rain on the wind" and a ghost ship stalks the waves with silent oars and oarsmen, pages 209–14. Follow with *The Green Years* by Cronin and *Greenwillow** by Chute for stories of other unusual boys growing up. *The Green Hills, and Other Stories* by Macken and *The Hands of Cormac Joyce* by Wibberley reflect other moods of Irish life, while Loti's *An Iceland Fisherman** continues the theme of lives shaped by the sea.

MARKANDAYA, KAMALA

Nectar in a Sieve

1955. Day.

Rukmani's marriage was arranged by her parents when she was twelve, according to Indian custom. The villagers felt she had married beneath her, but since she was the fourth daughter, her father's shrinking income could not be stretched to provide a dowry for her. Only a poor man would take a poor wife. Accustomed to a nice home, she was dismayed at the mud and thatch hut to which Nathan took her, but she soon learned from neighbors that he had built it proudly with his own hands. She was glad she had not revealed her disappointment upon her arrival.

114   Together they worked the land as tenant farmers, hoping to have

their own farm some day. They did own two bullocks and a milch goat, and from each harvest they stored some rice in their small stone-lined granary. Rukmani even planted a small garden near the hut and grew pumpkins, beans, sweet potatoes, brinjals, and chillies. Happiness increased with the birth of their daughter, Irawaddy, but then for several years there were no more babies and Rukmani worried. When Ira was seven, the first boy was born, and in the next four years four more boys came into the world. With six children to feed, the family could no longer afford to eat all the vegetables they grew. Rukmani took some to the village to sell and when she could, she put away a rupee or two against the time of Ira's marriage. They had to sell the goat and could not afford to buy milk for the children. Suddenly industry came to their community; houses were pulled down and a new tannery was built. At first the villagers shied away from the newcomers who worked in the tannery. When Ira was fourteen, a go-between found a husband for her, and she was given as fine a wedding as Rukmani and Nathan could afford. That year the monsoon broke early; the crops were ruined and they had to dip into their savings to buy food. After five years Ira returned home because she was barren and her husband needed sons. When Arjun, the oldest boy, was in his early teens, he went to work for the tannery much against his mother's wishes, and before long the second son joined him. With their money the family began to live well again. Rukmani had taught her children to read and write, and this ability made her sons leaders at the tannery. Eventually they led the workers to ask for more money; management retaliated by taking away their lunch period, and the employees struck. But a strike was not the answer because there were many others eager to take their jobs. The workers went back, and after a time the two boys had a chance for jobs in Ceylon. When Rukmani said good-by to them, she knew she would never see them again. Then drought came, and once again there was no food. One son went off to the city as a servant. When the situation became really desperate, Ira turned to prostitution in a vain effort to feed her baby brother. When the owner of their land sold the farm to the tannery, Rukmani and Nathan had no means of support. Ira went to live with her brother Selvam, who was by this time studying medicine with the village doctor, and the old couple decided to go to the son in the city. Upon arriving there, they found he had disappeared. Without money for food or the journey home, they went to work in the stone quarry, but privation and despair killed Nathan. He died in Rukmani's arms murmuring, "Have we not been happy together?" and she was able to answer, "Always, my dearest, always."

Life in an Indian village is determined by the earth-cracking droughts and the monsoon floods, and thus far nothing can be done to control them. This gentle couple, who struggled so bravely to make ends meet, were defeated almost from the beginning. Their story, unflinchingly real and moving, is told with compassion and is a triumphant vindication of the human spirit. *Nectar in a Sieve* appeals to young adults who are mature readers.

Effective in a book talk are the scenes of the wedding and the wedding trip, pages 11–14, and Rukmani's encounter with a cobra, pages 23–25. A likely companion is *The Good Earth* by Buck for its picture of people of the soil; also *Let the Hurricane Roar* by Lane for a bride's struggle with the elements, and *Chemmeen* by Sivasankara for the way another Indian girl coped with tragedy.

MARQUAND, JOHN P.

The Late George Apley

1937. Little.

Born in 1866 on Boston's Beacon Hill, George Apley was brought up in the orderly, proper way befitting a resident of that age and address. He said once of himself, "I am the sort of man I am, because environment prevented my being anything else." After a proper adolescence he was enrolled at Harvard—an experience destined to mold him further into a gentleman of honor, distinction, and social position. During his undergraduate years he did make the acquaintance of an eccentric or two, but a letter from his father firmly counseled him to cultivate the "right" people, those worthy of a member of the respected Apley family. Only once did George feebly try for freedom—when he fell in love with a little Irish girl from South Boston. His family terminated this affair, and she was never openly referred to again. A trip to Europe in the company of his aunt, uncle, and a girl cousin who had also been seriously interested in the wrong person served to provide new interests and restore his vigor before he entered law school. After serving in the Apley Mills for a time, George took his uncle's advice and entered a law firm. He also married Catherine Bosworth, daughter of a family in his parents' social set. The two families provided them with a summer cottage, a winter house, and all the comforts. George settled down to the

116

life of an elite, with membership in all the best clubs. His own two children, John and Eleanor, worried him because they seemed inclined to rebel and escape the family mold. John married a charming divorcee—happily of an old and established family. They eventually provided the Apleys with a grandson who was immediately enrolled by wire at Groton. Eleanor married an undistinguished Midwestern journalist, who displeased her father because he would not stay in Boston and work in the family business. As the years passed, Apley's principles never waivered and he defied prohibition as an abuse of his rights. He resented the large fortunes accumulated by the uncultured and uneducated. When George was warned by his doctor of heart failure, he put "his house in order" and passed away in gentlemanly fashion in December, 1935. Before he died, he was reassured by the fact that John had decided to move his family from New York to Boston, and it seemed likely that the Apley traditions would be preserved for at least another generation.

This is a delightful satire on Boston and its rigid mores. It also portrays the lack of understanding between generations and the futility of attempting to mold youth in older behavior patterns. Written in biographical style with frequent use of letters, this novel with its subtle humor and irony appeals only to the very astute young person.

The novel is best introduced to individual students rather than to a class. Readers who enjoyed Galsworthy's *The Forsyte Saga** might be interested in this family story. *The Magnificent Ambersons* by Tarkington is another story of an important family, but here the son, in departing from the familiar pattern, arouses the enmity of the community.

MARTIN, BETTY

Miracle at Carville

1950. Doubleday.

This is the true story of an attractive girl who writes under the assumed name of "Betty Martin." Nineteen and engaged to be married, she was supremely happy; then her world crumbled. It was at a family Christmas party that her uncle, a doctor, told her the results of a recent physical examination. She had leprosy. Two weeks later, accompanied by her mother and Robert, her fiancé, she was driven along the twisting Mississippi River road to Carville National Leprosarium, which she entered under an assumed name, lest word that she had contracted this dread disease get back to her family's neighbors and acquaintances. For a time Robert wrote faithfully, and as Betty responded to the first treatments everyone was encouraged and felt she would soon be discharged. As time passed, Robert's letters became more infrequent, and when she returned home for her second Christmas leave her fiancé told her that although he wanted to, he could no longer love her, and the engagement was broken. Initially Betty had remained aloof from the other inmates, but as it became apparent that her stay was to be an extended one, she began to make friends with the other patients. Soon her acquaintance with one of the young inmates, "Henry Martin," deepened into love and marriage followed. With the aid of their parents they left Carville without being discharged. After more than five years of freedom, Henry's condition required medical attention, and they returned to the hospital. The illness of both of them had progressed, and it began to look as if the only release from Carville was death. As they learned more about Hansen's disease (as the illness is now officially called), they became more interested in helping each other and all members of the Carville settlement; larger projects than their personal dreams gave them a reason for living. Finally, during World War II, the breakthrough in the treatment of Hansen's disease came. The use of sulfone drugs brought amazing results. Henry began to improve; Betty reached the end of her twelve tests with the much coveted negative response. At last, after twenty years, they left Carville together to start the life they had looked forward to for so many years.

Girls who like nursing stories or books about handicapped persons find this an intriguing adult study of prolonged illness.

The opening chapter and the first few weeks at Carville make a good book talk. *No One Must Ever Know* is a sequel dealing with the Martins' problems of adjustment to the outside world. Similar titles are Farrow's *Damien the Leper* and Burgess' *Who Walk Alone*.

MAUGHAM, W. SOMERSET

Of Human Bondage

1915. Doubleday.

Orphaned at the age of nine, sensitive, lame Philip Carey went to live with his uncle at the vicarage of Blackstable, sixty miles from London. The pompous vicar was a penny-pinching, smug individual lacking in human understanding. Philip grew up in

118

a sterile atmosphere, becoming ever more hostile and bitter about his clubfoot. At eighteen, having come into a small inheritance, he persuaded his uncle to allow him to go to Germany to study. There he met several young men whose discussions convinced him that the rigorous religious training of his youth was the cause of his unhappiness and spiritual suffocation. As he denied the existence of God, he denied his own love-starved youth and experienced a feeling of idealistic freedom. He began to discover that he was born in bondage and became free of one emotional shackle only to be enchained again. His enduring enslavement was to his ideals, which gave him a recurrent "pang of bitterness because reality seemed so different from the ideal." He studied art in Paris, but after two years gave up the idea of being an artist and went back to London to study medicine. There he met the unscrupulous, amoral Mildred Rogers, a crude, uneducated waitress. He transferred all of his romantic idealism to her, and once again became enslaved by his own passions. She spurned his proposal of marriage because of his lack of money and went away with another man. Later when she returned to London, penniless and pregnant, Philip took her in and cared for her until her child was born. Then she left him again, and Philip rededicated himself to his work and to his new friend Athelny. One day he came upon Mildred in the street and realized that she was earning her living as a streetwalker. He was sorry for her and took her in as his housekeeper. Mildred professed her love for him and became insanely angry when he repulsed her. She virtually destroyed the apartment and his possessions before she left him. When Philip was forced to give up his medical studies for lack of money, the Athelny family took him in and helped him find employment. Then the death of his uncle provided him with an inheritance which allowed him to finish his medical education. Although he was more than thirty years old when he graduated, he still held on to unrealistic, romantic dreams of the future. He planned to become a ship's doctor and sail around the world before he settled down to a permanent practice. But through his intimate association with Sally Athelny, the daughter of his friend, Philip finally realized that he really wanted a home, a family, and security. He had tried to live in the future; now he wanted to enjoy the present.

Mature readers follow this long autobiographical novel with interest. Here is a young man's search for a way of life. The thoughts and actions of a frustrated and confused boy are told with mature wisdom and understanding. The book traces Philip's **119** development from uncertainty and bewilderment to maturity and spiritual freedom, when he is finally able to achieve a satisfying philosophy of life and face the future with confidence, courage, and humor. It is an unusually long book, but it is one of the rare psychological novels which appeals to boys probably even more than to girls.

To introduce the story to individual readers, discuss Philip's life in Germany and his attempts to understand himself and his place in the future, pages 107–55. Other autobiographical novels are *David Copperfield* by Dickens, *The Way of All Flesh* by Butler, and *Clayhanger* by Bennett.

MAUGHAN, A. M.
Harry of Monmouth
1956. Sloane.

Young Hal, son of Henry, Earl of Lancaster, experienced a childhood full of bitterness and loneliness. His first heartbreak came at the age of six, when his beloved mother died. Four years later his father was banished from the country because of a quarrel with the reigning Richard II. Virtually an orphan, Hal was taken to court as a kind of hostage and came to admire the King, his father's cousin. Soon Henry returned to England, gathered the dissatisfied nobles about him, and seized the throne in 1399. Within six months Richard died, presumably of a wasting fever, but Hal heard rumors that his father had starved the former King to death. Hal was sent to Oxford to continue his education, but when trouble broke out in Wales, the fourteen-year-old boy, as Prince of Wales, had to help put down the rebellion. The great soldier, Lord Percy, was given the task of teaching Hal the ways of war and guiding him in the defeat of the Welsh. Hal was terrified as any teen-ager would be in his first battle, but Percy was firm since he knew that a usurper would always have uprisings to quell. The time came, however, when Percy himself plotted against Henry, and Hal was forced to defeat his old friend and teacher. During the years that followed, Hal became a riotous fellow and a drunkard, refusing to marry Anne of Burgundy, his father's selection for him. Doubts about his father and dislike of his own role as heir to the throne seemed to be the reason for Hal's drowning his unhappiness, but he was always ready to lead an army with skill when necessary. When King Henry IV died, Hal was at his side, trying even then to solve the mystery of Richard's death. The Hal who ascended the throne in 1413 as

Henry V soon became a different person. The new King was compassionate, honorable, and as devoted to his followers as they were to him. When it became clear that France must be stopped from raiding English coastal cities, Hal and his forces landed at Harfleur and laid siege to the city. Sickness struck his troops, but Harfleur fell and Hal pushed on toward Calais. The ensuing conflict at Agincourt, in which six thousand English soldiers defeated a French army about six times that size, cemented the love of his people for Hal. Eventually he negotiated a marriage with Katherine de Valois, daughter of the French King. Hal had fallen in love with her portrait, and fortunately she returned his affection. He never saw the heir she bore him, however, since he was destined to die on French soil while in his thirties.

Henry V seemed to have every good quality a great king should possess, and it is little wonder that he was one of England's most-beloved rulers. Young people with any liking for history read this book with deep feeling.

For book talks describe Hal's early heartbreaks and then mention the Battle of Shrewsbury, when Hal saw his friend, turned traitor, die at his feet, pages 1–15, 31–47, 76–93. Other dramatic incidents include Hal's coronation, beginning on page 180, and the Battle of Agincourt, beginning on page 293. *Within the Hollow Crown* by Barnes is the story of Richard II, and *The Gentle Falcon* by Lewis tells of Queen Isabella, Richard's child bride. Shakespeare's *Henry V* and *Richard II* give another writer's view of the same events and persons.

MAXWELL, GAVIN
Ring of Bright Water
1961. Dutton.

When he moved into Camusfeàrna about five years after World War II, the author found the cottage on the northwest coast of Scotland a perfect temporary retreat from the mad pace of the world. Isolated, primitive, and unfurnished, the small house became habitable as boxes, boards, and other usable items cast up on the beach were turned into furnishings. With his dog Jonnie as constant companion, Maxwell observed the wild animals and birds, studied the fascinating aspects of the sea, and enjoyed the occasional visits with his nearest neighbors, the MacKinnons. The first part of the book is devoted to beautiful descriptions of the landscape, beaches, waterfalls, and wild life. It was the loss of Jonnie that created in the author a desire for another kind of pet, for no other dog could replace his favorite. While traveling in Iraq, Maxwell encountered a rare variety of otter which appealed to him, and he decided to take one back to England. Mijbil was to become a most fascinating pet and comrade, but the agonizing, yet afterward amusing, trip home by air was an experience to remember. When it developed that Mij was of a race of otter not yet classified by zoologists, Maxwell had the distinction of adding his name to that of the new subspecies. Life in a London flat was a challenge to the otter whose ingenuity, curiosity, and impish activities were exasperating at times even though they were highly entertaining. When it came time to leave the city, Mij was delighted with the train. At bedtime he arranged himself on his back with his head on the pillow and his arms outside the bedclothes, just as Maxwell did. The next morning, when the attendant brought tea, he stared at Mij and asked if it was tea for one or two, sir? In time they reached Camusfeàrna where the otter adapted himself to the wilderness setting with little trouble. The reader is so thoroughly entranced with the intelligence, mischievous antics, affection, and personality of Mij that his violent death after a year's time is a real loss. Maxwell, after unsuccessfully trying to replace the otter, obtained other animals but these proved to be unsatisfactory. Then a minor miracle brought about his meeting with Edal and her owners, who had to leave England and were looking for a good home for her. She was a different variety of otter but equally captivating.

Young adults who like books about the out-of-doors and about animal-human relationships warm to this beautifully written narrative. The quiet style of writing in the first part of the book, however, limits the appeal to a reader who appreciates descriptive writing with little action.

If one of the episodes about the otters is used for a book talk, be sure the listeners understand that the animals are discussed only in the last part of the book. It may be better to introduce the book to individuals rather than to groups. The return trip to London with Mij, pages 82–98; the problems of apartment living, 99–103; and the train trip, pages 113–115, are suggestions for book talks. Follow this with *Strange Animals I Have Known* by Ditmars, *They Never Talk Back* by Trefflich, *My Zoo Family* by Martini, and the "Elsa" books by Adamson, such as *Born Free.** *The Incredible Journey* by Burnford is another appealing animal story, while *Seal Morning* by Farre tells of a girl and her aunt in a lonely section of Scotland who have quite a number of unusual animal companions.

Face to Face

1957. Little.

Blinded by meningitis when he was only three, Ved Mehta had no memory of color, light, or the faces of family or servants. His father, a doctor in the Public Health Department of India, understood and accepted the tragedy, but his mother hoped for a miracle. Dr. Mehta, determined that his son should not become a blind beggar, sent the little boy at the age of five to the Dadar School for the Blind where he learned to get along by himself and with other boys. This period was marked not only by intellectual progress but by continuous childhood illnesses. After three years Ved returned home as he had learned all that Dadar could teach him. He was accepted into the play of the other children in his neighborhood and enjoyed rooftop kite flying with his friends. When following the kite, they had to jump from roof to roof, and Ved followed his companions by sound. In the evenings he gathered with all the children around the grandmother to hear folk tales or her stories of earlier days. He often accompanied his father on business trips. When the doctor was busy, his servant acted as Ved's guide, and they took long walks together during which the man explained the villages, people, and politics of India. He also read the *Ramayana* to the boy, which made a great impression on him. Ved's schooling was also advanced by the "dinner-table school." Since his sisters were in college and had much to discuss and many questions to ask, they talked around the cleared dinner table, and Ved listened. He also attended Emerson Institute where he learned a little Braille, English vocabulary, and history. About this time Ved began to write to schools for the blind in the United States in the hope of studying abroad. When he was finally accepted by the Arkansas School for the Blind, arrangements were made for Ved to live with a blind musician and his wife in New York until school began. These people welcomed him, introduced him to America, and made him feel at home. After two weeks he went to Arkansas where everything seemed strange at first. His quick mind, well-developed "facial vision," and sense of humor helped in his adjustment, and he graduated from high school a year ahead of his class. He managed to finance a college education and went to study at Pomona College in California, where he was elected to Phi Beta Kappa in his junior year. Convinced that his future lay in India, he went for graduate study to Balliol College at Oxford

123

University and from there returned to India. His affection for America will undoubtedly draw him back, however.

This is a story of courage and humility, of gratitude and aspiration. Ved Mehta is sensitive and brilliant and his sense of humor disarms the reader, who has admiration rather than pity for him. Because the book tells a great deal about Indian life and customs, it appeals to the more mature reader.

For a book talk tell a little about Ved's background and then add his experience of repairing and riding a bicycle, pages 40–42. His plane trip to the United States and his visit with the De Francos in New York also catch interest, pages 207–23. The training to develop facial vision and Ved's unusual ability to use it are found on pages 249–60. *I Can Jump Puddles* by Marshall, which tells of an Australian boy, crippled by polio, and his efforts to overcome his handicap, is another title for the mature reader. *My Eyes Have a Cold Nose* by Chevigny, *The Stars Grow Pale* * by Bjarnhof, and *The World at My Finger Tips* by Ohnstad are other books with the theme of blindness.

MICHENER, JAMES A.

The Bridge at Andau

1957. Random.

On October 25, 1956, the chafing of the Communist yoke on the necks of the Hungarian people became unbearable. A revolution, poorly organized and destined for failure, erupted in Budapest and electrified the world. Growing in part out of rejected student demands to broadcast complaints over censored Radio Budapest, the wave of unrest spread quickly. Hungarian soldiers and factory workers joined the hysterical mob which attacked the radio headquarters, newspaper offices, and bookstores to destroy the sources of detested propaganda and get rid of the hated AVO. The Russians killed and wounded many of the rebels, but the ferocity and suddenness of the attack forced them to withdraw. For five days the city was free, and the people talked of establishing a socialist government, retaining some of the practices of a Communist state but having free elections and other democratic procedures. But suddenly one morning the peace of Budapest was shattered by four thousand Russian tanks, set on destroying the city. To help in the destruction came 140,000 of the most ruthless soldiers in the Soviet army plus planes, rockets, and flame throwers. Against this might the Hungarian freedom fighters had only some homemade gasoline bombs, a few rifles, and gren-

124

ades, but they dug in and began killing Russians and destroying the tanks sent against them. The Russians, who were senselessly slaughtering peaceful civilians, said they were liberating the Hungarian people from a few capitalist-inspired mobsters. Escape seemed the only hope for many—both the hunted revolutionary leaders and the dissatisfied who wanted to start life again elsewhere. A tiny, rickety, wooden footbridge provided a thin avenue of escape for a few hectic weeks. Spanning a canal on the border between Hungary and Austria, the structure had been built for farmers, but across it were to pass thousands of fleeing Hungarians seeking asylum in free Austria. About twenty thousand people from nearly every walk of life crossed the bridge named for Andau, the nearest Austrian village. After this symbolic link with liberty was destroyed, thousands more refugees found other means of escape until about 200,000 freedom seekers left their homeland. The men who had been courted most by the Communists were the ones who led the revolt. These were the factory workers of Csepel and the university students on whose loyalty the Russians had counted.

The part played by teen-agers in the revolution appeals to mature young adult readers, who may be shocked into examining their own feelings about fighting for freedom. The tense, suspenseful writing about an event already beginning to fade from memory makes exciting reading and recaptures the impact of a daring rebellion.

Book talks are plentiful, with the beginnings of the uprising, pages 3–8, and the description of the bridge, pages 197–98, as promising episodes for setting the mood of the story. *April Morning** by Fast and *Celia Garth** by Bristow contain some of the same flavor of the struggle against tyranny. *Boy on the Rooftop* by Szabo is a personal reminiscence of the same revolution. Other mature books with symbolic bridges include *A Single Pebble** by Hersey and *The Bridge of San Luis Rey* by Wilder.

MILLER, ARTHUR
The Crucible
1953. Viking.
Witchcraft in Salem, Massachusetts, is dramatically portrayed in this story of self-righteous fanaticism revolving about a serving girl's personally motivated lie. As the play opens, ten-year-old Betty Parris is in a coma and seems to have been bewitched. Her father, the Reverend Samuel Parris, questions his niece, Abigail

Williams, whom he has seen dancing in the forest with Betty while the slave woman, Tituba, sang incantations over the fire. Abigail swears this was just for fun, not for casting spells on anyone, but her uncle does not trust her. The Reverend John Hale has been summoned from the town of Beverly to assist in determining the cause of Betty's strange behavior. Instead of helping, he actually makes the situation worse by asking leading questions. Tituba quickly adopts the actions he suggests in his interrogation, implicating others in a hysterical, semihypnotic manner. Abigail and several young girls join in the frenzy as if they had been mesmerized. The people accused as witches are arrested, and a court is set up to try them with Abigail and her companions as the witnesses. The girls obey Abigail whom they believe to be a witch with strange powers because she drank blood. When John Proctor and his wife learn of it, she urges him to expose Abigail but he hesitates, knowing the girl will reveal him as an adulterer. The first day of the trial many more people are accused and arrested. One confesses; another is condemned to die. The Proctors' servant, Mary Warren, is among the witnesses, and it is obvious that the mass hysteria has taken possession of her, too. Elizabeth Proctor is sure that Abigail has manufactured this scheme of witchcraft to eliminate her as John's wife so that she can take Elizabeth's place. Other people seize this opportunity to get even with enemies, and many accusations are made. After Mrs. Proctor has been in jail for over a month, John goes to Abigail in desperation and demands that she withdraw her accusation against his wife. She refuses, and John tells her he will expose her as a whore. As the trials proceed and seventy-two death warrants are signed, it is obvious that the judges are biased and anxious to find witches. The powerful scene in the court when John accuses Abigail, and she pretends to see a spirit in the form of a bird attacking her, is a good demonstration of mental suggestion. As the play draws to a close, Reverend Hale attempts to get confessions from those condemned to hang. A confession means a pardon, but John Proctor refuses to give the court a written statement and without it he must hang.

This play is recommended for mature senior high school students who are interested in early American history. The story behind the play is especially good because it gives the background of the seventeenth-century witch hunts in New England. The play can also be used with a discussion group.

A book talk can be based on Act I, Scene 1, which takes place in Betty Parris' bedroom. Suggest *The Elegant Witch* by Neill and *The House of the Seven Gables* by Hawthorne as other books with somewhat similar themes. *The Witchcraft of Salem Village* by Jackson is an easy factual book on the subject.

MORLEY, CHRISTOPHER

The Haunted Bookshop

1919. Lippincott.

When red-bearded Roger Mifflin retired from his horse-drawn traveling book wagon and the journeys chronicled in Morley's *Parnassus on Wheels,* he opened a secondhand bookshop on Gissing Street in Brooklyn—a store "haunted by the ghosts of all great literature." Assisted by his charming, well-nourished wife Helen and comforted by Bock, their canine Boccaccio whose Carnegie-style kennel was called the "Reading Room," Roger continued to find life in the world of ideas and ideals stimulating and rewarding. Into the placid shop, better known as "Parnassus at Home," came Aubrey Gilbert representing the Grey-Matter Advertising Agency. Aubrey's plan to sell advertising was thwarted by Roger's dislike of formal publicity, but he remained to eat "Eggs Samuel Butler" and to discover the delights of imaginative bookselling. Aubrey soon found another, less bookish pleasure at the bookshop in the person of Titania Chapman, daughter of Roger's old friend, wealthy George Chapman. Mr. Chapman, hoping that Titania would gain some practical business experience and shake off the effects of finishing school, had apprenticed her to Roger as a clerk. Her presence gave the shop a glamor which Aubrey found irresistible. During his frequent pilgrimages to Gissing Street, Aubrey stumbled upon an assassination plot which revolved around the disappearance and reappearance of a copy of Carlyle's *Oliver Cromwell* from the bookshop. A chef from a New York hotel and the local druggist, Weintraub, became involved in the book's wanderings, and as circumstances developed Aubrey was sure Titania was in danger. Assuming the role of amateur sleuth, he was nearly killed before he found evidence which seemed to implicate Mifflin in the scheme. When Roger was called away to Philadelphia, Aubrey trailed him only to discover his innocence. The pair rushed back to Brooklyn in time to rescue Titania and Helen. Roger's dreams were fulfilled when Mr. Chapman established a fleet of Parnassuses to sell books in distant rural communities. Aubrey won a post in the Chapman firm and had every hope of marrying the boss's daughter.

The charm of this slight mystery is in the inimitable, bookish character of Roger Mifflin. His numerous quotations and allusions to books arouse the curiosity of most imaginative young adults and give them a picture of the almost lost art of personalized bookselling.

Too much revelation of the plot and the intricacies of the conspiracy would spoil the story for a prospective reader, but the brief description of the shop on pages 11–15 and a glimpse of the mystery surrounding the copy of Carlyle could constitute an introduction. A companion to Morley's *Parnassus on Wheels,* this mystery could lead to more involved suspense novels such as Stewart's *Nine Coaches Waiting** or the Sherlock Holmes stories by Doyle.

MORRIS, EDITA

The Flowers of Hiroshima

1959. Viking.

In this short, moving account of the aftereffects of the atomic attack on Hiroshima, Yuka-san, a young Japanese woman, tells of her family and a young American businessman, Sam Willoughby. Much as Mrs. Miniver became the symbol of all that was enduring in England, so Yuka-san may become the symbol of all that is courage for the proud Japanese people. Fourteen years after the bombing, Sam came into Yuka-san's troubled life. Eager to know about the ways of the Japanese people, he decided to live with her family rather than at a hotel. Here he watched Yuka-san as she served as an anchor for her whole family, though she herself bore the scars of the radiation burns she had received at the time of the bombing. Her husband, Fumio, was dying from the effects of radiation; her young sister, Ohatsu, was unable to marry her sweetheart because his parents feared the effects of the bomb on the couple's children. Yet in spite of these calamities, Yuka-san showed a brave, cheerful face, hid her sorrows in her heart, helped and comforted friends in the neighborhood, and tried to keep the terror of her position from her friend Sam. He, in the meantime, began to realize how much the Nakamura family and their friends had been affected by the bomb dropped by his countrymen. He had many chances to remember the philosophies of his own doctor-father as he shared the life of this courageous family.

Yuka-san's narration gives an insight into the oriental mind and character which interests young people. At first the book

128

appears to be sentimental in tone and mood, but this effect evolves into an understanding of the Far Eastern attitude. Mature girls like it very much.

Very effective book talks may be based on the chapter describing Ohatsu's visit to her future parents-in-law, pages 163–75, or the first part of the book which tells how Sam met Yuka-san and why he took a room in her house. A stronger, factual version of the bombing is found in *Hiroshima* by Hersey and *No High Ground* by Knebel. *Alas, Babylon** by Frank and *On the Beach* by Shute are other fictional accounts of the aftereffects of nuclear bombs. A happier glimpse of Japan will be found in Bosworth's *The Lovely World of Richi-san** and in *Rain and the Feast of the Stars* by Hatsumi.

MOSCOW, ALVIN

Collision Course

1959. Putnam.

On the night of July 25, 1956, the Swedish ship *Stockholm* was off the New England coast, outbound from New York, plowing along toward Copenhagen. Inbound from Italy, running a similar course on her final leg of the trip to New York, steamed the Italian luxury liner *Andrea Doria*. Both ships were equipped with every possible safety device and were commanded by experienced seamen. On the fog-wrapped *Doria*, the officers watched the Swedish ship on their radar screen without plotting her approach. The officer on duty on the *Stockholm's* bridge saw the other ship on his radar equipment, and as the vessels drew closer he charted their courses. He did not plan to adjust his own until he saw the *Doria's* lights. When the other ship was finally sighted, it was very close and suddenly turned across the *Stockholm's* path. A crash was inevitable, and the supposedly unsinkable Italian liner went to the bottom of the sea with a loss of more than fifty lives. For many of the 2,000 persons on both ships, chance played an important role in survival at the moment of impact. One couple was spared because they had ordered a second cup of coffee. This kept them from returning to their cabin which was obliterated by the collision. A teen-age girl was lifted out of her bed on the *Doria* by the *Stockholm's* bow and pinned in its wreckage until rescued by a seaman, who, moments before, had left the forecastle because of seasickness, thereby escaping being crushed with his messmates. Heroism, cowardice, the mad scramble for the lifeboats—all added their part to the disaster and rescue operations. 129

The stories of dozens of passengers are told succinctly and dramatically as the suspense builds. The details of the trial which followed provide a fascinating account of the factors contributing to the accident, and the documented evidence is presented with impartiality.

Good readers in junior high school like this book, and it may be introduced successfully to average readers in senior high who like action narratives. Anyone who has read or seen the film version of Lord's *A Night To Remember* will read *Collision Course* with interest.

Base book talks on a brief description of the collision plus a few details concerning passengers on the *Doria;* Chapter 6 contains several tellable incidents. *Johnstown the Day the Dam Broke* by O'Connor, *Tiger on a Leash* by Moscow, Gallagher's *Fire at Sea,* and *Miracle at Springhill* by Lerner are also accounts of disaster. Other rescue stories to suggest are *Skeleton Coast* by Marsh, *Rescue!* by Arnold, and *The Grey Seas Under* by Mowat.

MOWAT, FARLEY

The Dog Who Wouldn't Be

1957. Atlantic-Little.

It happened during the 1929 drought in Saskatoon, Saskatchewan. The Mowat family, which included a young son Farley, had been for a whole month without a dog. Then one afternoon when the father came home from work, he was greeted with, "Isn't he *lovely,* darling, and so *cheap* . . . I've actually saved you a hundred ninety-nine dollars and ninety-six cents." ($200 was the price of the retriever father had wished to buy.) Mother presented the small, nondescript, bedraggled pup she had bought at noon for four cents from a small boy who had come to her door. Named Mutt, the dog failed to show any retriever characteristics, although both father and son struggled desperately to teach him. In fact, he did not seem to want to admit that he was a dog, but considered himself just another member of the family. One day, near the end of the hunting season, Mutt discovered what a retriever should do and proceeded to demonstrate his prowess in a number of humorous episodes. Climbing ladders to chase cats, chewing gum, and leaning so far out of the rumble seat of the family car that Farley had to hold onto his tail were among the antics he performed. The author had other pets besides Mutt, and he includes some stories about snakes and his owls, Wol and Weeps. The owls loved to ride perched on the back of the rumble seat, bouncing up and down, while Mutt rode between them wearing his motoring goggles.

This especially appealing "boy and dog story" interests any reader who likes humorous tales. It is reminiscent of *Cheaper by the Dozen* by Gilbreth and *Old Yeller* by Gipson.

Book talks leap from every chapter, but the bath episode, pages 24–37; the bet on Mutt's retrieving ability in Chapter 6; the goggle incident, pages 141–47; and the skunk trouble in Chapter 14 are especially fun to tell. This book will lead to reading in other animal fields as well as in the dog kingdom. Suggest *Born Free** by Adamson, *Thrills of a Naturalist's Quest** by Ditmars, *Wild Voice of the North* by Carrighar, *The Incredible Journey* by Burnford, and *Ring of Bright Water** by Maxwell.

MUNTZ, HOPE

The Golden Warrior

1949. Scribner.

Edward the Confessor, King of England from 1042 to 1066, had no children, but there were several willing candidates ready for the succession. Bishop Brihtwold had had a dream early in Edward's reign in which St. Peter supposedly said, "The Kingdom of the English belongs to God; after Edward He shall provide a King according to His pleasure." Earl Godwin, until he died in 1052, was the strongest man in the Kingdom, the power behind the throne. Upon Godwin's death Harold inherited his father's titles and lands and took his place with the King. In gratitude for a miraculous cure of an ailment which had wasted him for a long time, Harold strove to do what he thought was just and right for England and was well loved by the common people. He was curious about William, Duke of Normandy, who was sometimes mentioned as Edward's successor, and when Harold was shipwrecked on the Normandy coast, imprisoned, and held for ransom by a minor noble, he appealed to William for aid. William graciously paid the ransom and welcomed Harold and his men as his guests. Harold did not realize that he was actually William's prisoner until he received an urgent message from England summoning him home as soon as possible. He was surprised and shocked to find that the man he had admired so much should be so lacking in integrity as to deny him the right to return home. In order to obtain his freedom Harold had to swear that he would help William gain the throne of England 131 when Edward died. Harold knew that an oath made under pressure was not binding, but when he found that the covered article on which he had sworn was not a sacred jewel—as he had supposed—but the bones of a saint, he was dismayed, since this kind of oath was more binding than an ordinary one. He was also forced to leave his young brother as hostage and to become betrothed to William's daughter, Agatha. It was a heavy price to pay for freedom and eventually brought about his downfall. When Edward died, the Great Council chose Harold as King, and he broke his oath to William. Now known as Harold II, he ruled from January to October, 1066, when he marched south to meet William at the Battle of Hastings after having suffered great losses in his victory over the Northmen at Stamford Bridge. Harold and his brothers fell on the field of battle, and England passed into Norman hands.

Mature high school students enjoy the superb characterizations of the two protagonists: Harold and William. The stories of the battles at Stamford Bridge and Hastings have an epic quality and make the historic characters and events come alive for the reader.

A weird incident to relate is Harold's encounter in the forest with the Old Woman who bit his hand and brought a strange sickness upon him, pages 45–57. Pages 110–41 tell of Harold's shipwreck and his rescue by William, of the months spent in Normandy, and of his oath to help William gain the throne of England. Other accounts of the days of the Norman Conquest are *The Conquerors* by Costain, *The Fourteenth of October* by Bryher, *The Last Englishman* by Weenolsen, and *Harold, the Last of the Saxon Kings* by Bulwer-Lytton.

NATHAN, ROBERT
Portrait of Jennie
1939. Knopf.

> Where I come from
> Nobody knows
> And where I'm going
> Everything goes
> The wind blows
> The sea flows—
> And nobody knows.

132 These were the words sung tunelessly in the dusk of a winter evening to the discouraged young painter, Eben Adams, by a small girl he had stopped to watch playing hopscotch in Central Park. She was well dressed but in an old-fashioned coat, gaiters, and bonnet. After Eben spoke to her, they walked through the park together, talking. She said that her name was Jennie Appleton and that her parents were actors playing at the Hammerstein Music Hall. With a shock Eben remembered that the theater had burned down years before, when he was a boy! When they reached the end of the park, Eben said good-by to Jennie. "I wish you'd wait for me to grow up but you won't, I guess," she said, and a moment later was walking away down the Mall. Back in his studio, Eben sketched a portrait of Jennie as he remembered her in her quaint clothes in the park. This seemed to mark the beginning of his popularity as an artist, for three days later he sold the sketch. From time to time Eben saw Jennie again, and always she seemed to be taller and older than he remembered her. His skill seemed to improve, especially when he was painting Jennie, and she came to his room occasionally to pose for him. He took the finished painting to the art dealer who had befriended him, and the man was so impressed with the masterpiece that he gave Eben $300 on account, hoping to sell "Jennie" to a museum or private collector. Months passed before Jennie came again to spend a whole day. This time she was a young lady and was being sent to France to school for two years. Eben spent the summer on Cape Cod, and in late September in a great hurricane Jennie appeared to him again, struggling futilely to escape the clutching sea. Eben tried to save her, but she was torn from his arms by the monstrous waves.

This is a strange tale—a story of mixed time sequences and an odd air of dream and unreality; and poetic evocation of the poignancies of life and love moving in the irreversible stream of time. Girls who like fantasies are captivated by this charming book.

Great care should be taken with this delicate story when attempting a book talk—so much depends on the way in which it is told. A lengthy description is dangerous lest the mood be lost. The first two meetings may be used, stressing Jennie's desire to grow up fast and emphasizing the strangeness of the two occasions. The fantasy theme runs through *Lost Horizon** by Hilton, *Tryst* by Thane, and *Green Mansions** by Hudson. *Outward Bound* by Vane and *Voice of the Lute* by Baner may also be used as follow-ups. *Gramercy Park* by Brooks tells of another little child in the same period in which Jennie lived but does not have the mysticism.

OGBURN, CHARLTON, JR.

The Marauders

1959. Harper.

Complete with a map of the 1944 Burma Theater, this book is a record of Merrill's Marauders, as they were named from their commanding officer—a tale of this rough, tough, resourceful, almost free-lance fighting arm of the U.S. Army which was sent to rid the Burma area of the Japanese and clear the Ledo Road for convoys. When the Army first planned "Galahad," as this infiltration was called, word went out for volunteers. Though they knew it would be a tough assignment, they came from everywhere: technicians, fighting men, gunners, men with a sense of adventure or bored with the positions they held. In the case of the author, he volunteered because he liked a warm climate. They were incorporated as the 5307th and grew through the hardships and the untold rigors they faced to a close friendship and loyalty to one another. As they crossed India, they had a "feeling of being an advanced rivulet of a current of history," and they perceived the deep hostility that India felt for them as soldiers. When the regiment pushed into Burma, they were given the job of getting behind the Japanese and cutting the Kamaing Road. Mud, rain, lack of food, confusion at the command level, and sickness were the constant conditions under which the guerillas moved, and fear stalked them like a living thing as they slogged their way through disease-infested jungles held by the enemy. Supplies came to them from airdrops, but between times they were underfed on K-rations or starving. Relentlessly the Marauders pressed on, no matter what the support from other American regiments, no matter what errors the allied Chinese made, no matter that they were all growing weaker with dysentery and other ills. They made their way to seemingly unachievable goals along the Kamaing Road; they climbed an impossible mountain to surprise the Japanese and succeeded; but steadily, surely, their ranks became decimated, and they were finally disbanded when some of the men actually fell asleep during the fighting.

Not written with sensationalism, the factual details piled upon details have an impact that no fictionalized account could have. Perhaps the most striking thing about Ogburn's book is the revelation of human courage in the face of conditions that seem beyond the bounds of human endurance. The book appeals to mature boys and to World War history students.

Introduce the book to individuals rather than use it for a book talk. *Burma Surgeon* by Seagrave and *The Flying Tigers* by Whelan may also be suggested. *A Thousand Springs* by Chennault gives a good view of the situation between Stilwell and Chennault from the Chinese side of the Hump.

OLIVER, JANE

Sing, Morning Star

1956. Putnam.

This dramatic story of Malcolm III, eleventh-century King of Scotia, is a sequel to the events immortalized in Shakespeare's *Macbeth*. When Duncan was murdered, his wife with her two sons, Malcolm and Donald Bane, fled to her brother, Siward of Northumbria. There she left the elder child Malcolm, who was his father's heir, but she and the baby returned to her home in Denmark. Malcolm grew up with the idea of avenging his father's death and regaining the throne from Macbeth. At the age of seventeen he returned to Scotia with Siward's forces, and at Dunsannin Macbeth was defeated but escaped only to meet death at Malcolm's hands three years later. Upon the death of Siward, Malcolm went south to Winchester as his uncle's heir to claim the earldom and pay homage to Edward, King of England. Edward, however, gave Northumbria to Tosti, son of the favored Earl Godwin, and Malcolm had no choice but to return to Scotia and try to consolidate his kingdom. When Edward died, Harold was named king, but he reigned only a few months before he was defeated and killed at the Battle of Hastings by William, Duke of Normandy. Edgar the Aethling was named king by the Saxons, but William quickly deposed him. Unhappy with his lot in England, Edgar with his mother and two sisters, Margaret and Christine, set out for Hungary where they had formerly lived. When a raging storm forced them into a harbor near Malcolm's stronghold, they became his guests. Malcolm fell in love with the gentle Margaret who gave up her dream of convent life to become his queen. Their life together ran a stormy course, for although Malcolm loved his wife dearly, he could not give up entirely a life of battle and struggle. Margaret tried to lead him in the paths of peace and often she succeeded. Together they performed many kind deeds, improved living conditions for their people, and built churches. But when the battle cry sounded, when an unjust act was to be avenged, Malcolm became the rough warrior and refused to heed the impassioned pleas of his queen. Finally

135

Rufus, a ruffian without honor or integrity, succeeded William to the throne of England and tricked Malcolm into a premature death.

Mature readers who favor historical fiction find this an excellent picture of the early Norman period in English and Scottish history, enhanced by the love story of Malcolm and Margaret.

Begin book talks by mentioning that this is a sequel to *Macbeth;* give Malcolm's background and his ability to inspire action, pages 81–85; and tie in the circumstances which led to Malcolm's romantic meeting with Margaret. Follow up with *The Golden Warrior** by Muntz, *The Conquerors* by Costain, *The Last Englishman* by Weenolsen, and Oliver's *The Lion and the Rose,* although the last title is about an entirely different period in Scottish history.

OPIE, JUNE
Over My Dead Body
1959. Dutton.

". . . I wished with all my heart that people would not worry themselves wondering what life had in store for me. Dead or alive, no one knows the answer to that." Perhaps these lines symbolize best the courage of the young New Zealander, June Opie, who contracted polio while enroute to England. Within a few hours of her arrival in London, she was so completely paralyzed that she could move only her left eyelid. For a long time she did not know what her disease was; even when she was put into an iron lung she did not suspect polio. When she discovered by accident what her trouble was, she hated her body—but not for long. She was determined to do anything and everything that would make her strong again. A courageous, almost detached view of her plight made June a delight to the sisters and doctors at St. Mary's Hospital where she lived for a year. Her wonderful sense of humor and her desire not to be a bother to anyone endeared her to the whole staff, and nurses and doctors who had no connection with her case often came to see her. "Jimmy," an ingenious but uncomfortable plaster bed, became an almost human and frequently humorous element in the often grim hospital routine. Friendships with other patients and a determination to recover helped her succeed in conquering despair and illness. A romance which shows signs of maturing into marriage also adds appeal to the book.

136

Girls from junior high school up who are interested in medicine and related vocations or in reading about handicapped people are fascinated by this story.

"Jimmy's" advent, pages 96–105; the fabulous old patient Gran, pages 154–57; and the description of Christmas in Chapter 16 can be used for introducing this personal history. The incident over June's knitting, pages 224–25, has humor as well as a picture of her determination to succeed. Suggest *My Left Foot* by Brown, *The Miracle Worker** by Gibson, and *Interrupted Melody* by Lawrence for other stories of conquered handicaps. Use *The Man Who Lived Twice** by Barnes and *I Can Jump Puddles* by Marshall with the more mature readers.

ORWELL, GEORGE

Animal Farm

1954. Harcourt.

Shortly before he died, Old Major, the pig, told the assembled farm animals of a dream in which he foresaw a rebellion that would free them from the tyranny of Man. Inspired by this prophetic vision and organized by Snowball, Napoleon, and other swinish revolutionaries, the animals eventually rebel and drive out lazy, besotted Farmer Jones and his family. A communal system is instituted by the pigs, who soon master the arts of reading and writing and proceed to transform Manor Farm into a classless Animal Farm. Man can no longer slaughter animals at will, and a life of animal prosperity leading to eventual retirement seems assured. Seven Commandments of Animalism, including such precepts as "All animals are equal" and "No animal shall sleep in a bed," are inscribed on the barn wall. For the benefit of sheep, hens, and the less brilliant animals, the rules are reduced to a single maxim: "Four legs good, two legs bad!" Objections from the fowl are quieted when they are convinced that wings count as legs; only Man is bad. When an attempt by Farmer Jones and his friends to retake the farm is rebuffed, Napoleon takes the credit and plots to eliminate Snowball and make himself leader of the animals. He and his cohorts establish themselves in the Jones home and begin to treat the "comrades" as slaves. Traitors are executed by the vicious dog guards, and as the totalitarian state slowly evolves, the Commandments are altered and history is changed to suit Napoleon's plans. "All animals are equal, but some animals are more equal than others"

137

eventually is all that remains of the lettering on the barn wall. The pigs learn to walk on their hind legs and wear human clothing, so the new chant becomes, "Four legs good, two legs better!" When at last humans come to confer with the pigs, the animals peering in through the windows find that they cannot distinguish between the faces of the enemy and their own leaders. A new totalitarian state has been born.

Young people enjoy this satire mirroring the dangers which beset societies led into revolution by unscrupulous individuals, who create new regimes worse than the old.

A book talk can be built around the changed Commandments, using the pigs' justification for sleeping in beds as an example, pages 75–77. Interested readers are often eager to follow this title with other satires. *Gulliver's Travels* by Swift, *Platypus at Large* by Kelen, and *Take Me to Your President* by Wibberley provide similar satiric approaches to human foibles. Orwell's *Nineteen Eighty-four* and Huxley's *Brave New World,** both of which are more mature, may be recommended if the librarian has read them.

PAGE, ELIZABETH
The Tree of Liberty
1939. Holt.

About 1760 Matthew Howard, a young frontiersman, fell in love with Jane Peyton, and they were married in spite of the objections of the girl's wealthy Tidewater family. Marriage did not change Jane's aristocratic views about the importance of family and social class, and she found it difficult to accept the neighbors near their wilderness plantation, Albemarle Hall. On the other hand, Matthew found it impossible to accept Jane's opinions on the Virginia House of Burgesses to which he was elected. Matt and Tom Jefferson, friends since boyhood, favored rebellion against England, and Jane could not understand their attitude. As tensions increased between the colonies and the mother country, relations between Jane and Matt became more strained. When the children came along, one boy looked like the Peytons and thought like a Howard, and the other boy was just the opposite. As the war drew closer, Jane took the children to her brother at Elm Hill, and Matt enlisted. Later the two boys joined their father with the American forces. James, the younger son, who became Colonel Hamilton's clerk, favored Hamilton's aristocratic ideas while Peyton, who had always idolized Jefferson, became a dispatch rider. This difference in viewpoint also served to divide the family until an emergency proved the strength of blood ties. Before the war was over, Peyton had married a little French girl with his father's and Lafayette's help, and Matt and Jane were reconciled. When peace came, James stayed with his uncle at Elm Hill to help him restore the plantation, and Peyton studied law so that he could support his wife and twin sons. Jefferson became Ambassador to France and he took Peyton along as his private secretary. Matt, Jane, and their daughter Mary had returned to Albemarle Hall where Mary fell in love with George Norton, the overseer's son. It broke Jane's heart to think of her daughter married to such a backwoodsy, uncouth, and common young man. But Matt forbade his wife to interfere. Mary was as happy in her cabin home as she had been in the luxury of Elm Hill. When Matt was sent to Richmond for the session of the House of Delegates, Jane went with him, and once more they could not see eye to eye concerning the establishment of the new government. The colonies had separated from England because of taxation, and now the poor people refused paying tax to the new government. Matt was on their side while Jane declared that the government had to have money. Later the family split over the Hamilton-Jefferson controversy. There are wonderful word pictures of the Jefferson household and of Peyton's family when they returned from their years in France. Bitterness over government policies separated the Howards time after time, but underneath they were devoted to one another. The reader follows this unusual family through three generations, sharing their heartbreak and their happiness while watching the young nation struggle to grow into a strong United States.

This superb novel is for the good reader because of its length and its splendid picture of the early days of this country. The great leaders come alive as they battle for their beliefs and as they relax in their family groups. Because of the romance girls like it, and because of the historical background and the fact that men number among the leading characters, boys find it equally interesting.

For a book talk introduce Matt and Jane and their divergent views or tell the humorous incident of Lafayette's assistance to Peyton in winning Adrienne's hand, 250–59. Several stories relating to historical events and ideas can also be used, such as James's discussion with Hamilton, pages 412–16, and Matthew's discussion of Jay's treaty with James Madison, pages 364–65.   139

Suggest *Northwest Passage* and *Rabble in Arms* by Roberts as other mature presentations of these early years. *Gone with the Wind* by Mitchell gives an equally vivid picture of a different period—Civil War times.

PATON, ALAN

Cry, the Beloved Country

1948. Scribner.

"These hills are grass-covered and rolling, and they are lovely beyond any singing of it. . . ." A native preacher from these hills of South Africa, the Reverend Stephen Kumalo, is called to Johannesburg to rescue his sister who has fallen into evil ways. As his brother John and his only son Absalom have also gone to the city and have not been heard from, he decides to use the money saved for his son's education to seek them out. He finds his sister who has become a prostitute, and she promises to return to their village with him. His brother has prospered, but his son Absalom has joined a group of young delinquents and has left a trail of misdemeanors. He has even served a term in a reformatory. Here he was a model prisoner and became a friend of the white social worker who found work for him and made arrangements for him to marry the girl who was expecting his child. Just as he seems to have reformed, Absalom disappears. Shortly after this, Arthur Jarvis, a young white attorney whose interest and sympathies are with the natives, is shot to death in his home. The police accuse Absalom of the crime, and he confesses to firing the shot—not from malice but from fear. Although a famous lawyer defends the boy, Absalom must hang for his crime. Ironically, Reverend Kumalo is aided by the dead man's father, who is finally beginning to embrace the views of his murdered son, becoming sympathetic toward the natives and particularly toward the burdened minister. Reverend Kumalo offers to give up his pulpit, but his congregation, knowing his true goodness, will not allow it. The elder Mr. Jarvis helps the natives who are suffering from drought by furnishing milk and food from his farm and promises further to promote the construction of a dam which will prevent future water shortages. He plans to help train the farmers in new methods and even promises a new church building for Reverend Kumalo. Thus his son's ideals and plans are to be carried out in spite of his untimely death.

The first appeal of this book is the singing rhythm, and the reader progresses through the almost Biblical style to comprehension of the forces at work in South Africa. The story is a classic tragedy. Mature readers appreciate the great sensitivity to human feelings and emotions, the depth of the story, and the well-portrayed characters.

For book talks use the second chapter almost word for word, deleting the few sentences unnecessary for telling. This will establish the problem. Or use the conversation between the condemned son and his preacher father, pages 204–8, or the scene where the white father reads his dead son's article on understanding South Africa, pages 173–76. *Venture to the Interior* by Van der Post, *Blanket Boy* by Lanham, and the author's *Tales from a Troubled Land* can be used as follow-ups. *Flamingo Feather* by Van der Post also shows a deep understanding of African problems and real sympathy for the natives. *Jamie* by Bennett, the story of a white boy and his native friend on a farm in South Africa, is comparable to Paton's books in beauty and sensitivity.

REMARQUE, ERICH MARIA
All Quiet on the Western Front
1929. Little.

Just out of school and only nineteen years old, Paul Baumer and his companions are in the front lines of the German army during World War I. Paul tells in short, stark sentences the soldiers' reactions to fear, hunger, shellfire, sickness, and danger. To those who face death so young, it is not an adventure; it is instead futility and disillusionment. When the bombardments start and the recruits are frightened, the older men keep an eye on them. One young boy goes mad, climbs out of the trench, and has to be tied to be kept from committing suicide. The men retreat and attack again with the trenches nearly flattened from the shelling. When they finally get reinforcements, there are only thirty-two men left from the original company of two hundred. Relief arrives, and Paul goes home on a fourteen-day leave to see his sister and his sick mother. When people ask about the war, he is at a loss how to answer them. When he returns to his company, he finds his friends Kat, Tjaden, and Kropp; Haie has been killed. Alone in a shell hole during an attack Paul crawls out to try to find his friends but has to seek cover in another hole. When a body falls in on him, Paul stabs it and then, tormented by his actions, tries to relieve the suffering of the dying man. Later Paul and his companions are assigned to guard a heavily bombarded village where **141** a valuable supply dump is located. When Albert and Paul are wounded, they persuade the doctor to keep them together. Albert loses a leg, and Paul is on crutches. Eventually Paul returns to his company. The war continues endlessly. Muller is killed and Paul inherits his boots. Kat is wounded and Paul attempts to carry him through the lines, but just as he brings him to safety, a piece of shrapnel kills Kat. In October, 1918, on a day when all is quiet on the Western front, a stray bullet kills Paul.

This arresting novel is one of the few classics of World War I. Its youthful point of view, grim humor, and vivid detail make it popular among senior high school boys.

A description of the different comrades would be a good introduction, and if one wanted to use a single chapter the first is probably most suitable. Paul's return home to see his mother, pages 152–88, or Paul in the shell hole with the French soldier, pages 218–28, might also be used for a book talk. As follow-ups suggest *They Fought for the Sky* by Reynolds, *What Price Glory?* by Anderson and Stallings, *Journey's End** by Sherriff, and *The Red Badge of Courage** by Crane.

RÖLVAAG, OLE EDVART

Giants in the Earth

1927. Harper.

With his head full of dreams for the future, Per Hansa moved his wife Beret and their three children—Ole, Anna Marie, and Hans Kristian—from Minnesota to Dakota Territory and staked out his claim near the land of Hans Olsa at Spring Creek. Strong and resourceful, he worked against overwhelming odds to establish a home for his family. A man of many moods and enthusiasms, he worked from before dawn until after dark, cultivating the land and building his sod house. Beret, uprooted from her native Norway, found the prairie lonely, bleak, and savage. She was haunted by a nameless dread of the relentless elements around her and could not understand the pleasure that her husband and children took in this rugged country. Her chief preoccupation was to escape from this terrible land. When the Indians came and camped nearby, Per Hansa had the courage to visit them. There he discovered an Indian with blood poisoning whom he was able to help, although Beret protested and was afraid. That summer he destroyed some markers put down earlier

142

on his neighbors' lands by Irish settlers. Beret discovered the deception and was haunted by the deed. Later it turned out that the Irish had never filed their claims and had no right to the land, but still Beret found it hard to forgive Per Hansa for his transgression. As the seasons passed, Per Hansa had to fight all the natural elements of this raw, wild land: snow and wind, cold and rain, and plagues of marauding grasshoppers. Yet he always seemed to come out on top and because of his resourcefulness was usually ahead of his neighbors in any undertaking. Beret grew queer as time went on and was obsessed with the idea that evil controlled their lives. When Hans Olsa was dying, she insisted that her husband go out into a blizzard to get a minister. This was Per Hansa's final struggle with the harsh elements of the prairie, for he was destined not to return.

Per Hansa typifies the hardy settler who exulted in hardships and the struggle with the soil. Beret, on the other hand, symbolizes the brooding melancholy of many of the pioneer women who had to brave danger and desolation to make homes for their families. Although this is a bitter and realistic story, the human spirit always triumphs, and the sacrifices of the early settlers have never been told more vividly. Boys and girls who are mature readers appreciate this "saga of the prairie."

There are many scenes worth reading or telling: the description of the building of the sod house, pages 49–55; the care of the sick Indian, pages 76–85; Per Hansa's struggle with a blizzard, pages 262–75; and the plague of grasshoppers, pages 341–44. This book could follow *Let the Hurricane Roar* and *Free Land* by Lane, *A Lantern in Her Hand* by Aldrich, and *The Edge of Time* by Erdman. As follow-ups use *Peder Victorious* by Rölvaag and *O Pioneers!* by Cather.

ROMULO, CARLOS P.

I Walked with Heroes

1961. Holt.

The real hero of this autobiography is Carlos P. Romulo himself—teacher, soldier, journalist, Pulitzer-prize winner, and diplomat. Although he is a man small in physical stature, he is a giant in mind and heart. It is impressive to see a very sensitive man have his ideals shattered by reality and yet keep his optimism and his faith in humanity. Carlos Romulo was born in a small town in the Philippines, the son of a well-to-do Spanish-Malayan family.

He believes that at least part of his success in life is due to the fact that he had a happy childhood surrounded by loving, understanding, intellectual adults. When he was in junior high school, his father was elected governor of the province and the family moved to the capital and later to Manila. Shortly after the first move Carlos discovered girls, and he did his first writing as a result: love letters and poetry. This gave him the courage to try for publication. In high school he also engaged in debate and oratory, two more skills he used to advantage in his adult life. He had already made up his mind to be a teacher, but while still in high school he began work as a cub reporter on the Manila *Times*. His first assignment was the Senate, and thus he became interested in politics. Later came four years at Columbia University where he earned a M.A. degree. On his return home he met the girl he married and theirs has been a very happy life together. Romulo went on to become in turn a college professor, editor in chief of two newspaper chains, army general, diplomat, and president of the General Assembly of the United Nations. In each period of his life he worked with and came to know well the prominent men of the Philippines as well as world leaders, and these are the heroes to which he refers in the title. He remarks that his happiest moments have had a trace of tragedy and his proudest hour was touched by comedy. For example, at his first session of the General Assembly he had to sit on three New York City telephone books in order to be seen by the delegates.

The author has an easy style of writing and a well-developed sense of humor. He is very matter-of-fact about his unusual accomplishments. Both boys and girls who are interested in world affairs, the United Nations, or the Philippine Islands enjoy this book.

For a book talk give an idea of the man's unique career and tell some of the small incidents which show his great ability and sincerity. Describe his job on the *Cable-News* when he was only sixteen years old, pages 82–86, or his first news story on President Quezon, pages 86–92. Amusing are his first date in America, pages 141–43, and the story of how William Howard Taft saved him from marrying the wrong girl, pages 151–54. Reading this book makes one want to read some of Romulo's others, such as *Crusade in Asia* or *The Magsaysay Story. The Ugly American** by Lederer is a natural follow-up. *In the Days of McKinley* by Leech describes how the Philippines won their freedom, and *Bare Feet in the Palace* by Keith is another story of the Philippines which appeals especially to girls.

ROSTAND, EDMOND

Cyrano de Bergerac; a new version in English verse by Brian
   Hooker

1923. Holt.

The nose of the famous French guardsman, Cyrano de Bergerac, was of such amazingly heroic proportions that the man's
very behavior was shaped and directed by it. His courage, which
seemed almost foolhardy, and his ability to compose poetry even
during a duel more than compensated for his ugliness. Cyrano
was not a man to be taunted or disparaged without dire consequences. Beneath the braggadocio and swaggering courage, however, lay a sensitive soul yearning for but one prize—the love of
the beautiful Roxanne. Her exquisite features, so much a contrast to his, made Cyrano despair that she could ever care for one
so gross. He nurtured his devotion deep beneath his gruff soldier's
exterior until a meeting planned at her request brought him to
the point of hoping that she might actually care for him. Unfortunately, her purpose was to plead for his protection of a
young popinjay named Christian, with whom she fancied herself in love. All the guardsmen were Gascons, and they were accustomed to making life miserable for an outsider like Christian.
Cyrano promised to look out for the young soldier and, discov-
ering that Christian loved Roxanne and was unable to put his
feelings into words, Cyrano agreed to write his love letters for
him. Because of their beauty and emotional presentation, Roxanne fell deeply in love with the image they created, and Cyrano
was forced to see another man win the prize he coveted. Roxanne
and Christian were married following a scene in which the concealed Cyrano spoke for the inarticulate Christian, and not five
minutes after the wedding the guardsmen were ordered immediately to the front. Cyrano promised to look after Christian and to
see that he wrote his young wife every day. Cyrano kept his
promise as well as he could, and when Christian was killed during an attack, Cyrano kept his secret. Roxanne went into deep
mourning and entered a life of seclusion without realizing that
she loved Cyrano rather than the dead boy. During the long
years of her isolation, Cyrano visited her regularly. Only after a
mortal injury and at the point of death did he accidentally reveal his feeling by reciting Christian's last love letter, so faded
that the writer alone could have known the contents. Too late,
Roxanne realized that she loved Cyrano, but the old soldier
died happy in the knowledge that his devotion had triumphed 145

over his ugly face. Consistent to his ideals, he met death on his feet with his sword in his hand.

This drama set in seventeenth-century Paris is full of the court intrigue of the time, and the classic love story enlivened with the hero's comic, impulsive escapades appeals to both boys and girls of high school age. The plot may seem exaggerated, but the dramatic presentation and reality of the characters make "suspension of disbelief" easy.

A description of the first scene, in which Cyrano composes a sonnet during the duel, and a mention of his plan to become ghost writer for Christian could introduce the story without spoiling the surprise ending. Other titles with unrequited love themes include *Tryst* by Thane, *Portrait of Jennie** by Nathan, *Ethan Frome** by Wharton, and *An Iceland Fisherman** by Loti. The excitement of this period of French history can be continued in Dumas' *The Three Musketeers.**

SAINT EXUPÉRY, ANTOINE DE
Wind, Sand and Stars
1949. Harcourt.

A new breed of men was cast when pilots were created, and the author reflects upon their lives and what impels them to risk themselves repeatedly and without regret. Two of these men he admired tremendously: Mermoz, who initiated night flights and pioneered the mail routes over the Andes and across the ocean, and Guillaumet, who was lost in the Andes for more than a week when his plane was caught in a bad storm. The author's enthusiasm for flying is dramatized in his descriptions of his own flights, crashes, and narrow escapes. He flew the mail over the Sahara and across the Andes in all weather conditions. He knew danger and loneliness, but he reveled in the beauty he saw and the rapture he felt. One of his most memorable experiences was on the Paris-Saigon flight. He and his companion, Prévot, became lost, flew down through the clouds to find a landmark, and crashed into a gentle slope in the desert. Both escaped alive. In the days following they knew the desperation and terror of being lost, suffered terrible thirst, and were crushed by false hopes when mirages deceived them into thinking help was near. Finally when they saw the Bedouin who rescued them, they thought that even he was a mirage at first. Saint Exupéry discusses the early planes, the elements and the comradeship of the pilots, as well as his adventures in Spain during the Civil War. Through all of

146

this he has woven philosophical musings, often speaking poetically about those thoughts which touched him deeply.

Because *Wind, Sand and Stars* is concerned fundamentally with human relationships and motives, it is not dated. The boys and girls who read it forget that they are earthbound as they accompany the flier who finds a meaning in life as he explores the skies. The book's adventures appeal to those who want action, but the beautiful language and meditative passages make it more appropriate for the poetic, sensitive individual.

Incidents useful for book talks include the episode in which French aviators purchased and freed the slave Bark, pages 152–68, and the description of Saint Exupéry's crash in the Libyan desert, pages 173–236. Use the book with *Night Flight* by the author, *The Spirit of St. Louis** by Lindbergh, *The Lonely Sky* by Bridgeman, and *Fate Is the Hunter** by Gann.

SCHARY, DORÉ

Sunrise at Campobello

1958. Random.

Beginning with the fateful day, August 10, 1921, when Franklin D. Roosevelt was stricken with infantile paralysis, this play details his trials of body and spirit through bleak days of invalidism until his triumphant political comeback on June 26, 1924, when he nominated New York governor, Alfred E. Smith, for the Presidency of the United States. Demonstrating to the world what an indomitable will could do, he changed the course of his own life and ultimately the events of American history. The play opens in Campobello, New Brunswick, Canada, where the Roosevelt family was enjoying a pleasant vacation. Their happy, boisterous life was suddenly changed by the illness that struck the father. In the thirty-four months which followed, all of the main persons of the Roosevelt entourage are clearly characterized. His friend, Louis Howe, made careful preparations to keep up F.D.R.'s courage. Eleanor, the shy, awkward young wife, developed as a woman as she devoted herself to building up her husband's spirit and his career. The dominating will and influence of his mother, Mrs. Sara Delano Roosevelt, are revealed in a high-tension, emotion-packed quarrel over Franklin's determination to pursue a political career.

This dramatization of a life of great courage and determination appeals to both boys and girls in senior high school.   **147**

A brief synopsis of the play or the dramatic reading from any one of the short, forceful scenes piques the interest. Act I, Scene 2, the conversation between Howe and Mrs. Sara Roosevelt, makes good dialogue for two people to read aloud. Other books about Franklin Roosevelt are *Affectionately, F.D.R.* by his son James, *A Good Fight* by Gould, *The Human Side of F.D.R.* by Harrity, and *When F.D.R. Died* by Asbell. For the drama of another struggle against a handicap, suggest Gibson's *The Miracle Worker.**

SHERRIFF, ROBERT C.

Journey's End

1929. French.

Young Lieutenant Raleigh, fresh from base training, arrived as a replacement in a dugout of the British army in March, 1918. Despite the danger, Raleigh's chief emotion was happiness because the commander, Captain Stanhope, had been his hero since public-school days. A middle-aged officer, Lieutenant Osborne, tried to prepare Raleigh for the tough, hard-drinking, cynical officer which Stanhope had become. Stanhope himself feared what the boy might write home to his sister, Stanhope's fiancée, so he censored his letter. But in the letter he found only praise of the man who was his continuing hero. As the company prepared for a German attack, the Colonel told Captain Stanhope that he must send out a raiding party to capture some German prisoners who might give them information. To lead the dangerous daylight raid he suggested Osborne because of his experience and Raleigh for his youth and vitality. Osborne realized the danger of this effort; Raleigh looked on it as a great adventure. The successful raid procured the prisoners who gave valuable information, but Osborne and some of his men were killed. The callous acceptance of this tragedy upset Raleigh whose brief experience in the trenches had not taught him the protective concealment of feelings. In the battle the following day Raleigh was badly wounded, and Captain Stanhope, in telling of his coming evacuation to a hospital, became once more the friend and hero that Raleigh so admired. Raleigh died, and Stanhope resumed his defense against the Germans.

This realistic picture of trench life in World War I reveals devotion to duty, courage, and the depths of human suffering. The secondary theme of friendship and admiration of a younger man for an older one is like a fine thread running through the play.

Merely stating the setting and theme will arouse reader interest. However, there are several scenes that might be used to characterize Stanhope, Raleigh, and Osborne. In Act II, Scene 1, Osborne reads the letter Raleigh had written to his sister about his assignment to Stanhope's company. In Act III, Scene 1, Raleigh and Osborne develop a warm friendship as they talk of home and the future. In Act III, Scene 3, Stanhope and Raleigh reestablish their fine relationship of former days. Other stories of stark realism disclosing human nature under the stress of war are *All Quiet on the Western Front** by Remarque, *A Walk in the Sun* by Brown, and *The Gray Captain** by Wheelwright.

SHERWOOD, ROBERT E.

Abe Lincoln in Illinois

1938. Scribner.

As a young man, Abraham Lincoln had no self-confidence even though his friends believed that he was destined for greatness. He was in debt, he could not seem to achieve success in business, and he was uncouth and uncultured. His friends, however, saw a future for him in politics, and even the cultured and wealthy Ninian Edwards conceded that Lincoln had possibilities. When Mary Todd came to visit her sister Elizabeth, Ninian's wife, Lincoln was among the eligible young men who were invited to meet her. Although she could have had any of the gentlemen, she chose Abe Lincoln before he had even thought of marriage. She decided he would go far, particularly if she were by his side. As a young politician in New Salem and Springfield, Lincoln seemed to have little to say. He bided his time and listened, so that when he gave an opinion it was a well-considered one. At first the professional politicians underestimated him. They thought he was clever but felt that when it came to important political moves, he would follow their instructions. They were wrong, and Abraham Lincoln was elected President of twenty-six states, eleven having decided to secede from the Union. The play ends as the Lincoln family boards the train for Washington, where the man from Illinois was to face the issue of appeasement or war.

The twelve scenes of this play are the highlights of Abraham Lincoln's life as a young man, a family man, and a politician in Illinois. Young people identify themselves with his uncertainties and fears, and understand his struggle with himself and the desire to withdraw from his destiny.

149

For book talks show Abe in Rutledge's tavern, joshing the wild-cats of Cleary's Grove out of murderously trouncing Ninian Edwards, who has come to urge Lincoln to run for the state assembly, Scene 2; let Lincoln's political views vibrate as he answers Judge Stephen A. Douglas, Scene 9; share Lincoln's relationship with his sons and Mary when the committee of Eastern politicians come to get his views before nominating him for the Presidency, Scene 10. The Lincoln family will also be found in *Love Is Eternal* by Stone, *I Mary* by Randall, *Life of Abraham Lincoln* by Lorant, *The Day Lincoln Was Shot** by Bishop, and *The Last Days of Lincoln* by Van Doren.

SHIRER, WILLIAM L.

The Rise and Fall of the Third Reich

1960. Simon & Schuster.

On November 10, 1918, a thirty-year-old Austrian named Adolf Hitler was in a military hospital recovering from temporary blindness when word came that the Kaiser had abdicated and fled to Holland. Like millions of his fellow countrymen, Hitler could not believe that Germany had been defeated. He blamed the traitors at home for the surrender and then and there decided to commit his own career to politics. Quite by accident he became involved with the National Socialist party, which had only about forty members in 1919. Small as it was, this group represented the nucleus from which the Nazi party developed. The depression gave Hitler the chance he needed. Believing that the Nazi movement could do the most for them, many German industrialists paid substantial sums toward its support. By the beginning of 1931, Hitler had gathered around him a little band of fanatical, ruthless men who would help him in his final drive for control of the government. Three years later he had gained complete domination of Germany. By sheer effrontery he confused other governments until he had rearmed the country and started his program of conquest. The Allied powers took no action, being too divided and too unwilling to recognize what was happening in Germany. As early as 1925 Hitler had published *Mein Kampf,* which outlined his plan for world domination. The sales had been very meager; no one could possibly take seriously the ideas it promulgated. If the Allies had done so and acted, World War II might have been averted. Now it was too late. With control

150

of Germany, Hitler began to carry out his plan. Austria, Czecho-slovakia, and Poland fell to the Nazis; Denmark, Norway, and France soon followed. World War II had begun. At this point the author devotes about three hundred pages to descriptions of the early German victories and the eventual turn of the tide toward the Allies. With direct quotations from testimony at the Nuremberg trials, the grisly details of inhumane treatment of slave laborers and the extermination of the Jews are laid before the reader in all their horror. The account ends with the death of Hitler and the speedy fall of the Third Reich.

Boys who are serious thinkers find this monumental work challenging and read it eagerly and critically, fascinated by the gullibility of the Germans and the blindness of the Allies. The balanced, objective presentation brings alive an evil regime which is almost legendary to young adults.

The book offers much meat for discussion and is best introduced to individuals or small groups. *Mein Kampf* by Hitler is an interesting companion volume, while Mr. Shirer's bibliography will aid those who want to pursue the subject in depth. *The Guns of August** by Tuchman and *Exodus** by Uris present other views of Europe in turmoil.

SHUTE, NEVIL
Pied Piper
1942. Morrow.
John Sidney Howard, a widowed English solicitor of nearly seventy who had lost his son in the R.A.F. at the very beginning of World War II, returned to the village in the French Jura where he and his son John had vacationed in happier days. As time passed and German troops invaded Norway, Denmark, and the Netherlands, Mr. Howard decided to go back to England while there was still an opportunity. As he moved toward home, his journey began to resemble that of a Pied Piper by request. First came two little English children of a League of Nations official, then the ten-year-old niece of the French hotel maid in Dijon. When the German invasion of France put an end to public transportation, the old man and the children were forced to walk. With a discarded perambulator purchased at a farm where they stopped for a drink of water, the pitiful group pushed on. Little shell-shocked Pierre joined them, then a Dutch toddler **151**

named Willem, and last of all the bitter Polish orphan boy. Success seemed assured until one of the children lapsed into English in front of a German soldier. The entire group was imprisoned, and Howard was questioned as an English spy. They were released only when Howard promised to take the German major's niece out of France with the group.

This suspenseful, tender novel appeals to older readers who want a war story with a different touch. The horror of war is mentioned, but the underlying theme is one of gentleness and compassion.

The librarian may use a summary to introduce the situation and main characters and then tell of Howard's acquiring the French and Dutch orphans, pages 96–99 and 126–30. *Diary of a Young Girl* by Frank is the story of another child during the war. *Our Share of Morning* by Burmetz tells of a mother, father, and small, crippled daughter who attempt to escape from the Gestapo in Austria and France. *And Four To Grow On* by Palmer and *The Family Nobody Wanted* by Doss are other stories of orphan children befriended. *Father Flanagan of Boys Town* by Oursler and *A Shirttail To Hang To* by Day also deal with the problems and care of homeless children.

STEWART, MARY

Nine Coaches Waiting

1959. Mill.

Linda Martin, an alert, intelligent English girl who spoke French like a native, had been accepted by a French family, the De Valmys, as a governess to nine-year-old Philippe. The little boy's parents had been killed recently in a plane crash, and he had been living in an isolated château in the French Alps with his uncle and aunt. A vast estate would come to the boy when he became fifteen. Several puzzling incidents occurred after Linda's arrival at Château Valmy, and as time went on she overheard some disturbing conversations, but it was the little boy who troubled her most. He seemed so pathetically thin and withdrawn, perhaps because the love and affection he had received from his parents, a favorite uncle, and an old nurse had been removed by circumstances or intention. Linda was much attracted to Philippe's cousin, Raoul, who occasionally visited his parents at the château. While in the village on an errand she also met

William Blake, an English forester camped in the mountains above Valmy. The trust she instinctively felt toward him was not misplaced, as the unfolding plot reveals. A series of near-fatal accidents, each cleverly planned, confirmed her suspicion that someone was trying to kill the little boy. Her smuggling of Philippe out of the château in the middle of the night, a wild chase through the mountains, and their successful hiding for twenty-four hours provide mounting suspense. The mystery ends with a satisfactory solution and a love interest for Linda.

This romantic mystery set in modern France fascinates high school girls who are fond of *Rebecca* by Du Maurier and Stewart's earlier book, *Madam, Will You Talk?*

Philippe's brush with death, pages 148–50, will stimulate interest in reading the book. Use *Jane Eyre* by Brontë as well as the more recent title, *Mistress of Mellyn* by Holt, to answer the request for a similar story.

STONE, IRVING

The Agony and the Ecstasy

1958. Doubleday.

Michelangelo's family, "the Buonarroti, were not only stingy, they were enemies of art because they despised the men who created it." But Michelangelo was determined that nothing would prevent his being an artist. He did a sketch for Ghirlandaio, and the artist was so pleased with the boy's talent that he paid for the privilege of teaching him. Michelangelo's progress was rapid, but he soon found that he was more interested in sculpturing than in painting. One day he learned that Lorenzo de' Medici had decided to restore to Florence its former greatness in sculpture and had persuaded the great Bertoldo to help him. When Michelangelo heard of it, he asked his good friend, Granacci, "Have you ever wanted anything so hard you couldn't bear it?" Shortly thereafter Lorenzo asked Ghirlandaio to send his two best apprentices to the Medici school to work under Bertoldo. The artist was angry because he needed his assistants, but he released Granacci and Michelangelo. Although Michelangelo became Bertoldo's favorite pupil, no word of praise or award was given to him for a whole year while he worked at drawing and modeling. He saw less worthy students rewarded and felt that he had failed to please his teacher and master. Suddenly he was 153 called to Lorenzo's study to be told that he had real talent and had passed the period of testing. He was offered a place in the Medici palace and a weekly allowance. Now he had an opportunity to associate with some of the outstanding scholars in Italy, and he did his first original work in marble. One after another, opportunities came to him but not always for sculpture. After Lorenzo died, Michelangelo went to Rome where he was to live and work for much of his life. One pope after another commissioned him with assignments, which often made him unhappy because they took him away from his beloved sculpturing. A particularly trying time came when he was asked to paint the ceiling of the Sistine Chapel. He worked for eight months and was not satisfied with what he had done. When he asked for permission to change the theme, Pope Julius consented but said he could not understand Michelangelo's request to do five or six times more work than necessary when he detested painting. Michelangelo replied, "I hardly understand myself. I only know that since I must paint that vault I cannot bring you something mediocre, even if that is all you have asked for." His final triumph was the design and construction of the dome of St. Peter's Cathedral in Rome. Three women influenced Michelangelo's life: for Contessina, Lorenzo's daughter, he had a spiritual love; his love for Clarissa was purely physical; his mature affection went to Vittoria Colonna. But none of these loves could surpass his passion for the feeling of the hammer and chisel against the gleaming white marble.

The author, Irving Stone, by immersing himself in the art and wars of the period, in the intrigues and decadence of the popes, in the struggles and hopes of the people of Florence and also of Rome, and by studying the terrain of Italy and the skill and necessities of marble carving, has managed to free the spirit and grandeur of Michelangelo as Michelangelo himself freed his statues from the blocks of marble. Mature readers are enthusiastic about the story.

The introduction of young Michelangelo and his extraordinary talent will interest some young people. For others use the occasion of the spending of his first allowance. He wanted to buy gifts for his good friends the Topolinos, stonecutters in the hills outside Florence, and Contessina helped him choose them, pages 113–15. Or tell the episode involving the ceiling of the Sistine Chapel, pages 428–44. Interested readers might try *Romola* by Eliot, *The Romance of Leonardo da Vinci* by Merejkowski, and *Rembrandt* by Schmitt.

STOWE, LELAND

Crusoe of Lonesome Lake

1957. Random.

While working as a roving reporter for the *Reader's Digest,* the author flew to Lonesome Lake in British Columbia to interview Ralph A. Edwards, a modern frontiersman and pioneer. So impressed was he by the story of this remarkable man's life that he decided to write this book about him. Ralph Edwards had a limited formal education, but his experiences while he was growing up convinced him that he wanted to have his own farm adjacent to a lake and mountains. For four years he worked on a farm in California and spent his free time poring over books on agriculture. In 1913, at the age of twenty-one, he applied for and was granted a 160-acre preemption in the Atnarko Valley. Although it was the dead of winter, he found a tough young trapper who knew the country and would guide him in. The spot he decided upon had everything he wanted. In three days the pair erected a small cabin, and Ralph began to chop down the virgin timber which covered his land. By springtime he was able to plant a small garden before leaving for "outside" to earn money for supplies. Patiently for several years he pushed back the wilderness until he had room for a very large garden and orchard plus a comfortable three-room Norwegian-type cabin. He allowed neither loneliness nor hardship to dim his view of the future. No matter what obstacle presented itself, he found a way to solve it by using his "fertile imagination, his remarkable powers of observation and an unusually retentive memory." These problems included making his own canoe and boat, moving twelve-foot cedar logs to the cabin site without a horse, getting cattle over the mountains and down to the farm, and importing machinery bit by bit and putting it together. In 1923 he found a sturdy, pioneer-type girl who was willing to share his isolation. Later, because no school was available to their three children, Ralph and his wife taught them, eventually having to study hard to keep ahead. Always eager to modernize the farm, Ralph experimented with a water wheel to generate electricity and eventually built his own sawmill. He grew wonderful fruit and vegetables after finding the varieties which thrived in that climate. Since a market was too remote, he set to work to learn enough about mathematics, engineering, navigation, aircraft design, and aerodynamics to enable him to build his own seaplane. In the process he designed an innovation in seaplane floats which later was adopted by the U.S. Navy. Although this family's busy life has been filled by incredibly hard work, they have found time to enjoy their surroundings, the animals and birds, and particularly the trumpeter swans which winter in their valley.

Ralph Edwards' experiences inspire boys to use their own ingenuity to overcome problems, while girls can enjoy the story, too, because Ethel Edwards and Trudy are also remarkable people. An additional value is the importance of books in this "most memorable" man's life.

For book talks there are many exciting episodes which a librarian can use. One October, when the children were small, the cabin burned, pages 83–87; pages 138–40, Ralph set out for town with only a .22 and was cornered by a pack of five wolves. Facing a grizzly bear, pages 140–42; the attack by a steer, pages 88–92; and the "Ding-blasted Trail," pages 145–50, are all tellable. The beautiful saga of the coming of the trumpeter swans and their care by Trudy is an outstanding chapter. For follow-ups use *Icebound Summer* by Carrighar, *Ring of Bright Water** by Maxwell, *Three against the Wilderness* by Collier, and *Driftwood Valley* by Stanwell-Fletcher.

SUCKOW, RUTH

The John Wood Case
1959. Viking.

Seventeen-year-old Philip had always been proud to be called John Wood's son. His father's loving devotion to Minnie, Philip's semiinvalid mother, was almost a legend in the small Iowa town of Fairview. Their marriage had been a sensation—the strikingly handsome man and the frail, ethereal girl so close to death who seemed to live on in the warmth of John's love. Such a perfectly balanced partnership, blessed with a sturdy son, appeared almost too ideal to exist. Could any husband be so anxious to care for his wife? For many people, John was a personification of the Christian virtues he supported so faithfully in his local church, where he was respected perhaps more than the young minister. Philip had grown up nurtured by this encompassing love and religious atmosphere without becoming self-righteous or resentful of his father's position in the community. He excelled in school and sports while bearing his share of the household duties cheerfully, almost eagerly. His selection as valedictorian of the high school class was an honor nearly everyone had expected and wanted for John Wood's son. Elaine Merriam, young grand-daughter of Colonel Merriam, John's employer, was another prize which some felt that Philip would win one day. Her delicate, introspective nature appealed to the young man, perhaps because she so closely resembled his mother. Marriage was something that Philip anticipated, but he realized that college was in his future and that the wealth and prestige of the Merriam clan might work against his hopes. Life seemed good and the future bright for these people living in the untroubled atmosphere of the early nineteen hundreds. It was the contrast between this serene, happy picture and a suddenly revealed crime which shattered the composure and peace of Fairview. The fact which astounded everyone, especially Philip, was that John Wood was a thief. His desire to provide extra comforts for Minnie had driven him to speculate and then to take large sums from his employer's business to cover the resulting losses. When an audit revealed the discrepancies, John was quick to admit his guilt and resign, but the community was stunned. Those who loved him said he had acted out of love for Minnie, and those who had been suspicious, perhaps jealous, of his selfless devotion were quick to condemn. Minnie's fierce, almost feverish defense of her husband only compounded the agony of the church leaders who tried to clear the air and settle the problem. Even when Colonel Merriam, the employer, refused to prosecute, it was clear that Philip had become an outcast with most of his friends and could neither claim Elaine nor pursue a college career with such heavy family debts to repay. His initial decision to drop out of the graduation exercises changed when he realized that he had become the head of the Wood family and should therefore stand before the audience and try to reclaim some of their lost respect. Feeling shut out of his parents' life when they turned to each other in their grief, Philip felt completely alone until Colonel Merriam's wife demonstrated her love for him by a gift of money and an heirloom. Philip then gained spiritual strength to face the prospect of moving to another town where he could help rebuild his parents' happiness and perhaps realize some of his own plans for the future.

Older young adults recognize the agonizing search of a teenager for maturity and self-realization.

The description of Philip's room, his parents, and the happiness which surrounded them, pages 3–13, could be used to set the mood of the novel in a book talk, followed by a brief statement of the crime and its consequences for Philip. *Death Be Not Proud** by Gunther, *The Human Comedy* by Saroyan, and

*Bridge to the Sun** by Terasaki echo the theme of a family shaken by tragedy.

TEALE, EDWIN W.

Autumn across America

1956. Dodd.

For several years Edwin and Nellie Teale toyed with the idea of traveling with the seasons, describing the United States as they found it at various times of the year. The first opportunity came one spring when they traveled 17,000 miles from Florida, zigzagging north as spring moved ahead of them to the Canadian border. The account of this first journey was given in *North with the Spring.* In *Autumn across America* they started from Monomoy on Cape Cod and drove west across the northern part of the United States, ending in Monterey, California, after a 20,000-mile trip. Their excursions were carefully planned so that they found the most interesting people to visit and the most unusual places and things to see. Edwin Teale not only describes the countryside through which they pass, but he also gives glimpses of the history of national phenomena. Whether the Teales are following the route of Lewis and Clark, discussing comets with a noted amateur comet collector, experimenting with the woolly bear caterpillar's sense of direction, seeing the Badlands by moonlight, observing the harvester ants on the Custer battlefield, marveling over the Craters of the Moon in Idaho, or beachcombing amid the tide pools on the Oregon coast, their fascinating experiences are described with a vividness which makes the reader a participant. There are new stories of John Burroughs, Charles Darwin, W. H. Hudson, Kit Carson, and Jim Bridger. In the depths of the Washington forests one day a birdcall makes them think of Rima of *Green Mansions.* They watch a monarch butterfly start for a thirty-five-mile flight across the water of Lake Erie and marvel at its courage and the pleasure it has as it dips close to the waves. As they travel, Mr. Teale inserts bits and pieces of information such as an ecological tale of seaweed, its sudden destruction, and the consequent death of fish and scallops that depended upon it for food; how bird feathers are attached and how hawks use the high air drafts; the story of the almost extinct trumpeter swan which has a home in the Wyoming Rockies; the Great Salt Lake and the strange tale of the buffalo gnats that the Indians collected and dried.

158   This book speaks to many kinds of readers, but it appeals espe-

cially to young adults who have enjoyed experiences in the out-of-doors.

Book talk possibilities include the description of the pikas, or rock rabbits, and their amazing customs, pages 170–79; the search for Poncho, a German shepherd belonging to a deaf-mute elk hunter in the mountains of Oregon, pages 225–30; the dipping bird walking on the water, pages 285–86; and the moment at Point Reyes when the Teales saw the ebb of the tide and autumn slipped away, pages 362–63. For other nature books use *North with the Spring, Journey into Summer, Dune Boy,* and *Grassroot Jungles* by Teale, *The Singing Wilderness* by Olson, and *One Day on Beetle Rock* by Carrighar.

TERASAKI, GWEN
Bridge to the Sun
1957. Univ. of North Carolina Pr.

Gwen was twenty-three when she left her home in Johnson City, Tennessee, and went to visit her aunt in Washington, D.C. During a reception at the Japanese Embassy, she met Hidenari Terasaki, secretary to the Ambassador. He was very attentive and eager to answer Gwen's many questions about Japan. The next day she received a package of Japanese books and pictures, a fan, a small container of green tea, and some yellow roses. This was the beginning of their courtship, and within a year they were married and on their way to Japan. They realized that their international marriage would bring complications, but they were confident that their love for each other would enable them to surmount any difficulty. After eight months Terry was assigned to Shanghai. The assignment was a difficult one because he did not approve of the arrogance of the Japanese soldiers who occupied parts of the country. When war broke out in Europe, and Germany tried to make an alliance with Japan, relations between the United States and Japan became tense. In 1941 the Terasakis and their daughter Mariko were transferred to the United States. Terry was convinced that Japan could not win a war and tried to bring about better relations. All his planning was in vain; Pearl Harbor was attacked. It did not occur to Gwen to desert her husband; instead, she took Mariko to join the group from the Japanese Embassy when they were interned. After many months they were exchanged for American internees and sent back to Japan. Life there during the war was strenuous. The family suffered from a shortage of food, from ill health, hard   **159** work, and the lack of a safe, permanent home. But people were good to them and shared whenever they could. Terry's health began to fail when the war began, and it steadily declined thereafter. At the end of the war he became the liaison person between the Emperor and General MacArthur, and grew to admire both men. When Mariko reached college age, it was decided that she and her mother should go back to the United States to live with the grandparents. A tightly knit family group was broken, and not long afterward Terry died.

Girls especially like this story of life in Japan during World War II. It offers a sharp contrast with the way the Japanese were treated in the United States during the war.

To introduce the story tell of Gwen's meeting with Terry and their courtship, pages 4–13. Other appealing stories of Japan are *Rain and the Feast of the Stars* by Hatsumi, *Windows for the Crown Prince* by Vining, *The Lovely World of Richi-san** by Bosworth, and *The Flowers of Hiroshima** by Morris. For more accounts of international marriages suggest *My Heart Lies South* and *Where the Heart Is* by Treviño, *I Married a Korean* by Kim, and *A Thousand Springs* by Chennault.

THACKERAY, WILLIAM M.

Vanity Fair [1848]

Dodd.

When Amelia Sedley returned home to London after six years of "improvement" at Miss Pinkerton's Academy, she could sing, dance, embroider, and spell as well as any seventeen-year-old girl who had ever graduated from that honored establishment. Traveling with her was a friend named Becky Sharp, whose opinion of the school was summed up in her parting act of throwing her gift dictionary back over the fence as the carriage drove off. Becky had been half student, half teacher because of her ability to speak the French language with a Parisian accent and because of her poverty, but Amelia had been the darling of the whole school because of her sweetness and charm and her father's money. Amelia took Becky home to visit her and treated her with every kindness. She even gave her a large collection of her own very slightly worn dresses so that Becky, on her way to being a governess in Sir Pitt Crawley's home, might have a presentable wardrobe. Becky repaid Amelia by flirting with her brother Joseph. While Becky maneuvered, Amelia renewed her lifelong admiration for handsome but inconstant George Osborne, who was more

160

interested in his own foppish appearance and his position than in any woman. Becky lost the security she might have had in Joseph, but she felt she could do better than marry George whom she had stolen from Amelia. She went to her post at the Crawley home where she soon determined to become its mistress. A little too impatient, she decided to marry Rawdon Crawley secretly, and in a short time found she might have had Sir Pitt himself—a much better catch. Amelia had married George who continued to gamble and play around with society women until he was killed at the Battle of Waterloo. Then Amelia isolated herself, dwelling upon his supposed devotion until Becky pointed out his infidelity. Realizing that she had been mourning an illusion, Amelia turned to her husband's friend William Dobbin, who had long cherished the hope of winning her hand. Becky was never without a scheme for future conquests, and although at one time she sank to the point of bankruptcy, she managed to maintain herself in suitable circumstances until the end of her life.

This long, richly descriptive novel is an excellent period picture of the manners and mores of the eighteenth century and the posturings and strivings of middle-class society. Older girls who have enjoyed Dickens and the Brontës find this a fascinating glimpse of two eternal types of women: the realist schemer and the sentimental innocent.

An introduction of Amelia and Becky and a hint at their romantic problems are enough to interest mature girls in reading the story. For other studies of human nature in novel form try *Pride and Prejudice* by Austen, *Jane Eyre* by Brontë, *Tess of the D'Urbervilles* by Hardy, and *Eugénie Grandet** by Balzac. The heroine of *Gone with the Wind* by Mitchell resembles Becky in many ways.

THANE, ELSWYTH

Washington's Lady

1960. Dodd.

Martha Custis who had been married at seventeen and widowed at twenty-five was left with two small children. Eighteen months later she met and was courted by the tall, diffident officer, George Washington, whom she married on a January day in 1759. Happily, he was devoted to her little Jack and Patsy, and the children adored their new Papa. As a member of the House of Burgesses, Colonel Washington attended the Assembly in Williamsburg that winter, and finally in April they came home to Mount Vernon, his estate on the Potomac, where for more than ten years they were happy with their country life and the building up of their estates. The years passed quickly as Martha's children grew up and the family alternated between Mount Vernon and Williamsburg. Politically the times were disturbed, and Martha Washington watched her husband becoming gradually absorbed into the "relentless trend of events" as the British imposed taxes and Boston had its tea party. Militia companies were forming all over the colonies, and George ordered a new uniform. In a short time he was named as a representative to the First Continental Congress in Philadelphia. These were difficult days for Martha. Her daughter Patsy died in her teens; her son Jack married young and established his own home; now her husband was going away and, if conditions became critical, he might be gone for a long time. Her fears were realized when the Second Continental Congress asked Washington to take command of the American Army and to go immediately to Boston. He wrote Martha that he hoped to be home by Christmas; surely when the King saw that the colonies meant what they said, changes would be made and peace would return. But in November Washington sent for Martha to join him in Cambridge. With her carriage packed with good things for the table at headquarters she set off with Jack and his wife Nellie for the thousand-mile winter drive. This was a journey she was often to make to New York, Philadelphia, Valley Forge, and Morristown in the years which followed. Whenever the General was to be in residence for a considerable period of time, he sent for Martha. While at Mount Vernon she kept herself busy by overseeing the new developments which Washington outlined in his letters. It seemed that the time would never come when Washington would be able to take up civilian life again, but when the war was over, he returned to Mount Vernon. Before he was able to get his plantation back on a paying basis, he was asked to attend the Constitutional Convention in Philadelphia and before long was elected to the Presidency. The government was first established in New York and later moved to Philadelphia, where the Washingtons felt much more at home because of their frequent visits there during the war. After eight years as President, George Washington and Martha finally moved back to Mount Vernon. There followed two more years of building up their plantation and home and putting their affairs in order, and then Washington caught a severe cold and died. Martha followed him within three years.

Washington's Lady reveals Martha and George Washington as real personalities, engaged and involved in all of the activities of the country life of the landed gentry, concerned over the problems of the children, entertaining and enjoying their neighbors and friends, managing and furnishing the estate and house at Mount Vernon—yet always ready to serve their country in war and peace. This perhaps is one of the few intimate pictures of Martha Washington, who felt with her husband that their private life was not a subject for public curiosity or investigation. Girls, especially, enjoy the events of colonial and revolutionary America seen through the activities of Martha Washington at Mount Vernon and wherever else her husband's career took her.

As an introduction tell the story of Martha and George's first meeting and courtship, pages 3–15. Her journey to army headquarters at Cambridge is a good example of Martha's courage and devotion, pages 83–88. Her first visit to Washington's headquarters at Cambridge can be used in a book talk also, pages 93–135. For another factual account of the period there is *The Family Quarrel* by Thane. *Man from Mt. Vernon* by Boyce and *George Washington* by Cunliffe give other views of the first President and his lady. For novels of the period there are *Dawn's Early Light* by Thane, *Rabble in Arms* by Roberts, *Farewell to Valley Forge* by Taylor, *The Tree of Liberty** by Page, *Janice Meredith* by Ford, and *Yorktown* by Davis. *Our First Ladies* by McConnell is excellent for the roles played by Presidents' wives.

TOLSTOI, LEO

Anna Karenina [1877]

Modern Library.

Coming from Petersburg to save her brother's marriage, Anna Karenina shared a compartment with Countess Vronsky. When they arrived in Moscow, Anna met the old lady's son, a dashing young officer. It was love at first sight. Moving in the same social circle they saw each other frequently, and before long they were deeply involved. Forgetting her duty to her husband and son, Anna abandoned herself to an affair that was soon choice gossip in both cities. Eventually she told her husband who tried to bring her to her senses, but after the birth of her daughter, she left with Vronsky. Her husband refused to give her a divorce. Scorned by her former associates, lonely for her son, Anna finally came to doubt Vronsky's love, and in an almost deranged condition she threw herself under a train. As a contrast to and parallel with the main theme, is the story of Levin and Kitty. Kitty had refused Levin, thinking herself in love with Vronsky, but after she realized that she had lost him to Anna, she accepted Levin. He was a sensitive, perceptive person who wanted to understand man's role on earth. He was concerned about the plight of the peasants, was impatient with the bureaucracy of government, and mistrusted religion. All these doubts tortured him. His devotion to his land, his great love for his wife, and his slowly developing pride in his baby son were strengthening forces in his life. In contrast, Anna's passionate love for Vronsky was her ruin. Tolstoi, skillfully weaving his many threads together into a tapestry of Russian life, shows how Anna and Levin separately react to their environments. Step by step the author builds the novel to its logical end—Anna's suicide and Levin's understanding of himself.

For the mature high school reader interested in European history who is able to follow the intricate subplots and many characters, *Anna Karenina* is a moving and absorbing novel. Its value is twofold: a highly moral theme of inevitable punishment for sin and a picture of the times and mores of a somewhat decadent society.

Because of the leisurely way Tolstoi sets the stage for action, most episodes are too long for use in book talks. However, the scene of Kitty at the ball may be used. Her complete pleasure with her gown, her partners, and her popularity is followed quickly by her heartbreak as she watches Anna and Vronsky and realizes their love for one another, pages 102–12. Before introducing this incident, give the audience some information about the main characters. Other titles which may be suggested are *War and Peace* by Tolstoi, *Tess of the D'Urbervilles* by Hardy, and *Vanity Fair** by Thackeray.

TUCHMAN, BARBARA

Guns of August

1962. Macmillan.

Dateline—August 4, 1914: German troops marched into Belgium, and the guns of August set off a conflagration that was to sweep around the world. Europe was like a heap of swords piled as delicately as jackstraws—one could not be pulled out without disturbing the others. This war had been in preparation for years, and it was no secret that Germany meant to invade France. Germany intended to concentrate her troops on the right wing and, swinging through Belgium, catch the French from behind. The French, on the other hand, planned to break through into Germany with their center and left lines and sever the German right wing from its base, thus winning a smashing victory. France's belief in her ultimate success was strengthened by agreements with England and Russia, but neither ally was ready when August, 1914, arrived. Germany was thrown off balance by unexpected resistance from the Belgians who, despite unpreparedness, stood their ground and fought at Liége, gateway to Belgium. The rigidly planned German timetable was delayed, and the Belgians paid the penalty. The French lines ran into surprisingly strong German defenses, and that part of their army would have been wiped out if the Germans had carried out their original plan. The Russians attacked on the Eastern front before they had worked out their supply lines. In spite of this they forced the Germans to retreat, and the German general asked Headquarters for help. In order to save the situation Von Moltke transferred two whole corps from the Western Front, thus weakening that front. The help was not actually needed because the Russian ammunition had given out. Half starved and exhausted, the Russian soldiers pulled back. Indecision, unpreparedness, and flagrant errors made a calamity of the first thirty days of the war on all fronts and forecast the senseless destruction of men and matériel which was to follow.

The mature young adult who enjoys history appreciates this intensive, documented study of the background and early weeks of World War I. The participants are drawn objectively, and the story is told with authority and a dramatic flair. Much of the book reads like a novel, and superior students find it stimulating and revealing.

A book talk might outline the German and French plans and show how the French expected their élan vital to carry them to victory, Chapters 2 and 3. Chapter 17 pictures the senseless brutality and tragic waste involved in the destruction of Louvain. Other books related to World War I are All Quiet on the Western Front* by Remarque and Journey's End* by Sherriff. The Zimmermann Telegram by Tuchman gives the story of the United States' entry into the war in 1917. The Rise and Fall of the Third Reich* by Shirer, D-Day* by Howarth, The Longest Day by Ryan, and Day of Infamy by Lord are mature accounts of the type of planning and preparation made in World War II.

URIS, LEON

Exodus

1958. Doubleday.

It was November, 1946. Mark Parker, an American correspondent, had arrived in Cyprus for a reunion with an old friend, Kitty Fremont, who had been widowed by the war. The British had set up detention camps on the island for Jewish refugees from World War II, all anxious to settle in Palestine. The Palestinian agents of the Mossad Aliyah Bet, an illegal immigration organization, were determined to set their people free. So the stage was set for melodrama, tragedy, and heroism as the story of the origins and establishment of the Jewish nation unfolds. Brigadier Bruce Sutherland, the British military commander on Cyprus, had been ordered to avoid trouble and detain the refugees until the government decided what to do with the Palestine mandate. When Ari Ben Canaan with his coworker, David Ben Ami, and Mandria, a Cypriot taxi driver, planned the daring escape of three hundred Jewish children on the *Exodus,* a battered refugee ship, Mark Parker's newspaper story of the operation aroused public opinion to force the British to let the ship go in safety. Kitty, who was a nurse, was drawn into the Zionist cause. She met young Karen Hansen Clement, a refugee from Germany, and saw in her a resemblance to her own small daughter who had died of polio. Kitty was also attracted to Ari Ben Canaan whose strength and courage overwhelmed her. Accompanying the children on the *Exodus,* Kitty arrived in Palestine and was assigned to a youth village. Flashbacks give the reader a detailed picture of Hitler's Germany and the Russia of the czars and commissars. Dov Landau had spent his boyhood in the Warsaw ghetto; was saved from the gas chambers because of his skill as a forger; and, embittered and desolate because of the tragic fate of his family, finally reached the Promised Land. Karen's experiences had been less difficult than Dov's. Her father, a brilliant German professor, had sent her off to Denmark when life became frightening under Hitler's regime. There she was adopted by the Hansens. Surrounded by love and understanding, she nevertheless felt after the war that she must find her family, and so, after hardship and suffering, she finally arrived in Palestine. It was Karen who taught Dov the futility of hate, and Dov, following a terrifying role in Israel's fight for freedom, became part of the new generation which would rebuild Israel. The story of

Ari's father, Barak Ben Canaan, and his brother Akiva and their escape from Russia has a heroic quality. In Palestine they were to spend a lifetime in service to their country—restoring the land, struggling for freedom, fighting for the partition of Israel at the United Nations, and scouring Europe for needed arms and supplies to fight the Arabs. Ari and his sister Jordana accepted war and strife as their heritage and lived completely for their country. With the recognition of Israel as an independent state, the British were forced to withdraw, and a bloody future lay ahead because the Arabs had no intention of allowing the Jews to take over. Only when the Maccabees and Palmach and Haganah troops united against a common enemy were they able to achieve a hard-won victory. Many valiant fighters were dead, but Kitty and Ari were left with a future that might bring them some personal happiness.

Profanity, sex, and gruesome war details make this a book for mature high school students. The drama, the tragedy, the heroism of the characters—both real and imaginary—give the story heroic proportions and the quality of an epic.

The introduction of the book to individual students may be best, but several incidents lend themselves to book talks. The story of Operation Gideon, the daring and successful attempt to take the children to Palestine on the *Exodus,* pages 167–96; the rescue of Akiva and Little Giora (Dov) from the British jail, pages 441–48; the evacuation of the youngest children from Gan Dafna before the Arab attack, pages 514–22, are suggested. Another story of the Warsaw ghetto fighters is told in *The Wall* by Hersey and in Lampell's adaptation of the Hersey novel into a play by the same title. *The Diary of a Young Girl* by Frank and *All But My Life* by Klein provide similar accounts of Jewish wartime experiences. *Cast a Giant Shadow* by Berkman is the biography of Mickey Marcus, the American who united the Israeli fighting groups under one command. Although this man was almost irresponsible with money and was a heavy drinker, he had a genius for organization and the ability to accomplish the impossible.

WEST, JESSAMYN

The Friendly Persuasion

1945. Harcourt.

Near the banks of the Muscatatuck in Indiana, Jess Birdwell, a Quaker, built his white clapboard house. Here he lived with his good wife Eliza, who was a preacher, and a houseful of children.

Jess farmed the land he loved and sold fruit-tree seedlings far and wide. People trusted him and respected his beliefs. Jess and Eliza, with their children growing up about them, aged with grace and the knowledge that they had done their best to follow their persuasion. Harmony was not always present, however, especially on the day that the organ, which had caught Jess's fancy during a trip to Philadelphia, arrived. Aware that this instrument would be frowned upon by his wife and the congregation, he still insisted upon having it, and Eliza finally agreed to let him place it in the attic. When the Ministry and Oversight Committee unexpectedly came to call, their daughter Mattie was playing softly overhead. Jess astounded his guests by launching into one of the longest and loudest prayers ever given. Reverend Godley of the Bethel church and Jess had a friendly feud over which had the fastest horse. The minister's horse usually won until Jess traded for a half-Morgan that would not let anything pass her. During the Civil War their son, young Josh, heard of Morgan's raiders and the havoc they wrought as they plundered the countryside. He joined the Home Guard in spite of his Quaker faith and the opposition of his parents, and although he did not have to kill, he learned about fighting and dying. He knew that he had stood in the front line even though he was afraid.

The Friendly Persuasion is a series of sketches which give an episodic effect rather than a strong plot to the story. Each tale, complete in itself, adds to the total picture of Jess and Eliza Birdwell and their children. There are warmth and wisdom, gaiety and suspense, and always the lovely, gentle, ethical essence of the American Quaker. Both boys and girls who liked *Mama's Bank Account* by Forbes or *Greenwillow** by Chute enjoy this simple novel about a farm family a century ago. Almost any reader will enjoy the humorous incidents, but only a more mature person will appreciate the thoughtful episodes.

Several of the sketches would be suitable for reading or telling. Mattie's impromptu organ recital in Chapter 1, or Eliza's venture into court on behalf of her goose Samantha in Chapter 3, are amusing. Moving incidents are Labe and Josh's discovery that their neighbor, old Alf, hides his loneliness in pretense, Chapter 2, and the uncovering of the buried leaf and the message from Great-Uncle Jordan Birdwell in Chapter 5. Other families and their problems are depicted in *Papa's Wife* by Bjorn, *Applesauce Needs Sugar* by Case, *Cheaper by the Dozen* by Gilbreth, *The Family Nobody Wanted* by Doss, and *The Roosevelt Family of Sagamore Hill** by Hagedorn.

WHARTON, EDITH

Ethan Frome

1911. Scribner.

Mattie Silver's was the only happy face, the only hope in Ethan Frome's life. For years his wife's fretfulness and ill health had made his existence one long, lonely misery. Illness was something Ethan could understand and accept, but he was baffled by Zeena's ailment, supposedly brought on by caring for Ethan's dying mother. No doctor could pinpoint the trouble, and no amount of patent medicine seemed to quiet her continual complaining. It was evident that Zeena enjoyed her "sickliness" as a means of keeping Ethan close to her, if only through pity. Love was something he had never felt for his wife. Loneliness and gratitude for her help during his mother's decline had made marriage appear proper and charitable, but love had never been in his heart. This void might not have mattered so much if Ethan had never met Mattie, Zeena's cousin. Destitute and alone, the young woman had been grateful to come to the Fromes' New England farm when Zeena's doctor suggested that she needed help with the housework. What could be more perfect for a self-made invalid than a poor relation who could double as nurse and servant without pay! As the months passed, however, Zeena began to realize her mistake. She saw that the innocent, winsome Mattie was a ray of joy in Ethan's barren life. Fresh and sweet, she was the kind of girl Ethan could have married for love if he had not been trapped by circumstances years before. The shy mutual admiration between Mattie and Ethan grew almost against their wills. When Zeena suddenly arranged to replace Mattie with a hired girl, Ethan thought seriously of leaving with Mattie, but the shame of deserting his wife in the middle of winter forced him to abandon the idea. Driven to desperation by their impending separation, Mattie and Ethan decided to die rather than to live apart and attempted a double suicide by a dangerous sled ride down a tree-studded slope. Down they coasted, faster and faster, until a blinding crash against a large elm ended the descent, leaving the couple seriously injured. Twenty-four years later a snow-bound stranger who had heard bits and pieces of Ethan's story, was driven to seek shelter from a storm in the Frome farmhouse and discovered Zeena, then an old woman, caring for an ugly, shriveled hag—the once lovable Mattie. Disfigured and lamed, Ethan had been forced to bear the double burden of his spiteful wife and the crippled girl whom he had loved.

A tense, psychological tale, this is a special favorite with girls who like the unrequited love theme. The tragic, surprise ending is reminiscent of many O. Henry stories.

A description of Ethan as the narrator first saw him plus the few facts that the man learned about the smash-up, together with a brief description of Zeena and Mattie as a young girl, set the background of the story and create a suspenseful book talk without revealing the surprise ending. Suggest as follow-ups *Tryst* by Thane, *The Enchanted* by Coatsworth, and *The Return of the Native* by Hardy.

WHEELWRIGHT, JERE H.

The Gray Captain

1954. Scribner.

It was the summer of 1864, and Lee's hungry, shoeless, war-weary men knew they were beaten. The Army of Northern Virginia was making its last stand. First Lieutenant Thomas Brice, recently recovered from wounds received in earlier fighting, had just joined I Company, a ragged remnant of the Second Maryland Infantry, located at Cold Harbor. His new superior was Captain Stowell, a man of sixty, too old and tired to stand the strain of war much longer. Stowell's magnificent spirit held fast, however, and he watched over his men like a father. Beneath the outer, stern appearance of the disciplinarian there were compassion and understanding; subtly he tried to persuade Brice to follow his tactics. Even when the Lieutenant lost several men through carelessness, Stowell did not reprove him and later provided several chances for him to redeem himself. The real test for the older man came when Murray Stowell, the Captain's sixteen-year-old son, joined his father's unit. The boy had been spoiled and protected by his mother and faced difficulties in adjusting to the discipline of army life. Stowell would not give him special treatment and despaired of ever making a man of him. As the days wore on and the ever shrinking I Company made the difficult forced march to Charlottesville, Brice proved to the men that he was competent and worthy of their trust. They fought at the Monacacy River and then marched on Washington as part of General Jubal Early's army, hoping to capture the city in a surprise attack. Arriving a day too late, they were confronted by the hastily manned Union forts and realized that retreat was inevitable. Captain Stowell was wounded, and Lieutenant Brice knew at last that he soon would have to take over the command.

170

This excellent description of the life of the hard-pressed Southern infantry during the closing days of the Civil War is popular with boys. Not only the hardship, suffering, and heroism appeal to them but also the development of the characters, especially young Murray Stowell and Thomas Brice.

For a book talk use Brice's first assignment which resulted in the death of two of his men, pages 33–41, or the march to Charlottesville, Chapter 9. To Appomattox by Davis and With Sherman to the Sea by Foote may be suggested for further reading.

WHITEHEAD, DONALD F.

The FBI Story

1956. Random.

For almost a year John Dillinger led his gangsters on a bloody trail through the Midwest. Behind them they left seven wounded and ten murdered men, four bank robberies, three police arsenals plundered, and three jails from which prisoners had been loosed. The FBI could not go after the gang for any of these crimes because they were not violations of federal law. But when Dillinger crossed a state line with a stolen automobile, the G men entered the hunt and eventually got him. From the files of the Federal Bureau of Investigation the author has drawn many similar stories as he tells the history of this famous agency. On July 26, 1908, Theodore Roosevelt organized the Bureau of Investigation to help him fight big-business trusts and Western land thieves. It was then a disorganized and loosely directed agency, staffed mainly by political appointees. During World War I, it was poorly equipped to deal with German sabotage and espionage. Mr. Whitehead, in his complete but not sensational report, points out the early faults of the FBI, its development over the years, and its irreproachable, nonpartisan organization since the 1924 appointment of the present Director, J. Edgar Hoover. Hoover's first decision was to get rid of the political appointees and staff the Bureau with young lawyers and accountants. Appointments were based on merit, and promotions made on proved ability. During the thirties the agency gradually acquired full legal stature and official responsibility. Gangland murders and racketeering in the 1920's; complicated kidnappings, such as the Lindbergh and Greenlease cases; investigations of Communist activities and sabotage; and civil rights disputes are among the dozens of cases discussed and documented. Perhaps the most fascinating material is that relating to the meticulous scientific 171 methods of analyzing bits of evidence. Telltale partial finger-prints can be checked through complex files to pinpoint identi-fication, while heelprints, watermarks in paper, type specimens from nearly every typewriter model, and animal hairs and auto-mobile-paint samples are available for sorting out clues.

This thrilling account of many of the nation's most notorious crimes and criminals appeals to the teen-ager who likes true stories of adventure. The careers of G men intrigue all ages of readers.

Book talks can be developed from the discussion of the finger-print files in Chapter 15 and the scientific techniques outlined in Chapter 16. Baughman's *Secret Service Chief* is a less formal study of another investigative agency; *Treasury Agent* by Tully gives some of the most exciting crime stories in the files of the In-ternal Revenue Service, the Bureau of Narcotics, the Bureau of Customs, and the Secret Service. *Emergency!* by Lobsenz provides a picture of police rescue work in New York City.

WIBBERLEY, LEONARD

The Mouse That Roared

1955. Little.

Tucked in a European valley is the Duchy of Grand Fenwick, a tiny country five miles long and three miles wide. Scarcely changed since the fourteenth century, this kingdom is ruled by the lovely Gloriana XII. Grand Fenwick has only one industry, one export, and one source of revenue—a fine wine, Pinot Grand Fenwick. By the end of World War II the Duchy's population has increased to such an extent that the country's income cannot support the people, and it has to look for additional revenue. Several ingenious schemes are suggested, and the one finally de-cided upon is to make war on the United States and be defeated. Since the United States is always generous to conquered enemies, it would immediately send food, machinery, clothing, money, and technical aid to Grand Fenwick. The plan is to declare war on Monday, be vanquished on Tuesday, and be rehabilitated by Fri-day. The reason for war would be aggression by the United States. A wine manufacturer in California has been making an inferior wine and labeling it so that it closely resembles the real Pinot Grand Fenwick. This is certainly grounds for a conflict. A formal declaration of war is sent to the United States, but the clerk in the State Department who opens the envelope thinks it is a joke of reporters and carelessly loses it. When no reply comes, the Privy Council of Grand Fenwick sends Tully Bascomb and twenty brave men equipped with longbows to attack the United States. In a volley of arrows and a flash of broadswords and maces, the tiniest nation conquers the most powerful one, and the defeated United States remains unaware that a war has taken place! Grand Fenwick does more than put itself on a new financial basis; it brings peace to the world by devising a very interesting plan.

This is a hilarious and successful spoof on international politics. The humor and satire appeal to the mature and experienced reader.

For a book talk, a brief outline of Grand Fenwick's predicament and its plan for rehabilitation is enough to awaken interest. If more is needed, amusing incidents to tell are Tully's masterful assault on Columbia University, pages 118–29, and the discovery by the American President that his country has been defeated, pages 163–74. Other meaningful titles in this light, fanciful vein are *Take Me to Your President* by Wibberley, *Animal Farm** by Orwell, *Duty Free* by Coles, *Scruffy* by Gallico, and *Island Rescue* by Tickell. *The Mouse on the Moon* is a successful sequel to *The Mouse That Roared.*

WILLIAMS, ERIC

The Wooden Horse

1958. Abelard-Schuman.

Stalag-Luft III, near Sagan, Germany, was a prison compound for British officers during World War II. Despite its exposed position in a rectangular clearing in a forest guarded by high sentry towers and barbed wire, escape was the main concern of many of the prisoners. Suddenly the Trojan horse was the inspiration for a bold plan of a break for freedom. Peter Howard and John Clinton's ingenious scheme involved the use of a hollow, wooden, vaulting-horse which they built from scraps of lumber pilfered from camp construction supplies. Daily a group of prisoners carried the boxlike structure, when weather permitted, to the same place in the open yard and then lined up to vault. Eventually, when the German guards' curiosity had subsided, a man was carried out inside the horse and began to dig the opening for a tunnel. The sand removed from the hole was placed in drawstring bags made from trouser legs and hung on hooks inside the horse. At the end of each day's work the digger covered the entrance to the tunnel with boards and dirt. Then he carefully sprinkled 173 this with dry sand to camouflage it before he was carried back inside the horse. The tunnel was to be about 130 feet long when it was completed. This was a tremendous job, and the two men finally had to ask a third person to help in order to complete it within their time schedule. After many weeks of hard labor the moment arrived for the escape. Since only three men could ride out inside the horse at one time, and a fourth person was needed to camouflage the tunnel after the break, one escapee was concealed in the tunnel in the afternoon. That evening the vaulters carried the horse out again. This time the other two escapees entered the tunnel and the third man covered the entrance and disguised the boards. The last few feet had to be "moled" out, and the break was made just after dark while a diversion was created to draw the guards' attention to another section of the compound. Peter and John decided to remain together, travel by local trains, and stay at hotels disguised as French workmen being shifted from one factory to another. Philip, the third escapee, went to Danzig by fast express, immediately found a ship for Sweden, and stowed away. He waited in Sweden for his friends who took considerably longer. After days of frustration and fear, Peter and John were smuggled onto a Danish ship and finally reached safety in Sweden.

Most boys warm to this adventure story based on the author's own experiences during World War II. The only hard-cover edition in print, a slightly abridged version of the 1949 original, eliminates profanity and replaces British expressions with their American counterparts. Edited by the author, it retains the same suspense as the out-of-print edition and has perhaps been improved in the rewriting.

The prefatory note on pages 7–8 and a brief mention of the escape plan lure potential readers without revealing the whole plot in the book talk. If possible, show the diagrams of the man inside the horse and the tunnel construction. *The Long Walk* by Rawicz, *A Man Escaped* by Devigny, and *The Colditz Story* and *Men of Colditz* by Reid are similar accounts of escape by clever planning.

WILSON, DOROTHY CLARKE

Dr. Ida

1959. McGraw-Hill.

Ida Scudder was pretty and vivacious and she loved gay parties and fashionable clothes. Although the Scudder family had given over a thousand years of service to missionary work in India, Ida had no intention of continuing the tradition. When after eight years of education in the United States she was called home to India by her mother's illness, she had her eyes opened to the plight of the women of India—three women died because they could not be attended by a male doctor and there was no woman physician available. She announced the next day that she was going back to the United States to study medicine and that she would return to help the women of India. In 1895 she enrolled at the Women's Medical College in Philadelphia. Three years later she transferred to Cornell from which she was graduated. Before she could return to India, the mission board decided to give her a chance to raise money for a woman's hospital in Vellore. Successful, she returned to India, and for two years she interned at her father's mission. When the new hospital was opened, she took charge. She had only one untrained assistant to help her at first, as her father had died from cancer a short time before. Tirelessly, she battled the ancient Indian taboos and tragic ignorance to establish decent medical care for women. She performed her first major operation with the help of an untrained servant girl. She delivered babies in rude oxcarts. She fought an unending war against malaria, cholera, leprosy, and tuberculosis. She made several trips back to the United States where she worked unceasingly to raise money for a nursing school and later for a medical college at Vellore. She lectured and told stories of some of her Indian patients, and her audiences responded generously. Friends like Gertrude Dodd gave of their talents as well as of their money to make her dreams a reality. In 1957, at the age of eighty-seven, she could look around her—at the new Leprosy Research Sanatorium, the rural hospital health center, a radiation therapy ward, an out-patient dispensary, the eye hospital, a psychiatric department—and say very humbly, "God has been good to me." Dr. Ida loved life in all its fullness and fulfilled both family tradition and a destiny she little expected.

Because of the graphic descriptions of sickness, disease, superstitious practices, and life in India, this book is best for the mature boy or girl sincerely interested in medicine or missionary work.

A dramatic moment to read or tell is the event which led to Dr. Ida's choosing a career, pages 32–43. Among the many human-interest stories of people she treated and healed is the confinement case in a high-caste Hindu home where the patient was denied drinking water and fresh straw for a bed, pages 84–86.

Bamboo Hospital by Read is the story of another medical missionary family in India. *Take My Hands* by Wilson tells of a young Indian woman who became a doctor in Dr. Ida's hospital. Fisher's *To Light a Candle* describes a missionary in China and India teaching people to read. Bartholomew's *My Heart Has Seventeen Rooms** tells of another American woman's work in an Indian hospital.

Title Index

The books which are fully annotated are indicated by an asterisk (*) in front of the page number on which the complete annotation appears.

A
Abe Lincoln in Illinois, 16, *149
Across to Norway, 91
Act One, 13, *78
Adventure on Wheels, *56
Adventurous Alliance, 20
Affectionately, F.D.R., 148
Age of Innocence, 96
Agony and the Ecstasy, *153
Aku-Aku, 32, *84
Alas, Babylon, *58, 129
Albert Schweitzer: Genius of the Jungle, 73
All But My Life, 167
All Quiet on the Western Front, *141, 149, 165
All the Queen's Men, 97
Alone, 103
Ambassador's Report, *20, 104
Amedeo, 30
American Daughter, 9
American Tragedy, 50
American Way, 79
America's Concentration Camps, 11
Amrita, 101
Ancient Sun Kingdoms of the Americas, 32
And Four To Grow On, 152
And Promenade Home, 79
Angel Mo' and Her Son, Roland Hayes, 9, 89

Angel Who Pawned Her Harp, 86
Animal Farm, *137, 173
Anna and the King of Siam, 14, *101
Anna Karenina, 50, *163
Anne Sullivan Macy, 68
Ant Hill Odyssey, 47
Antarctic Scout, 103
Anything Can Happen, 107
Applesauce Needs Sugar, 168
April Morning, 40, *53, 125
Around the World Submerged, 10, 42
Arrowsmith, *107
Arundel, 52
At Home in India, 21
Atomic Submarine, 10
Atoms in the Family, *55
Autumn across America, *158
Away All Boats, 36, 57

B
Bamboo Hospital, 27, 44, 176
Bare Feet in the Palace, 144
Battle Submerged, 57
Bell for Adano, 48, *81
Bellevue Is My Home, *43, 108
Big Change, 112
Black Bull, *69
Blanket Boy, 141
Blood Brother, *10, 62
Blue and the Gray, 45
Book of Americans, 88
Book of the Seven Seas, 85
Born Free, *7, 71, 122, 131
Bounty Lands, *52
Boy on the Rooftop, 40, 125
Brave New World, *94, 138
Brave New World Revisited, 95
Bridge at Andau, 40, *124
Bridge for Passing, 25
Bridge of San Luis Rey, 84, 125

Bridge to the Sun, 14, 19, 157, *159
Brigadoon, 34
Broad Highway, 101
Broken Arrow, 11
Bull of Minos, 32
Burma Surgeon, 135

C

Caine Mutiny, 57
Captain Cousteau's Underwater Treasury, *36
Cars at Speed, 56
Cast a Giant Shadow, 167
Caves of Adventure, 85
Caves of Mystery, 85
Celia Garth, *23, 125
Challengers of the Deep, 10, *41
Cheaper by the Dozen, 69, 131, 168
Chemmeen, 116
Circus Doctor, 8
Citadel, 108
City of Bells, 34, 69
Clayhanger, 120
Colditz Story, 92, 174
Collected Lyrics (Millay), 60, 87
Collected Poems (Coffin), 60
Collision Course, *129
Come North with Me, 10
Complete Poems of Robert Frost, *59, 87
Conquerors, 132, 136
Count of Monte Cristo, 51
Crime and Punishment, *48
Crisis, 100
Crossing of Antarctic, 103
Crucible, *125
Cruise of the Cachalot, 113
Crusade in Asia, 144
Crusoe of Lonesome Lake, *155
Cry, the Beloved Country, 77, 106, *140
Cyrano de Bergerac, *145

D

D-Day; the Sixth of June, *89, 165
Damien the Leper, 118
Dance to the Piper, 79
David Copperfield, 46, 120
Dawn's Early Light, 163
Day Lincoln Was Shot, *15, 67, 150
Day of Infamy, 165
Days with Albert Schweitzer, 73
Death Be Not Proud, 40, *71, 157
Death Comes for the Archbishop, *29
Deep Range, 22
Deliver Us from Evil, *47, 73, 104
Désirée, 51
Diary of a Young Girl, 152, 167
Doctor Dan, 89
Doctor Hap, *26, 48, 108
Dr. Ida, 14, 21, 27, *174
Doctors Mayo, 20, 44
Dog Who Wouldn't Be, *130
Driftwood Valley, 156
Drums along the Mohawk, *51, 53
Drunken Forest, 71
Dune Boy, 159
Duty Free, 173

E

Earth Abides, 59
Earth Is Room Enough, 22
Easter Island, 85
Edge of the Sea, 37
Edge of Time, 143
Edge of Tomorrow, 48
Education of Henry Adams, 20
Education of Hyman Kaplan, 107
Einstein, 56
Elegant Witch, 126
Elizabeth and Essex, 97
Elizabeth the Great, *96
Emergency!, 172

180

Enchanted, 92, 170
Endurance, 80, *102
Episode of Sparrows, *68
Ethan Frome, 146, *169
Eugénie Grandet, *11, 161
Exodus, 151, *166

F
FBI Story, *171
Face to Face, 17, 68, *123
Family, 69
Family Nobody Wanted, 69, 152, 168
Family Quarrel, 163
Famous Auto Races and Rallies, 56
Fanny and the Regent of Siam, 102
Far from the Madding Crowd, 78
Far Shore, 90
Farewell to Valley Forge, 23, 163
Fate Is the Hunter, *64, 147
Father Brown Omnibus, 41
Father Flanagan of Boys Town, 152
Final Harvest, 60, 87
Fire at Sea, 130
Flamingo Feather, 141
Flowers of Hiroshima, 59, *128, 160
Flying Tigers, 135
Forsyte Saga, *63, 117
Fourteenth of October, 132
Free Land, 143
Friend to Friend, 104
Friendly Persuasion, *167

G
Gentle Falcon, 121
Gentlemen, Start Your Engines, 56
George Washington, 163
George Washington Carver, 9, *88
Gertrude Lawrence as Mrs. A, 13, 79
Giants in the Earth, 31, 81, *142
Gods, Graves, and Scholars, *31, 85

Golden Warrior, *131, 136
Gone with the Wind, 140, 161
Good-bye, Mr. Chips, 38
Good Earth, 25, 83, 116
Good Fight, 148
Good Morning, Miss Dove, 38
Good Shepherd, *57, 58
Good Years, 74, *111
Gramercy Park, 133
Grassroot Jungles, 159
Gray Captain, 45, 149, *170
Great Expectations, *45
Green Hills, and Other Stories, 114
Green Mansions, 63, 86, *92, 133, 158
Green Years, 114
Greenwillow, *33, 69, 114, 168
Grey Seas Under, 130
Gulliver's Travels, 86, 138
Guns of August, 112, 151, *164

H
H. M. Pulham, Esquire, 64
Half Mile Down, 37
Hands of Cormac Joyce, 114
Harold, the Last of the Saxon Kings, 132
Harry of Monmouth, *120
Haunted Bookshop, *127
Heart Is the Teacher, *37, 99
Hearth in the Snow, 28
Helen Keller, 68
Henry V, 121
Her Name Is Mercy, 41, 94
Hiroshima, 18, 59, 129
Home to India, 21
Honey-Pod Tree, 89
House of Exile, 25
House of Mirth, 96
House of the Seven Gables, 127
How Green Was My Valley, *109
Howl of the Malemute, 28

Human Comedy, 33, 157
Human Side of F.D.R., 148
Hyphenated Family, 74

I
I Can Jump Puddles, 124, 137
I Like Diving, 37
I Married a Korean, 160
I Mary, 150
I Walked with Heroes, *143
Ice Palace, 27
Icebound Summer, 28, 156
Iceland Fisherman, 17, 63, 81, *112, 114, 146
I'll Tell You a Tale, 70
Illustrated Man, *22
Immortal Wife, 100
Impossible Journey of Sir Ernest Shackleton, 103
In the Clearing, 60
In the Days of McKinley, 144
Incredible Journey, 122, 131
Interrupted Melody, 137
Invasion: '44, 90
Island Rescue, 173
It's Good To Be Alive, 89

J
Jamie, 141
Jane Eyre, 153, 161
Janice Meredith, 163
Jest Olga, 107
John Wood Case, 33, *156
Johnstown the Day the Dam Broke, 130
Jonathan Blair: Bounty Lands Lawyer, 53
Journey into Summer, 159
Journey's End, 142, 148, *165
Joy of Music, *14

K
Kenilworth, 97
Keys of the Kingdom, 26, 30, *40, 83
Kim, *100

King from Ashtabula, 83
Kingdom Within, 14, 17
King's Fool, 97
King's Rangers, 52
Kon-Tiki, 32

L

Lady in Waiting, 97
Lady with a Spear, 37
Lantern in Her Hand, 143
Last Days of Lincoln, 16, 150
Last Englishman, 132, 136
Last Nine Days of the *Bismarck*, *57
Late George Apley, *116
Laughing Boy, 11, 62, 76, 93
Leonard Bernstein, 15
Les Misérables, 50, 78
Let the Hurricane Roar, 116, 143
Life of Abraham Lincoln, 150
Life with Father, 74
Lion, 8
Lion and the Rose, 136
Listen! the Wind, 66
Little America, 10
Little World of Don Camillo, 41
Living Free, 8, 71
Living Treasure, 71
Lonely Sky, 147
Long Haul, 57
Long Walk, 92, 174
Longest Day, 90, 165
Looking Backward, 95
Loon Feather, 11, *60
Lord Jim, *35
Lost Cities, 32
Lost Horizon, 83, *85, 133
Lost Pharaohs, 32
Lost Worlds, 32
Love Is Eternal, 150
Lovely World of Richi-san, *17, 129, 160

M

Macbeth, 135, 136
Madam, Will You Talk?, 153
Madame Curie, 56
Magnificent Ambersons, 117
Magsaysay Story, 144
Make a Joyful Sound, 68
Making of the President, 1960, 112
Mama's Bank Account, 106, 168
Man Escaped, 92, 174
Man from Mt. Vernon, 163
Man in the Iron Mask, 51
Man Next to Me, 44
Man Who Came to Dinner, 79
Man Who Lived Twice, *12, 79, 137
Many a Voyage, 67, 100
Marauders, *134
Marble Faun, 50
Marching On, 40
Maria Chapdelaine, *80
Mary Emma and Company, 106
Mayor of Casterbridge, *77, 96
Mein Kampf, 150, 151
Men of Colditz, 174
Men under the Sea, 42
Miracle at Carville, 72, *117
Miracle at Springhill, 130
Miracle in the Mountains, 38, *97
Miracle Worker, *67, 137, 148
Mistress of Mellyn, 153
Moby Dick, 80, 113
Moneyman, 51
Moonlight at Midday, *27
Moonstone, *34
Mouse on the Moon, 173
Mouse That Roared, *172
Mrs. Mike, 27
My Antonia, *30
My Eyes Have a Cold Nose, 124
My Heart Has Seventeen Rooms, *13, 21, 101, 176

My Heart Lies South, 160
My Lady of Cleves, 97
My Left Foot, 68, 137
My Lord, What a Morning, *8, 89
My Several Worlds, *24, 26, 83
My Zoo Family, 8, 47, 122

N

Nation of Sheep, 104
Nautilus 90 North, *9, 42
Nectar in a Sieve, 101, *114
Nefertiti Lived Here, 32
Night Flight, 65, 147
Night They Burned the Mountain, 48
Night To Remember, 48, 112
Nine Coaches Waiting, 128, *152
Nine Tailors, 35
Nineteen Eighty-four, 95, 138
90° South, 103
No High Ground, 129
No One Must Ever Know, 118
No Room in the Ark, 8, 71
No Time for Sergeants, *106
None Shall Know, 63
Nor Scrip, Nor Shoes, 26
North to the Orient, 66
North with the Spring, 158, 159
Northern Nurse, 27, 94
Northwest Passage, 140
Nun in Red China, 94
Nun's Story, 30, 73, *93
Nuvolari, 56

O

O Pioneers!, 31, 143
Of Human Bondage, *118
Old Herbaceous, 69
Old Man and the Boy, 80
Old Man and the Sea, *79, 84
Old Yeller, 131

Oliver Twist, 46
Omnibus of Speed, 56
On the Beach, 59, 129
One Day on Beetle Rock, 159
Operation Deepfreeze, 10, 103
Operation Noah, 8
Ordeal by Water, 37
Oregon Trail, 30
Our First Ladies, 163
Our Share of Morning, 152
Our Son Pablo, 76
Out of the Silent Planet, 22
Outward Bound, 133
Over My Dead Body, 44, 68, 72, *136

P
Paint the Wind, 76
Papa's Wife, 168
Parnassus on Wheels, 128
Passage to India, 101
Peabody Sisters of Salem, 20
Peder Victorious, 143
Père Goriot, 12
Perelandra, 22
Phantom Fortress, 23
Pied Piper, *151
Pilgrim's Inn, 34
Plague, 108
Platypus at Large, 138
Poems To Read Aloud, *86
Portrait of a Lady, *95
Portrait of Jennie, 34, 93, *132, 146
Pride and Prejudice, 161
Profiles in Courage, 67, *99
Prophet in the Wilderness, 48, 56, *72

R
Rabble in Arms, 52, 140, 163
Rain and the Feast of the Stars, 19, 129
Rain on the Wind, 33, *113

Raisin in the Sun, *76, 106
Raleigh's Eden, 23
Ramona, 11, 30, 62
Rebecca, 153
Red Badge of Courage, 36, *39, 54, 142
Red Star over China, 25
Rembrandt, 154
Rescue!, 130
Return of the Native, 96, 170
Rice Roots, 104
Richard II, 121
Ring of Bright Water, *121, 131, 156
Rise and Fall of the Third Reich, 58, *150, 165
Romance of Leonardo da Vinci, 154
Romola, 50, 154
Roosevelt Family of Sagamore Hill, *73, 112, 168

S
Scruffy, 173
Sea of Grass, 31
Seadragon, 10
Seal Morning, 71, 122
Secret Service Chief, 172
See Here, Private Hargrove, 107
Serengeti Shall Not Die, 8, *70
Seven Miles Down, 42
Seven Science Fiction Novels, 22
Shadows on the Rock, 81
Shannon's Way, 108
Sherlock Holmes, 128
Shining Trail, 11, 62
Shirttail To Hang To, 152
Silas Crockett, 113
Silas Marner, 12
Sing, Morning Star, *135
Singing Wilderness, 159
Single Pebble, *83, 125
Six Feet Six, 100
Skeleton Coast, 130
Sledge Patrol, 91

Small Woman, *25, 27, 41, 83

Smiling Rebel, 23

Snakes Alive, and How They Live, 47

Snow Goose, *62

Song of the Sky, 65

South Town, 106

Spin a Silver Dollar, *75

Spirit of St. Louis, 66, *108, 147

Stars Grow Pale, *16, 124

Stars Look Down, 111

Story of My Life, 68

Strange Animals I Have Known, 47, 122

Submarine!, 37, 42, 57, 58

Subway to the Met, 9

Sunrise at Campobello, 74, *147

Surface at the Pole, 10, 42

Sycamore Men, 23, 52

T

Take Me to Your President, 138, 173

Take My Hands, 176

Tales from a Troubled Land, 141

Teahouse of the August Moon, 83

Tess of the D'Urbervilles, 96, 161, 164

They Fought for the Sky, 142

They Never Talk Back, 122

They Wrote on Clay, 32

This Hallowed Ground, 45

Thousand Springs, 135, 160

Thread That Runs so True, 38, 99

Three against the Wilderness, 156

Three Musketeers, *50, 146

Three Saints and a Sinner, 20

Three Tickets to Adventure, 71

Thrills of a Naturalist's Quest, *46, 131

Tiger on a Leash, 130

Times Three, 88

To Appomattox, *44, 67, 171

To Kill a Mockingbird, 77, *105

To Light a Candle, 176

Treasury Agent, 172
Tree of Liberty, *138, 163
Tryst, 63, 86, 92, 133, 146, 170
Twenty Years After, 51
Twisted Image, 104
Two in the Far North, 27, 29
2000 Fathoms Down, 42

U
Ugly American, 21, 48, 82, *104, 144
Under My Wings, 65, 109
Under the Greenwood Tree, 78
Under the Red Robe, 51
Undersea Patrol, 37, 57
Up from Slavery, 89

V
Valley of Decision, 64, 111
Vanity Fair, *160, 164
Venture to the Interior, 141
Vicomte de Bragelonne, 51
Victory over Myself, 89
Visibility Unlimited, 109
Voice of the Lute, 133

W
Walk in the Sun, 149
Wall, 167
War and Peace, 164
Washington's Lady, *161
Way of All Flesh, 120
We Die Alone, 80, *91
What Price Glory?, 142
When F.D.R. Died, 148
When the Legends Die, 11, 62
Where the Heart Is, 160
White Company, 51
White Witch Doctor, 73, 94
Who Walk Alone, 118
Wild Voice of the North, 28, 131

William Diamond's Drum, 54
Wind, Sand and Stars, 65, 109, *146
Windows for the Crown Prince, 102, 160
Windswept, *32, 64, 74
Winter Wheat, 31
Wish I Might, 72
Witchcraft of Salem Village, 127
With Sherman to the Sea, 40, 54, 171
Within the Hollow Crown, 121
Woman in White, 35
Wooden Horse, 92, *173
World at My Finger Tips, 124
World of Albert Schweitzer, 73
World of Amphibians and Reptiles, 47
Wuthering Heights, 46

Y
Yankee from Olympus, *19
Yankee from Tennessee, 53, *66, 100
Yorktown, 163
You Can't Take It with You, 79
You Come Too, 60
Yours with Love, Kate, 99

Z
Zimmermann Telegram, 165
Zoo in My Luggage, 47